Creating Mashups with Adobe Flex and AIR

Chris Korhonen, David Hassoun, John Crosby

D1614197

friendsof

DESIGNER TO DESIGNER™

an Apress® company

Creating Mashups with Adobe Flex and AIR

ISBN-13 (pbk): 978-1-59059-936-5

ISBN-10 (pbk): 1-59059-936-5

ISBN-13 (electronic): 978-1-4302-0537-1

ISBN-10 (electronic): 1-4302-0537-7

Printed and bound in the United States of America 9 8 7 6 5 4 3 2 1

Trademarked names may appear in this book. Rather than use a trademark symbol with every occurrence of a trademarked name, we use the names only in an editorial fashion and to the benefit of the trademark owner, with no intention of infringement of the trademark.

Distributed to the book trade worldwide by Springer-Verlag New York, Inc., 233 Spring Street, 6th Floor, New York, NY 10013. Phone 1-800-SPRINGER, fax 201-348-4505, e-mail orders-ny@springer-sbm.com, or visit www.springeronline.com.

For information on translations, please contact Apress directly at 2855 Telegraph Avenue, Suite 600, Berkeley, CA 94705. Phone 510-549-5930, fax 510-549-5939, e-mail info@apress.com, or visit www.apress.com.

Apress and friends of ED books may be purchased in bulk for academic, corporate, or promotional use. eBook versions and licenses are also available for most titles. For more information, reference our Special Bulk Sales–eBook Licensing web page at http://www.apress.com/info/bulksales.

The information in this book is distributed on an "as is" basis, without warranty. Although every precaution has been taken in the preparation of this work, neither the author(s) nor Apress shall have any liability to any person or entity with respect to any loss or damage caused or alleged to be caused directly or indirectly by the information contained in this work.

The source code for this book is freely available to readers at www.friendsofed.com in the Downloads section.

Credits

Lead Editor Clay Andres	**Production Editor** Ellie Fountain
Technical Reviewer Christophe Herreman	**Compositor** Lynn L'Heureux
Editorial Board Clay Andres, Steve Anglin, Ewan Buckingham, Tony Campbell, Gary Cornell, Jonathan Gennick, Matthew Moodie, Joseph Ottinger, Jeffrey Pepper, Frank Pohlmann, Ben Renow-Clarke, Dominic Shakeshaft, Matt Wade, Tom Welsh	**Proofreader** Nancy Bell **Indexer** Julie Grady
Project Manager Kylie Johnston	**Artist** April Milne
Copy Editor Kim Wimpsett	**Interior and Cover Designer** Kurt Krames
Associate Production Director Kari Brooks-Copony	**Manufacturing Director** Tom Debolski

To the millions of developers out there who continue to amaze me with their creativity!
—Chris Korhonen

To the thriving and supportive development communities out there and to my friends and family who make it all worthwhile.
—David Hassoun

To my Sara and Aidan and the rest of my family and friends who push me to make myself better and never stop teaching or learning.
—John Crosby

CONTENTS AT A GLANCE

CONTENTS

ABOUT THE AUTHORS

Chris Korhonen is a front-end developer and user experience designer with more than four years of experience creating both internal and web applications for Fortune 100 companies. Educated at the University of Durham and the University of Sussex, Chris has a solid programming background in Java and the fundamentals of computer science and software engineering. He has since shifted his attention to emerging front-end technologies including JavaScript, Flash, and Flex, specifically, to how they can be used to create an engaging and effective user experience. Originally based in Brighton, England, Chris has recently relocated to New York City. In his spare time, he enjoys photography, cooking, and sampling new and exciting beers.

David Hassoun is the founder RealEyes Media LLC (http://www.realeyes.com), a Colorado-based digital media firm focused on interactive motion media and advanced Flash/Flex platform applications. David has always had a passion for motion media, the power of video, and the challenges of usability and interactivity. David is an Adobe Certified Master Instructor, teaches advanced RIA classes at the University of Denver, is the Rocky Mountain Adobe User Group manager, and has taught and developed many successful advanced Flash/Flex application courses. As a consultant or while employed with other firms, David has done work for a wide range of companies such as American Express, Chase Manhattan, Qwest, Boeing, Macromedia, Adobe, U.S. Air Force, Bechtel/Bettis, Mitsubishi Electronics, and many more. David has performed many advanced code/technical/best practices reviews and has provided directional advice for international industry leaders over the past years including many technical, courseware, and application reviews for Macromedia/Adobe and their clients as an industry expert.

John Crosby, senior developer and partner at RealEyes Media in Denver, Colorado, has more than eight years of experience with web, server-side, and application development. A Certified Adobe Instructor, he has conducted training classes nationwide for Adobe Authorized Training Partners. He has also authored and/or provided technical review for multiple Adobe Official Curriculum courses as well as a number of nonofficial courses. A certified Flex, Flash, and ColdFusion developer, he has been involved in many large- and small-scale projects involving AIR, Flex, Flash, and ColdFusion. Aside from work, he is a wine enthusiast and classically trained chef and still enjoys the fire and knives of the kitchen, as well as the efforts of other chefs and cooks wherever he travels.

ABOUT THE TECHNICAL REVIEWER

Christophe Herreman is a software architect and developer living in Belgium. He mainly focuses on Flex-based rich Internet applications and likes to philosophize about object-oriented development. He is an active open source contributor and the author and lead developer of the Prana Framework (http://www.pranaframework. org). He has also been involved in other projects such as AS2lib, AMFPHP, and ARP.

You can find him blogging at http://www.herrodius.com.

ACKNOWLEDGMENTS

We would like to acknowledge the development community as a whole because without you, the technology would not be pushed to ever-higher levels and new directions. Open source libraries, forum discussions, and community events drive technologies and development, so thanks!

We'd also like to acknowledge the companies, individuals, and groups that provide the technologies, data, and APIs that allow everyone to create wildly useful, insanely cool, and totally off-the-wall applications. Their hard work and generous openness provide the information everyone can use to create these applications.

Finally, to Ben Renow-Clarke, Clay Andres, Kylie Johnston, Kim Wimpsett, Ellie Fountain, and everyone else at Apress/friends of Ed; Christophe Herreman; Jonathan Markwell at Inuda Innovations; Andy Mitchell at ProductiveFirefox.com; George Palmer at idlasso; Ribot & Ribot at . . . Ribot; Chris Hunt at Sapient; Paul Bennett, Glenn Crouch, Jose Barrera Ballesteros, Adam Moore, Graham Wall, John Newman, Catriona Hamilton, and Adam Whitehouse, who all provided advice and inspiration; James "Cliff" McCarthy at Artist Haus & The Werks, a fantastic mentor; Seb Dee-Leisle, Niqui Merret, Richard Willis, Jo Summers, Peter Passaro, Paul Booth, Lego Joe, and everyone else at Flash Brighton for building a vibrant and enthusiastic developer community; our friends and families and everyone else who has helped with creating this book. It couldn't have been done without you! Thank you!

INTRODUCTION

It is fair to say that one of the fastest-moving areas in technology, in terms of innovation and "coolness," is the Web. In the space of ten years, it has gone from being a near text-only medium to a platform upon which developers can create immersive and highly interactive experiences. The impacts on business, entertainment, and everyday tasks have been huge.

And just when a lot of people were thinking we had reached a peak, along came the concept of **mashups**, applications that combine information from more than one source into a single application. They empower users to view data in new and infinitely more useful ways, and they empower developers to push the limits of their imagination.

Adobe Flex and Adobe AIR provide a solid platform that enables developers to quickly and easily build mashup applications with proven toolsets and knowledge already in use. The Adobe Flash platform allows these applications to be deployed to an audience that has widely accepted Flash as a safe and powerful delivery platform.

I first started playing with AIR back when it was still referred to by the code name Apollo at the end of 2006. Having experimented with many cross-platform desktop technologies in the past, I was a bit skeptical as to whether AIR would really be any good. Usually a lot of compromises are made, or developers still need to produce lots of platform-specific code.

Pretty much the same day I got my hands on the SDK, I had to fly from Phoenix to London Heathrow. Having watched all of the decent movies on the outward flight, I was glad to have something to occupy myself, so I opened my laptop and fired up Flex Builder. By the time I had arrived in London, I had converted several widgets and web applications to run as AIR applications, and I was well on my way to creating some other dashboard applications.

What struck me almost immediately was that this was no different from building a web application using Flex, Flash, or even JavaScript. Applications were still written in a similar way, and even the additional AIR APIs available were straightforward and intuitive to use. Suddenly I realized that I could add "cross-platform desktop application development" to my list of skills.

AIR is a technology that has massive implications for developers. It has the potential to empower developers to create integrated experiences, taking interaction beyond the browser, and also to be a catalyst for innovation. As a result, this book is about exploring both the technological and creative sides of developing mashups; it provides inspiration about what is possible and is backed up by technical tips and guidance when working with Adobe Flex and AIR.

—Chris Korhonen

Who this book is for

This book is aimed at a broad range of people, whether they are web developers who have exclusively been working with HTML and JavaScript who want a view into complementary technologies or Flash developers who are interested in what both AIR and ActionScript 3.0 are and how they can be leveraged to create next-generation applications. In a general sense, it is for developers of front-end web applications who are looking either to enrich the user experience by incorporating data mashups or to take their skills and ideas to the desktop using AIR.

This book provides a gradual introduction to the technologies involved, addressing the basic concepts right through the specifics that should be considered when developing applications.

How this book is structured

The book is composed of 15 chapters providing information on specific topics related to developing mashups and desktop applications. It starts with the core concepts behind mashups and then covers the various technologies available before diving into the Flex framework and ActionScript 3.0. It then covers how you can realize the work in the previous chapters as desktop applications by using Adobe AIR and the key differences between developing for the Web and developing for the desktop.

Prerequisites

You should have Flash Player 9, the Flex 3.0 SDK, and Adobe AIR 1.0 SDK and runtime installed in order to compile and run the examples in this book. All are available for free download from Adobe's website (http://www.adobe.com).

Adobe Flex Builder 3.0 was used as the authors' development environment, which is available for purchase from Adobe. This is *not* required in order to build Flash, Flex, or AIR applications. The SDK is perfectly usable on its own or with your development environment of choice.

Layout conventions

To keep this book as clear and easy to follow as possible, the following text conventions are used throughout.

Important words or concepts are normally highlighted on the first appearance in **bold type**.

Code is presented in `fixed-width font`.

New or changed code is normally presented in **`bold fixed-width font`**.

Pseudo-code and variable input are written in *`italic fixed-width font`*.

Menu commands are written in the form Menu ➤ Submenu ➤ Submenu.

Where I want to draw your attention to something, I've highlighted it like this:

> *Ahem, don't say I didn't warn you.*

Sometimes code won't fit on a single line in a book. Where this happens, I use an arrow like this: ➥.

```
This is a very, very long section of code that should be written all ➥
on the same line without a break.
```

Downloading the Code

The source code for this book is available to readers at http://www.friendsofed.com in the Downloads section of this book's home page. Please feel free to visit the friends of ED website and download all the code there. You can also check for errata and find related titles from friends of ED.

Contacting the Authors

Chris Korhonen: chris@sourcebottle.net, http://sourcebottle.net/

David Hassoun: david@realeyes.com, http://david.realeyes.com/

John Crosby: john@realeyes.com, http://john.realeyes.com/

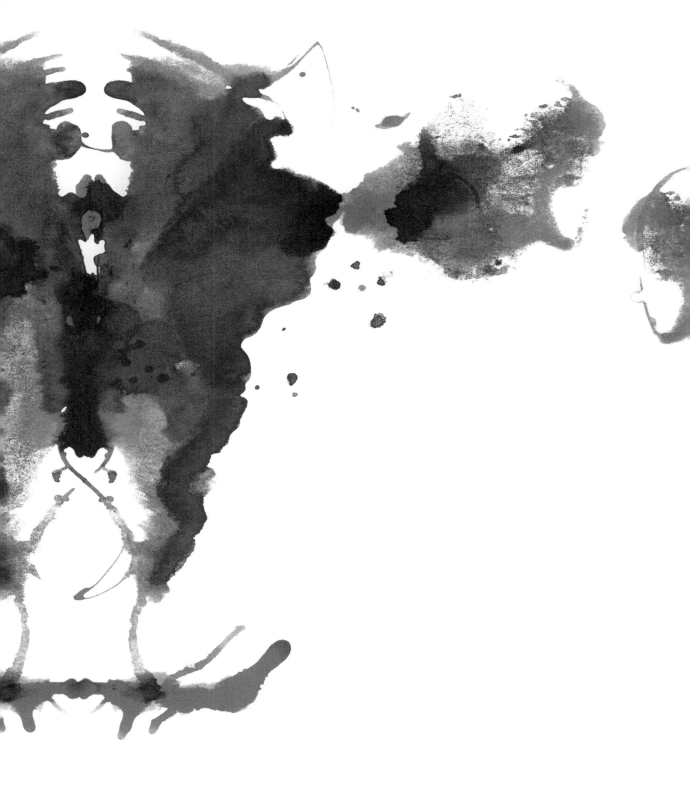

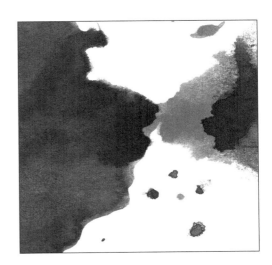

Chapter 1

INTRODUCTION TO MASHUPS

This chapter discusses how the Web has evolved into what you know today and how it has become a platform for applications and mashups.

A brief history of the Web

Before you begin looking at examples of mashups and what they can offer, it often helps to look back at the growth of the Web and the technological trends that have been significant in its development.

The origins of the Internet as it is today can be found in the Cold War era, which was a time when most people were more concerned about the threat of impending nuclear annihilation than the possibility of watching the antics of a skateboarding dog on YouTube.

This threat helped drive the development of interconnected computer networks and a communications infrastructure. During October 1969, the first node of ARPANET, an initiative by the U.S. Department of Defense and the grandfather of today's Internet, went online.

Over the next 20 years, networking efforts continued, with more mainframes and computers around the world being connected under a single networking infrastructure and with TCP/IP networking acting as a common communications protocol. At this time, the main users of these emergent computer networks were mainly the government and academic institutions, and they benefited from the ability to exchange data and transmit messages instantaneously.

> *TCP/IP stands for Transmission Control Protocol/Internet Protocol.*

One of the main drawbacks of this early "internet" was of course the technical barrier to entry—there were no web pages or e-mail clients; there were simply terminals where users typed commands, which demanded a certain level of technical savvy. This all changed in 1991, when researchers at CERN in Switzerland unveiled the World Wide Web, an application based on Tim Berners-Lee's work developing the Hyptertext Transfer Protocol (HTTP) and the Hypertext Markup Language (HTML). Nontechnical individuals could now browse through pages of information, with support for text formatting and images. This first web browser contained many familiar features that are still present in the browsers you use today, including browsing history and the Back and Forward buttons.

With the technical barrier to entry lifted, academia embraced the World Wide Web like never before. Sharing research papers and laboratory data was now easier than ever, and communities were brought together in ways never thought possible. Usenet, for example, brought together people from around the world with common interests and allowed for free discussion.

Through the early 1990s, the software improved, and interest continued to spread beyond the technical and academic communities. By 1996, the word **Internet** had become a household name, with businesses looking at ways through which they could use this emerging technology as a new medium to reach their customers.

Some companies simply created a basic home page that was a pointer to their offline operations. Others provided services—from simple mechanisms to communicate with new and existing customers to fully blown online shopping operations. And online advertising, in the form of basic banner ads, started appearing on the Web.

In the late 1990s, a new breed of company started to take advantage of this growth in public awareness—the start-up. Budding entrepreneurs were drawn to the Web because of the large amounts of venture capital available. Suddenly the market was flooded by masses of online-only companies that offered innovative products and services to customers worldwide. Within a few years, though, many had gone bankrupt.

One of the main reasons the dot-com boom went bust was not a lack of innovation but a lack of a feasible business model. Dot-com start-ups often operated on the "get big fast" principle, relying on investment to fund this growth. If the money ran out, then a fledgling company would soon find itself in trouble.

The other reason why many dot-coms failed has nothing to do with money at all. Simply put, the technology available could not support many of the more innovative ideas that were pitched, making it especially difficult to "get big fast." This can be broken down into two key areas:

- The battles fought between the two dominant web browsers, Microsoft Internet Explorer and Netscape Navigator, had left a legacy of incompatibility, which made it difficult to develop advanced web applications supported by compelling user interfaces. Ajax was not an option at this time, because it did not yet exist in a cross-browser form.

- Although the Internet existed, in many cases access to specific data was possible only from the site that owned the data. These isolated data stores meant that in the process of creating user experiences, developers often had to reinvent the wheel. For the user, it meant having to maintain copies of duplicate data across different online services.

Since the days of the dot-com boom, we have seen considerable change and growth. As of June 2007, approximately 1.13 billion people use the Internet (according to data from the Internet World Statistics website at http://www.internetworldstats.com/).

So, more than 1 billion people are connected. Although most of these people are located in the developed world, developing countries are seeing substantial growth in Internet usage as the infrastructure improves. Initiatives such as One Laptop Per Child (OLPC), run by MIT and backed by the likes of Google, will further contribute to this rapid growth—bringing the world closer together.

In addition, wireless connectivity is becoming more widely available and integrated into all manner of devices, from laptops to mobile phones to PDAs to fridges to beer mats! When traveling, you need not look any farther than the nearest Starbucks, where you can connect to the Internet over wi-fi and access your documents and e-mail. We are constantly connected, and the Internet has evolved into a ubiquitous platform that is ripe for innovation.

Of course, this is probably what investors and entrepreneurs thought during the dot-com boom, so what really has changed?

Ten years later, business models have been developed that have enabled many companies to prosper on the Web. Amazon is a prime example of this. But perhaps, more important, the technology environment has changed significantly:

- Web browsers are gaining maturity, and following the earlier "browser wars," vendors are now embracing open web standards rather than proprietary technologies. Although, as any web developer will tell you, things are still not perfect, they are moving in the right direction.

- The raw processing power of desktop computers has increased significantly, and custom hardware enables cinematic-quality visual effects to be rendered in real time. Developers can increasingly leverage these advances in order to create user experiences that significantly enhance the usability and learnability of an application.

- The Web is becoming an open platform that serves as an incubator for innovation. Increasingly, data sources are being opened up to developers. There is no need to reinvent the wheel, and data sharing is encouraged. We exist within a web of data, and our tools are APIs and code.

A web of data

Yahoo's Tom Coates coined the phrase "a web of data," using it to describe the current state of the Internet and the transition from many websites serving as isolated repositories of data to a much more interconnected model, which allows data to be shared and manipulated throughout the online ecosystem.

Imagine that you are the owner of a database full of restaurant addresses. You can display them in a list, sort them, filter them, and allow users to search through them; however, you cannot show your users where they are located on a map because you don't have any maps stored, and even if you did, you don't have the skills, time, or desire to create the logic that takes an address and pinpoints its exact location on a map.

Now say there's a second company that owns a wealth of mapping data that can be searched by address. Separately, you have two moderately useful websites; a user can search one, but in order to make sense of the data they find, they have to visit the second website.

Obviously, this is not the best experience from the user's perspective, because they need to visit two websites in order to find the information they need. When information is arranged in isolated silos, the user experience usually suffers.

If you examine the same scenario but with open data sources, you will see new possibilities for innovation. For instance, if the owner of the address data had access to mapping functionality, then they would be able to provide customers with customized maps for each address in the database.

The user would benefit because the information they are looking for is more readily available, without requiring visits to multiple websites. The benefits can work both ways, though; the owner of the mapping data might want to allow users to search for restaurants. A search term could be cross-referenced with restaurant names from the first database, and if there are any matches, then they could be displayed on the map.

And that is just the beginning.

Many developers have taken this much further, developing innovative new web applications by mixing different sets of data and functionality to create mashups.

Examples of mashups

> *"We don't have a corner on creativity. There are creative people around the world, hundreds of millions of them, and they are going to think of things to do with our basic platform that we didn't think of. So the mashup stuff is a wonderful way of allowing people to find new ways of applying the basic infrastructures we're propagating."*
>
> —*Vint Cerf, Google*

There are many different interpretations on what mashups are and what they mean for the Web, for innovation, and for creating value propositions for the user. In broad terms, a **mashup** is an application that consumes data from different sources and combines them in a single user experience. As you will see later, this can be in order to add value to the preexisting data or to take a more fun and creative slant.

In many ways, mashups offer a platform for innovation, where developers can demonstrate their talent and creativity without having to reinvent the wheel by accessing data sources that otherwise would not be available to them.

Although originally *mashups* was a term used to describe web applications that were built around one or more data sources, we are seeing them move from the web to the desktop as widget platforms and desktop technologies evolve. The concepts behind mashups, such as interacting with data sources, are being worked into applications that are available to run locally on the desktop.

Mashups present a great opportunity for web developers to innovate and demonstrate their creativity, with near limitless possibilities.

Data can be consumed from various sources, including the following:

- Public APIs
- Web services
- Data feeds (such as RSS)

Mashups have been embraced by many Internet companies, including Google, Yahoo, and Amazon, which have all provided various methods for developers to leverage the functionality of their web applications. Over the next few pages, you will see some of the most novel and innovative examples of mashups that are available on the Web.

Buzzword

http://www.buzzword.com/

Many users are deserting desktop applications and moving toward web applications for common functions such as e-mail and document creation.

In the past, this was somewhat limited because the experience that a web application can offer did not compare to the speed and quality of interaction provided by a desktop application; however, with the rise of client-side presentation technologies, Buzzword is a shining example of what is possible when you combine a powerful technology with the social and collaborative nature of the Web.

Recently purchased by Adobe, Buzzword is a web-based word processor written entirely in Flex, with full support for popular document formats and notable technical achievements such as an advanced text and document layout engine (see Figure 1-1).

Although not strictly a mash-up, Buzzword embodies many of the emerging social attributes of the Web, and at the same time sets the bar for client-side applications.

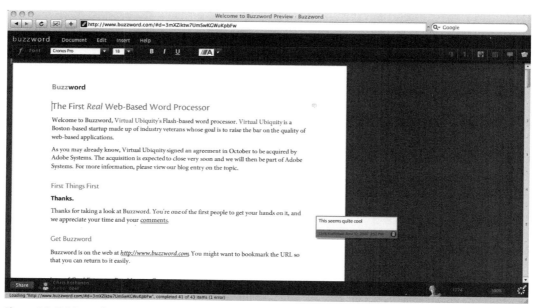

Figure 1-1. Editing a document in Buzzword

Picnik

http://www.picnik.com/

Following the trend of moving traditional desktop applications online, Picnik is a Flash-based application that allows you to edit photos and perform simple image-processing tasks all from the comfort of your web browser.

Recently, this functionality has been added to Flickr—you choose a photo, click the Edit Photo button, and edit your photos directly within the Picnik interface (see Figure 1-2).

Like Buzzword, Picnik demonstrates what is possible on the client side, as well as how web-based applications can be integrated with data sources as a mashup.

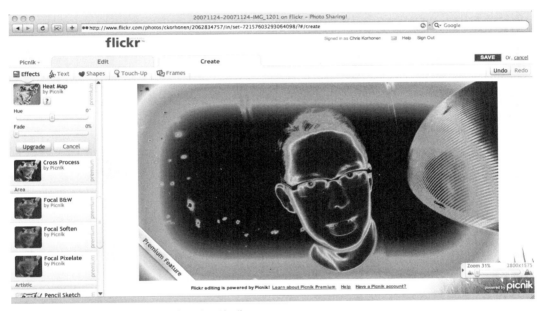

Figure 1-2. Editing a photo from Flickr, using Picnik

Chicago Crime

http://www.chicagocrime.org/

Ever wanted to find the safest route home after a late-night session in Chicago? If so, then Chicago Crime (see Figure 1-3) might be right up your street!

This classic mashup utilizes crime data from the Chicago Police Department and plots it on a searchable Google map (see Figure 1-4). Users can choose to view a particular geographic location or filter the results by crime type.

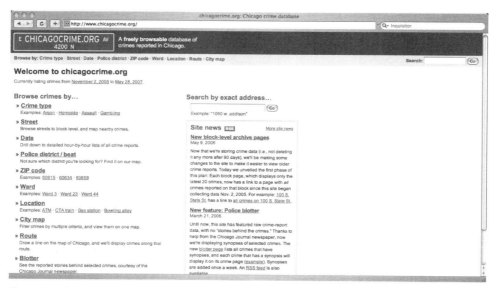

Figure 1-3. The main page of Chicago Crime, inviting the user to view data based on various parameters

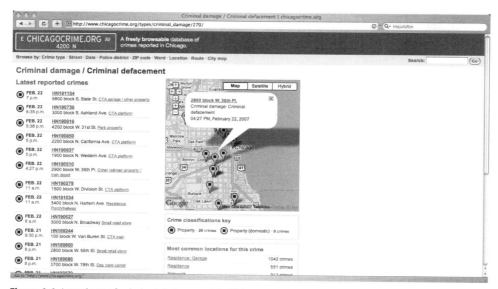

Figure 1-4. Locations of criminal defacement in Chicago

Flash Earth

        http://www.flashearth.com/

Flash Earth is an interesting example—rather than combining different types of data, it allows the user to choose between different sources of the same data (see Figure 1-5).

In this case, the application can retrieve data from the extensive collections of maps and aerial photos at Google, Yahoo, Microsoft, Ask.com, and NASA. As you would expect, a user is able to search and zoom (see Figure 1-6).

This mashup serves as a great tool for comparing the offerings from each of these data providers and for demonstrating the data-handling capabilities of Flash.

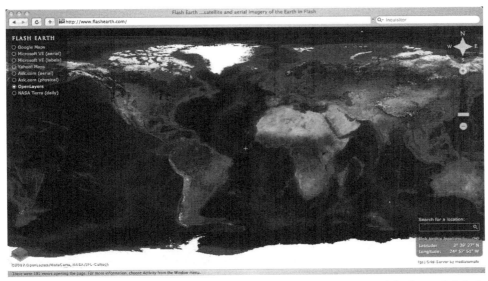

Figure 1-5. A bird's-eye view from the main screen of Flash Earth. Note the controls in the top left that allow the user to select their source of mapping data.

Figure 1-6. A zoomed-in view of central Brighton

Flappr

http://bcdef.org/flappr/

Flappr is built upon Flickr's APIs and is essentially an entirely new interface that can be used to access the photo-sharing website (see Figure 1-7).

This again demonstrates the impressive capabilities of Flash, transforming the user experience of viewing and browsing through large collections of photographs (see Figure 1-8).

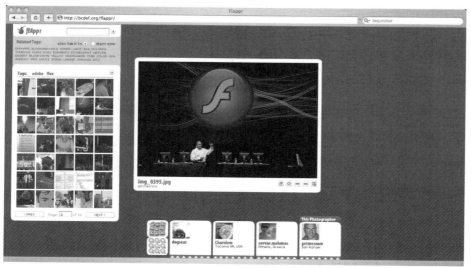

Figure 1-7. Flappr's alternative view on the data contained within Flickr

Figure 1-8. Browsing through a pile of photos

Flickr Sudoku

http://flickrsudoku.com/

Not all mashups need to be deadly serious. Flickr Sudoku demonstrates this, using Flickr photos as symbols on a Sudoku board (see Figure 1-9). Repurposing content in unexpected and often interesting ways is indicative of many of the innovative mashups found on the Web.

Figure 1-9. Flickr Sudoku

Adactio Elsewhere

http://elsewhere.adactio.com/

Have you ever wished you could collect all the information about a particular person in a one place? Well, JavaScript-guru Jeremy Keith has done just this. Adactio Elsewhere is a data aggregator that retrieves data of Jeremy's online activities from Flickr, Amazon, Del.icio.us, and Upcoming to name but a few (see Figure 1-10).

All this data is pulled from RSS feeds (Figure 1-11) or application APIs and presented in one easy-to-use, Ajax-powered user interface.

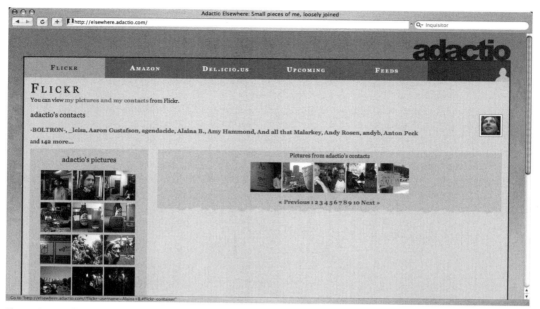

Figure 1-10. Adactio Elsewhere, aggregating an individual's many RSS and data feeds

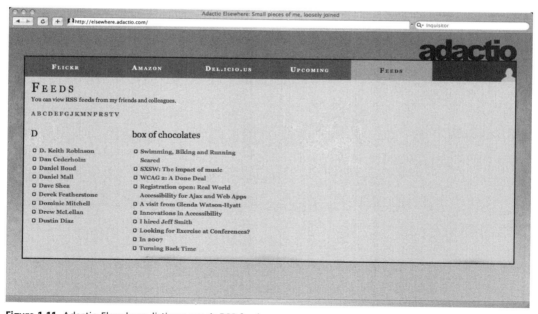

Figure 1-11. Adactio Elsewhere, listing a user's RSS feeds

Google offers a multitude of APIs for its range of web applications, including easy ways to integrate Google Maps and Google Search with your web applications.

Flickr, an online massively multiplayer photo-sharing website, gives developers almost complete access to its application functionality via APIs. From searching through photo collections to retrieving user profile data, the possibilities are endless.

Amazon has its entire product catalog accessible though various APIs. It also offers secure online storage and data processing services, which can be purchased as a commodity and consumed by your web applications by using web services.

Del.icio.us is a social bookmaking service with APIs that allow users to post and edit bookmarks. This data is organized and categorized through tags and can be syndicated as an RSS feed.

Opening your web application

Web application developers have several options when it comes to opening their application functionality and data to the hoards of mashup developers. Often, one of the simplest ways to facilitate the syndication and consumption of data is by publishing it as an RSS feed.

Feeds

RSS stands for Really Simple Syndication and is essentially an Extensible Markup Language (XML) document that conforms to a specific data schema. An RSS feed contains details of the feed publisher and can contain any number of items that correspond to web application data. This can include news stories, photos, listings, and much more.

The following is an example of an RSS feed:

```
<?xml version="1.0" encoding="ISO-8859-1"?>
<rss xmlns:media="http://search.yahoo.com/mrss/" version="2.0">
  <channel>
    <title>BBC News | Technology | UK Edition</title>
    <link>
        http://news.bbc.co.uk/go/rss/-/1/hi/technology/default.stm
    </link>
    <description>
        Visit BBC News for up-to-the-minute news, breaking news,
        video, audio and feature stories. BBC News provides
        trusted World and UK news as well as local and regional
        perspectives. Also entertainment, business, science,
        technology and health news.
    </description>
```

```
<language>en-gb</language>
<lastBuildDate>Mon, 25 Jun 2007 17:24:34 GMT</lastBuildDate>
<copyright>
    Copyright: (C) British Broadcasting Corporation, see
    http://news.bbc.co.uk/1/hi/help/rss/4498287.stm for terms
    and conditions of reuse
</copyright>
<docs>http://www.bbc.co.uk/syndication/</docs>
<ttl>15</ttl>
<image>
  <title>BBC News</title>
  <url>
    http://news.bbc.co.uk/nol/shared/img/bbc_news_120x60.gif
  </url>
  <link>
    http://news.bbc.co.uk/go/rss/-/1/hi/technology/default.stm
  </link>
</image>
<item>
  <title>Social sites reveal class divide</title>
  <description>
    Social networking sites are proving a good guide to
    socio-economic divisions in the US, reveals research.
  </description>
  <link>
    http://news.bbc.co.uk/go/rss/-/1/hi/technology/6236628.stm
  </link>
  <guid isPermaLink="false">
    http://news.bbc.co.uk/1/hi/technology/6236628.stm
  </guid>
  <pubDate>Mon, 25 Jun 2007 11:42:15 GMT</pubDate>
  <category>Technology</category>
</item>
<item>
  <title>Leader of net piracy gang jailed</title>
  <description>
    A Briton who operated a net piracy gang out of his
    Australian home is jailed in the US for 51 months.
  </description>
  <link>
    http://news.bbc.co.uk/go/rss/-/1/hi/technology/6237610.stm
  </link>
  <guid isPermaLink="false">
    http://news.bbc.co.uk/1/hi/technology/6237610.stm
  </guid>
  <pubDate>Mon, 25 Jun 2007 13:56:19 GMT</pubDate>
  <category>Technology</category>
</item>
<item>
```

```
      <title>California landing for Atlantis</title>
      <description>
        US space shuttle Atlantis touches down in California, after
        bad weather prevents a Florida landing.
      </description>
      <link>
        http://news.bbc.co.uk/go/rss/-/1/hi/sci/tech/6232320.stm
      </link>
      <guid isPermaLink="false">
        http://news.bbc.co.uk/1/hi/sci/tech/6232320.stm
      </guid>
      <pubDate>Fri, 22 Jun 2007 20:56:50 GMT</pubDate>
      <category>Science/Nature</category>
    </item>
    <item>
      <title>Computers 'can raise attainment'</title>
      <description>
        A study says high levels of computer technology can improve
        school results, but the picture is mixed.
      </description>
      <link>
        http://news.bbc.co.uk/go/rss/-/1/hi/education/6231704.stm
      </link>
      <guid isPermaLink="false">
        http://news.bbc.co.uk/1/hi/education/6231704.stm
      </guid>
      <pubDate>Sun, 24 Jun 2007 07:08:51 GMT</pubDate>
      <category>Education</category>
    </item>
    <item>
      <title>Yahoo sees advertising shake-up</title>
      <description>
        Yahoo is overhauling the way it sells advertising in the US,
        in an effort to help revive the business.
      </description>
      <link>
        http://news.bbc.co.uk/go/rss/-/1/hi/business/6236102.stm
      </link>
      <guid isPermaLink="false">
        http://news.bbc.co.uk/1/hi/business/6236102.stm
      </guid>
      <pubDate>Mon, 25 Jun 2007 06:45:30 GMT</pubDate>
      <category>Business</category>
    </item>
  </channel>
</rss>
```

This is an RSS feed from the BBC News website. The channel node contains information on the feed publisher including the feed name, description, associated URL, and published date. It also contains many <item> nodes that correspond to individual news stories, each with their own title, description, URL, category, and publication date. RSS feeds are often consumed by **aggregators**—desktop or web applications that monitor a list of feeds and present them within a single interfaces. Desktop examples include Newsfire, Sage, and NetNewsWire; the online equivalents are Google Reader and Jeremy Keith's Adactio Elsewhere. In addition, most major web browsers have built-in support for reading RSS feeds.

For users there is a clear benefit—rather than visiting multiple websites in order to keep updated with the day's events, you can simply subscribe to a number of feeds and view them together within a single interface.

Creating an RSS file is usually a process that can be automated within a given web application. For example, if you upload a new photo to a photo-sharing service such as Flickr, the application will store the photo in its database and at the same time update your home page and a separate RSS feed, reflecting the new content. An RSS aggregator would detect that a feed had been updated and download the update accordingly.

You can secure RSS feeds just like you can a regular web page, so for example if a feed contains sensitive data such as the contents of a user's inbox, then you can set it up to require a user to authenticate before viewing it.

Mashups take the concept of feed aggregation to the next level, with RSS providing a universally recognized format for data encoding. It negates the need for complicated, and often unreliable, techniques that essentially are performed by downloading an entire web page and attempting to extract specific pieces of data. This is often known as *screen scraping* and is often prone to error—if the content or structure of a page changes, then this data extraction is liable to fail. RSS and its standard data encoding hugely simplifies the use (and reuse) of data across different websites and applications.

> *As you work with RSS feeds, you will probably come across another type of feed, named Atom. Atom is another XML-based format for web feeds, and it addresses several of the shortcomings of the RSS specification. For all practical purposes of creating mashups, this is not something that developers need to worry about—both RSS and Atom feeds are XML documents and can be parsed in a straightforward manner.*

APIs

An application programming interface (API) is a way for third-party developers, in this case mashup authors, to leverage the functionality of another application. Usually when dealing with web applications, an API takes the form of well-specified functions that are accessible over a RESTful HTTP interface. In some cases, fully blown web services and SOAP messaging are used.

SOAP web services are based on an XML messaging format and allow for atomic elements of functionality to be exposed. Coupled with protocols that allow for service discovery and syndication, they were hyped as "the next big thing" and are commonplace in enterprise computing. Directories such as http://www.xmethods.net/ publish many of these services, which can be utilized by application developers, and many other derivative standards have been published and proposed around SOAP encompassing features such as the monetization of services and encrypted messaging.

Although promoted quite heavily in development environments such as Microsoft's .NET suite of products and languages, SOAP tends not to be used at the grassroots level by mashup authors—who instead see REST as the favored method of exposing application functionality, because it doesn't have much of the messaging overhead and complexity associated with SOAP.

The APIs you'll explore in this book are mostly REST-based, which is indicative of the majority of what is available.

> *A Representational State Transfer (REST) service is a model for web services based on HTTP, avoiding any extra overhead such as additional messaging formats or service descriptors. A REST service is represented as a URL and can be manipulated using standard HTTP GET, POST, PUT, and DELETE requests.*

API publishers usually provide application developers with formal API specifications that describe the methods available for usage, the required input parameters, and the outputs. These often provide access to functionality such as user authentication and the retrieval, creation, and modification of data within the application. For example, the Flickr API provides full functionality for searching through images and retrieving data (and metadata) associated with a single image.

For popular APIs, it is common to find third-party libraries that offer built-in support for given applications. These are often published as open source software, but you should review any licensing conditions before using them. For example, the Flickr API is documented extensively, providing support for multiple request/response formats including REST, JSON, and XML messaging (see Figure 1-12).

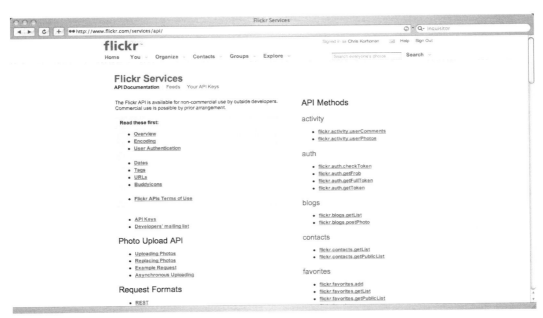

Figure 1-12. Some of the many API methods that are available to Flickr developers

The benefits of being open

Many companies and developers open their web applications, using a combination of APIs and RSS feeds, in order to create a platform upon which mashup developers can thrive. Depending on the web application, the reasons for this can be very different.

Innovation is encouraged

If you refer to the quote from Vint Cert earlier in this chapter, you can see that Google recognizes that it does not hold a monopoly on creativity. Many developers out there will, given the chance, find novel uses for data or functionality that the original programmers of an application may never have considered. An API gives programmers the tools to experiment and create new applications.

In some cases, this creative output can be fed back into the research and development process, stimulating new ideas and influencing the overall product direction. These ideas may be totally unexpected—I doubt that anyone in the Chicago Police Department anticipated seeing police reports plotted onto a Google Map!—and ultimately add considerable value to the data.

As a mashup developer, a lot of the fun lies in the ability to take different sets of data and create new views of that data. This could potentially add value; for example, by plotting information on a map, you add context that would otherwise be missing. Alternatively, combining data could ultimately provide a form of creative expression and entertainment.

Extended functionality

Following on from innovation, an API allows you to extend the functionality of a given web application, potentially in areas that might not be of interest to the application developers themselves but often are desired by a subset of the user base. For example, Housing Maps (http://www.housingmaps.com) extends the functionality of Craigslist, allowing classified advertisements to be viewed on a map.

Increased traffic

A mashup can often be the means though which people will be driven to a website or application. In fact, it could drive user registrations and ultimately increase the profile of the site in question. For example, the many mashups built around the Flickr feeds and APIs are a major factor in the site's popularity. Mashups help build brand awareness among the online community and often serve to differentiate websites from their competitors.

Often this can work both ways—if a respected brand launches an API interface to its services, then developers will be more inclined to check it out, compared to, say, a fledgling start-up. A good example of this is Amazon, and its various S3 web services, as a company renowned for integrity and reliability; its brand serves to reassure developers that its services are secure, scalable, and reliable.

In many cases, there are also opportunities for mashups to be embraced by the data provider themselves. For example, Flickr recently integrated the functionality of Picnik into its site—making it available to millions of users.

Communities

An API can be a way through which to develop a community around a particular web application. Just as you can see increased traffic by opening your application, you also get mashup developers flocking to your door. Embracing this can be crucial to the success of a web application because getting third-party developers to support an application can generate massive returns across the board.

If you look at social networking, sites such as Facebook and OpenSocial have been successful in developing huge communities of developers who are interested in building mashups and applications upon their platforms. This has really led to an explosion in functionality available to users and has also generated huge amounts of publicity.

Open data

Often, feeds and APIs serve a primary purpose—to allow access to the underlying data contained within an application. Offering this functionality promotes the principles of open data, giving the end user control of the data that is stored within your application. If they want, users can stop using the service and leave, taking all their data with them.

Alternatively, opening data tends to simplify data reuse across many different applications. If you look at the recent explosion of social networking websites, you'll see one major annoyance—the user is required to maintain the same profile data across multiple sites, so they end up having to spend additional time updating Facebook, MySpace, Bebo, and so on, each time they come across a new favorite song, for example!

APIs offer a means of decentralizing this, and already we are seeing examples of this; for example, the Facebook developer platform allows for easy mashups and integration with other data sources.

At the end of the day, yes, there is a risk that your users are perhaps less tied down to a single application, but surely this sets a challenge to developers to develop relevant and compelling applications that ultimately fulfill the needs of the user.

Internal mashups

Mashups also do not have to be public; instead, they can be inward-facing. By exposing the internal core services of an organization, you can make it easier for developers to build applications within a company's infrastructure and also simply reuse data across the enterprise. This can lead to significant cost savings and added value.

Yahoo takes this one step further with a concept called Hack Day. Simply put, a *hack day* is a day where employees are challenged to develop a prototype of an application and present it to their peers. Each application must utilize any number of the company's products, services, feeds, and APIs. Successful applications could potentially be developed into fully fledged products.

This approach to innovation helps breed creativity within the organization and serves to boost morale—giving developers the chance to do something fun for a day, outside of their normal duties and responsibilities.

Moneymaking opportunities

There is nothing set in stone that says an API should be freely available to everyone. If you are the owner of a data source that people are willing to pay to access, then there is nothing stopping you from exposing an API and requiring developers to pay for its usage.

In the United Kingdom, companies such as the Royal Mail have been doing this for many years; it allows other organizations to query its postal-code database for a small fee. Amazon also has adopted a similar model for its S3 (online file/data storage) service, charging users for disk space and bandwidth used.

Although the commoditization of data might not always be appropriate, it can be a dependable revenue source in those situations where it is.

Summary

In this chapter, you looked at the history of the Web and also saw how web application developers are opening their applications and data with APIs and data feeds. You also looked at the motivating factors behind this approach.

In the next chapter, you will learn about the technology choices you have when developing a mashup, and you'll take the first steps in mashup development.

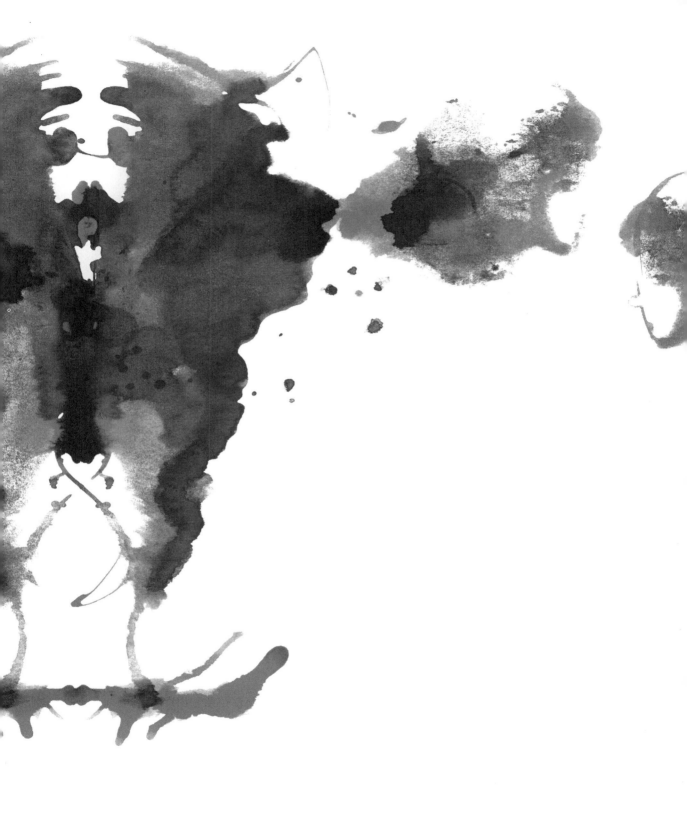

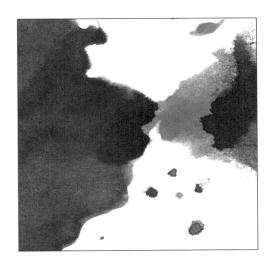

Chapter 2

TECHNOLOGIES TO MASH WITH!

In this chapter, you will look at the various technology options available to mashup developers when building mashups.

Web application development is not a simple task, as many a developer will attest. Back in the early days of the Web, the main challenge was maintaining page compatibility between Internet Explorer and Netscape. Over the past decade, we have seen pages evolve from static experiences to something much richer and more dynamic. With this evolution comes additional challenges and constraints that need to be considered when developing web applications.

The key issue to keep in mind is how a user is going to interact with your web application as you introduce richer functionality and new user interface paradigms. It is far too easy to get carried away with many of the client-side technologies that are available to developers, either by visually enhancing aspects of an application or by introducing dynamic data loading. At all stages, usability should be considered—what value does feature X add to the user? And conversely, how functional will an application be if a user is viewing it in a browser or on a device that does not support a certain technology?

If you look at the technology platforms that are used to deliver these rich web experiences, you will see two paths. On a foundation of Hypertext Markup Language (HTML) structure and Cascading Style Sheets (CSS) presentation, developers have embraced JavaScript as a means of delivering interactivity and rich functionality within the browser. In addition, plug-in technologies such as Adobe's Flash Platform are well regarded when it is necessary to deliver increasingly rich visual experiences to users.

Both of these technologies have their place when it comes to developing mashups and can be used to produce fantastic results, as evident in the examples you saw in Chapter 1.

Choosing whether to develop a mashup application using Flash or JavaScript is often a decision driven by the services you are looking to consume and the creative vision of what you are going to build. Secondary considerations might include the availability of server-side scripting, accessibility requirements, and usability.

Let's take a closer look at the available technologies so you can see the differences between them and what makes one more suitable to a certain requirement than another.

Working with JavaScript

Today, most websites tend to use JavaScript in order to add client-side interactivity and logic—whether it is simply to change the appearance of a button when the user hovers over it with their mouse or whether it is to create something much more complex such as an entire user interface in the vein of the Fluxiom web application (www.fluxiom.com; see Figure 2-1).

Figure 2-1. Fluxiom, online storage and media management

At the heart of Fluxiom is a scripting language based on the ECMAScript specification, with a syntax that should be familiar to anyone who has done any Java or ActionScript programming. The ECMAScript specification itself is an international standard, of which both JavaScript and ActionScript are dialects.

JavaScript is a universal technology, available in every major desktop browser and even on mobile devices such as the latest Nokia phones and, of course, the iPhone. Despite a spotted past of incompatibilities and proprietary functionality, the language has reached a point of maturity where it has become pretty much standardized in implementation, with various frameworks offering up conventions as to how developers should be using the language. The popularity of common component frameworks has also helped support its usage by developers across the Web.

Frameworks often provide developers with components and utility classes that can be leveraged when building more complex applications. They often reduce the amount of headaches that a developer has to deal with by implementing generic functionality such as object orientation, garbage collection, visual effects, and rich user interface components, while at the same time providing solutions to common cross-browser programming challenges (a diplomatic phrase for bugs!). This reduces development time and negates the need to reinvent the wheel when producing a simple web application.

Many frameworks are available, ranging from fully blown affairs encapsulating all of the utility functions that you will likely need when building a web application, including data communication and DOM manipulation, to simple reusable components that might implement a specific user interface element such as a slider or accordion. Depending on whom you ask, you will often get recommendations for different frameworks, and often their suitability will vary depending on the project. Of particular interest are MooTools (www.mootools.net) and jQuery (www.jquery.com); both provide a great deal of features given their small file size and offer exceptional performance.

In major projects, a framework is often considered essential, whether it be an off-the-shelf one such as those mentioned here or something homegrown. They often make larger projects more manageable, standardizing development and encouraging reuse.

The use of JavaScript in mashups is varied, because often it is necessary to augment it with server-side scripting that performs data aggregation and other pieces of logic/processing—both tasks that could have performance overhead if performed using JavaScript on the client. In these cases, JavaScript is used mainly to provide a rich, interactive user interface and to allow asynchronous communication with the server using the XmlHttpRequest object (a JavaScript object that is used to make asynchronous calls to a web server).

When developing more complex mashups using an HTML/CSS/JavaScript front-end, a server-side component to handle the aggregation of data from various sources or to store user preferences often becomes essential.

JavaScript also runs within a tight security model, restricting access to domains other than the one from which the script was loaded. There are ways around this; however, this can also impact connectivity with external application programming interfaces (APIs) and data services.

That said, it is possible to consume external data services using JavaScript as part of a web application with some creative workarounds. A good example of this is the incorporation of an interactive Google map within a web page.

Mashing Google Maps using JavaScript

Google provides a free API that allows developers to embed maps on web pages using JavaScript. Using this you can create a map of anywhere in the world and overlay it with additional data and functionality.

> You can take a look at the full Google Maps API reference at
> www.google.com/apis/maps.

You can use the Google Maps API for free provided you abide by the terms of service. The terms are pretty standard and place limits on traffic volumes (50,000 requests per day, per API key) and acceptable usage.

If you want to embed Google Maps on an intranet or nonpublic website, then Google offers an enterprise option for a fee.

To use the Google Maps API, you must register for a free API key. This is a straightforward process and is shown in Figure 2-2; you essentially have to agree to abide by the terms of service and also provide Google with details of the site where you want to use Google Maps.

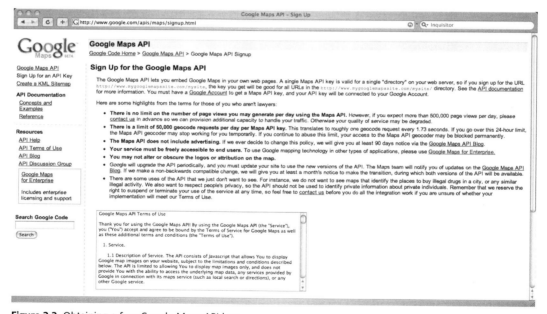

Figure 2-2. Obtaining a free Google Maps API key

It is worth noting that the API key is specific to a directory on your web server, so if you register with the URL www.mysite.com/maps, then the key will be valid only for pages within this directory or its subdirectories.

Once you have an API key, then you can begin creating your HTML page, with a header containing several items of JavaScript and the document body containing a simple heading and a <div> element that will contain the map:

```
<!DOCTYPE html PUBLIC "-//W3C//DTD XHTML 1.0 Transitional//EN"
        "http://www.w3.org/TR/xhtml1/DTD/xhtml1-transitional.dtd">

<html xmlns="http://www.w3.org/1999/xhtml" xml:lang="en" lang="en">
<head>
    <meta http-equiv="Content-Type" content="text/html; charset=utf-8"/>
    <title>Google Maps Example Page</title>
    <script src="http://maps.google.com/maps?file=api&amp;v=2&amp;
                    key=<KEY>" type="text/javascript"></script>
    <script type="text/javascript">

    function load(){
            if (GBrowserIsCompatible()) {
                var map = new GMap2(document.getElementById("map"));
                map.setCenter(new GLatLng(50.8333, -0.1333), 10);
            }
    }


    </script>
</head>
<body onload="load();">
    <h1>This is My Google Map!</h1>
    <div id="map" style="width:80%;height:500px;"></div>
</body>
</html>
```

This HTML page references the Google Maps JavaScript function:

```
<script src="http://maps.google.com/maps?file=api&amp;v=2&amp;
                key=<KEY>" type="text/javascript"></script>
```

For this to work, you should replace <KEY> with the API key that was provided during the registration process.

You will notice that this JavaScript code resides on Google's servers, rather than locally. This is true for two reasons—the first is that it allows Google to maintain control over its mapping functionality, ensuring that all sites using it are using the same version and not breaking the terms of use by providing a modified version of the code.

The second reason is because of technical constraints. Earlier in this chapter, we briefly touched upon the JavaScript security model and how you can make a request, using the XMLHttpRequest object, only to the server from which the JavaScript was originally served. If this code were hosted on a different web server, then it would not be able to asynchronously retrieve updated data or images as the user interacts with the map. By pulling this functionality from Google.com, it gets around this restriction and allows the free download of images and data.

The page's body contains a <div> element:

```
<div id="map" style="width:80%;height:500px;"></div>
```

This is simply a container into which the map will be placed. You can adjust the width and height of this container as required by your page design. In this example, you are simply defining a width of 80 percent and a height of 500 pixels.

With the necessary JavaScript loaded and the container element in place, you can now instantiate your Google map. If you examine the other <script> block within the page header, you can see you have an additional JavaScript function, which is called when the page is loaded:

```
function load(){
    if (GBrowserIsCompatible()) {
        var map = new GMap2(document.getElementById("map"));
        map.setCenter(new GLatLng(50.8333, -0.1333), 10);
    }
}
```

This function is using the GBrowserIsCompatible method provided by the Google Maps API to determine whether the user's browser is compatible.

Although the functionality of Google Maps is supported in most modern browsers, it is a good idea to include this check. If nothing else, it reminds you to ask the following question: "Do I need to provide an alternative experience for users who can't see the map?" This is perhaps a more important consideration if you anticipate that your site might be viewed using mobile devices or by users who are using assistive technologies or custom browsers.

If a user is using an incompatible browser, then that user will not see the map at all. In this instance, you might choose to display a message informing the user that their browser is not supported, if the map is at the core of the page functionality; or, you might just omit the map entirely, if it is simply being used to enhance the content of the page.

Next, you instantiate the Google map by calling the GMap2 method and passing it the element ID of the <div> container.

Before you can see the map on the page, you also need to provide a geographical location to use as a center point for displaying the map. You can do this by using the setCenter method and providing a location and a zoom level.

For this you use a GLatLng object—which contains a latitude and longitude coordinate. If you are looking for the coordinates of a specific location, such as New York City, you can usually obtain them from your favorite search engine.

If you do not specify a center point for the map, then you would simply see a gray rectangle on the page.

Figure 2-3 shows the end result of your efforts.

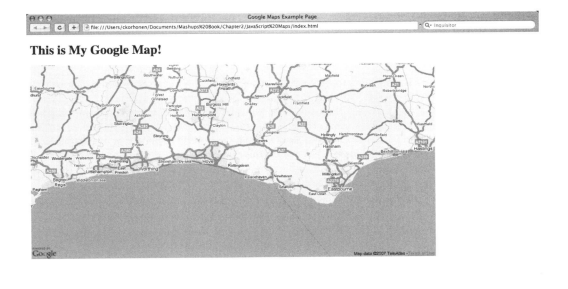

Figure 2-3. Your newly created Google map

Now that you have an interactive Google map, there are plenty of ways you could extend the functionality using the API and this example as a base.

For instance, you could do any of the following:

- You could add navigation controls that allow the user to pan/zoom.
- You could add markers to denote specific locations and provide further information in a clickable tooltip bubble.
- You could add custom icons to locations on the map.
- You could overlay information onto the map, such as location boundaries or paths.
- You could overlay information extracted from an RSS feed.
- You could add live traffic information to roads on the map.
- You could display driving directions between multiple points.

So far, we have touched on just a bit of the functionality offered by Google Maps; there is much more potential for developers to explore, especially when combined with other data sources and geographical data.

Simple mashups such as this can be very straightforward to implement and add a lot of value and usability to a given site. For example, when providing addresses, the addition of mapping functionality can provide value to users who want to locate a particular address. More sophisticated mashups could extend this and combine multiple data sources, such as taking event data from Upcoming (http://upcoming.org) and plotting venue locations on a map.

However, as you develop more complex mashup-based applications, it will become necessary to develop server-side logic and functionality in order to aggregate data and provide it to the client.

These are the key reasons for this:

- It keeps developers from having to deal with client-side cross-domain security restrictions that can restrict access to specific services and resources. For example, within JavaScript you can use the XmlHttpRequest object to make requests only to the same domain from which a JavaScript file originates. This places a reliance on code owned by the data provider or on the use of more nonstandard means of loading data. Similarly, in Flash applications, the data owner is required to provide a crossdomain.xml file on the remote server, specifically granting access to specific resources; without it, a Flash application cannot access data on a particular server. If the request is made on the server side, then these restrictions simply do not exist.

- It reduces the overhead on the user's processor. Because JavaScript code is interpreted and then executed on the client side, it is not well suited for CPU-intensive operations such as parsing large amounts of XML data. You cannot assume that all users have the latest CPUs and lots of memory, so you need to be careful to consider application performance.

In these situations where performance is a concern or where the developer does not have access to a web server that supports server-side scripting, then it might be prudent to consider other technology directions for your mashup.

Working with Flash

Flash is a platform upon which developers can produce and distribute multimedia content, such as web applications, games, and movies. Flash has been around for more than ten years and is currently owned by Adobe Systems following its 2005 merger with Macromedia.

Flash can be a very expressive medium, traditionally being used to create graphically rich movies and interactive experiences. It is also popularly used to create and deliver online advertising.

More recently, the Flash platform has gained popularity as a means to integrate video into web pages by using Flash Video (FLV) and also as a platform used to develop rich Internet applications (RIAs).

Adobe is currently shipping version 9 of Flash Player, as well as Adobe Flash CS3—a version of the developer environment that can be used to create content that takes advantage of the new features of the player, including the new ActionScript 3.0 scripting language that offers huge performance gains over ActionScript 2.0.

To view Flash content, users must have Flash Player installed on their systems. This is a fairly small download by today's standards and offers support to all major web browsers on Windows, Mac OS, and Linux platforms.

Unlike other web browser plug-ins, Flash Player has one major advantage—its ubiquity. It is a very mature platform that has widespread adoption. Statistics published by Adobe indicate that more than 98 percent of computers have a version of the player installed, and more than 90 percent of these are Flash Player 9, the latest major version.

This means that developers can produce content safe in the knowledge that they are not going to be excluding a large proportion of their audience. However, as any good web developer is keen to point out, it is always important to consider the experience that users without Flash Player will have.

> *Traditionally, there has been a lot of prejudice against the usage of Flash on the Web. Although some of this is deserved (because of the many unnecessary and gratuitous usages of Flash to deliver irrelevant and obtrusive intro animations and functionality), this is by no means representative of all Flash applications. Certainly not all developers are about swirly animations rather than the user experience!*

Under the hood

In early versions of Flash, developers were limited to timeline animation when it came to adding interactivity to their applications. In more recent releases, increased scripting support has been incorporated using a language called ActionScript.

Like JavaScript, ActionScript is based upon the ECMAScript specification. Both languages share a similar syntax, making it easy for developers to alternate between the two.

Within Flash, ActionScript is designed to be asynchronous, allowing multiple lines of code to be executed concurrently and using callbacks in order to pass data. A developer can define custom events and assign them to be dispatched during code execution, and listeners are assigned to monitor the application for events and to execute the appropriate code block.

You can create ActionScript using a simple text editor; however, the Flash integrated development environment (IDE) offers additional functionality such as syntax highlighting, code autocompletion, compiler integration, and a language reference. In addition, third-party IDEs such as FDT, FlashDevelop (see Figure 2-4), and SEPY offer ActionScript-specific support and functionality beyond what's found in the Flash IDE.

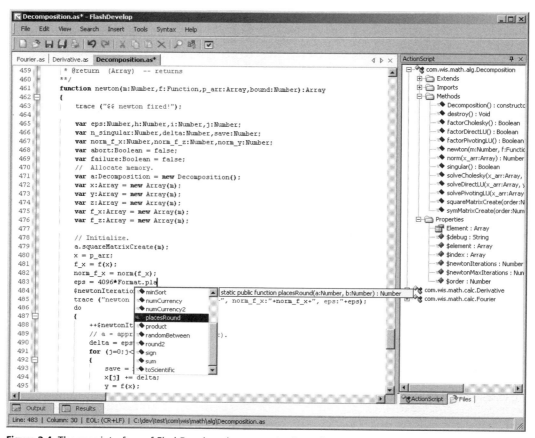

Figure 2-4. The user interface of FlashDevelop, demonstrating its code completion functionality

With the release of Flash Player 9, ActionScript made the jump from version 2.0 to version 3.0. This represented a major overhaul of the language's syntax and structure. In addition, ActionScript 3.0 uses a new compiler that transforms your ActionScript code into byte code and a new virtual machine in which the byte code is executed.

ActionScript 3.0 can offer developers a massive performance boost, offering performance approximately ten times faster than the equivalent ActionScript 2.0 code. In addition, it offers support for runtime exceptions, type checking, data types, and regular expressions—all functionality that aids developers when creating rich Internet applications and mashups that rely heavily on client-side data processing and visualizations.

There is also a vastly enhanced XML parsing engine, E4X, which reduces the complexity and lines of code required to manipulate XML documents.

Working with data

Flash offers many options when it comes to working with external data sources such as web services. XML is natively supported in both ActionScript 2.0 and 3.0. In addition, there are many other data formats that a developer can use when working with data:

- LoadVar objects, which consist of variable names and values, can be used when dealing with simple text strings.
- JSON, a method of encapsulating text and numerical data within native JavaScript objects, is perfectly usable within Flash, and its parsing is straightforward because of the shared ECMAScript syntax.
- ActionScript 3.0 is capable of directly manipulating binary data.
- Other techniques, such as SWX, which we will cover later in the book, provide a way of essentially serializing Flash objects and communicating data as a SWF, eliminating any parsing overhead.

Compared to JavaScript, Flash is also a lot more flexible when it comes to loading cross-domain files and resources, while also running within a security sandbox that mitigates most security risks. Imagine a Flash application hosted on www.mydomain.com. During the course of its execution, it makes an attempt to call a data service located at www.datadomain.com/services/myservice. Before the call is made, Flash Player makes an additional call to a cross-domain security file, www.datadomain.com/crossdomain.xml. This is a file that can be used to specify whether requests from a Flash application hosted on a specific domain are allowed to access resources on the web server.

For example, if you wanted to allow any application to use your service, you would create a crossdomain.xml file that looked like this:

```
<?xml version="1.0"?>
<cross-domain-policy>
  <allow-access-from domain="*" />
</cross-domain-policy>
```

You could also restrict access to your service so that it could be accessed only from applications on mydomain.com, like this:

```
<?xml version="1.0"?>
<cross-domain-policy>
  <allow-access-from domain="*.mydomain.com" />
</cross-domain-policy>
```

If a crossdomain.xml file does not exist or does not permit access, then any calls to that domain would not be made.

By default, Flash Player looks at the root of a given domain for the crossdomain.xml file. If the file is located in a different location, then you need to explicitly specify this in your ActionScript code during the initialization of your application using the following syntax:

```
Security.loadPolicyFile("http://www.domain.com/path/to/
    crossdomain.xml");
```

Unfortunately, this method returns no feedback as to whether the policy file has been loaded and access is allowed.

In the context of mashups, Flash can provide the developer with many opportunities for creating applications that are rich in both data and functionality. It is more flexible in the various ways that data can be aggregated, and although sometimes a hindrance, the cross-domain data-loading policies offer a less restrictive solution than technologies such as JavaScript.

Flash does present additional challenges. Specifically, if you are developing content for Flash Player, then you might be limiting your user base. It is also important to fully consider the usability of your application and how it fits within the standards and best practices for developing web application front-ends.

Working with Flex

Flex is a framework for developing rich Internet applications, and it is built around ActionScript 3.0 and Flash Player 9, currently version 3. The object of Flex is to provide functionality that allows developers to quickly and easily build rich applications that can be deployed on the Internet, while still allowing access to the expressiveness and visual capabilities of Flash.

The framework supports an XML-based language called MXML that can be used in the specification and development of user interfaces. To support this, it offers a wide variety of prebuilt UI components including buttons, text fields, data grids, graphs/charts, and components supporting drag-and-drop.

Other features also allow the developer to consume web services and work with XML data with ease. This gives the developer a powerful platform upon which they can mash up web services and create entirely new applications.

On the application architecture side, the move to ActionScript 3.0 and features such as the event-handling model allow for the development of much more well-structured and maintainable applications, leveraging industry-standard design patterns and architectural practices.

Flex applications can be developed either by using freely available command-line tools that are distributed as part of the Flex SDK or by using Adobe's commercially licensed Flex Builder (see Figure 2-5)—an IDE built upon the open source Eclipse platform.

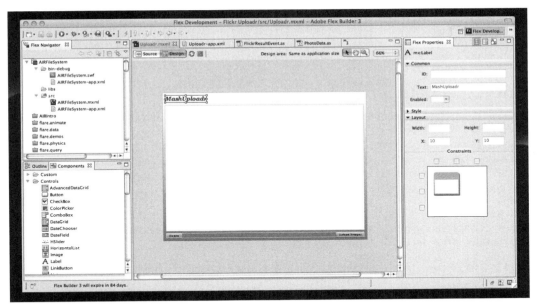

Figure 2-5. The Flex Builder IDE

Working with the Adobe Flash Platform

Flash and Flex are part of a much bigger picture when it comes to Adobe's long-term product strategy. Also part of this strategy is the Adobe Integrated Runtime (AIR), which we will cover later in this book.

This strategy comprises five key elements:

- Universal formats, including HTML, SWF, and PDF, with cross-platform reach and extending across many different operating systems and devices. This is not necessarily confined to the web browser, with the AIR platform serving as one example of liberating applications from the confines of the browser and making them available on the desktop.

- Platform abstraction, allowing for predictable application behavior and performance across all platforms, rather than other technologies that place dependencies on particular web browsers and platforms.

- Server-side applications, providing capabilities that can be leveraged by client applications in order to aid the development of compelling data-driven experiences.

- Extensive development tools, which are designed to integrate with design and development workflows, optimizing the production and development process.

- A sizable and enthusiastic community of designers and developers located around the world.

All these elements together go a long way to ensure that the Flash Platform is a stable and lucrative platform for developers that offers many opportunities to develop great applications and experiences.

Supporting products

Several supporting products are available as part of Adobe's Flash Platform that, depending on your requirements, might be worth considering when developing your Flash, Flex, and AIR-based applications.

Flex LiveCycle Data Services

This is an optional component that can be used to develop Flex applications that rely heavily on data stored on an application tier. Flex LiveCycle Data Services can be deployed on a Java 2 Enterprise Edition (J2EE) application server, and it supports many forms of data synchronization, including remote data push—where the server sends data to the client, rather than the client polling the server for updates, which can be very bandwidth intensive. Also included is built-in support for offline applications and occasionally connected clients.

Flex LiveCycle Data Services is licensed per CPU and can be a pricey option for smaller applications; however, enterprise customers might find this a more attractive option because they are more likely to use a selection of features.

When should you use it? When you are building a data-intensive application where performance is a high priority.

Any alternatives? If performance is less important, it might be worth looking at Flash Remoting (covered in a moment) or some of the open source alternatives such as Granite Data Services (http://sourceforge.net/projects/granite/).

Flex Charting

Flex Charting can be separately licensed from Adobe for a relatively small fee. It integrates with Flex Builder to provide a library of rich charting components that can be used to provide interactive data visualizations. These can be styled as required using CSS and extended to create totally new types of chart.

When should you use it? When you have the requirement to present data as a graph or chart.

Any alternatives? You can find some third-party components if you look around; however, few offer the same levels of customization.

Flash Media Server

Flash Media Server is Adobe's solution to the provision of streaming audio and video content, offering advanced features such as support for interactive and on-demand content. There is also support for live broadcasts and conferencing.

When should you use it? When you have a need to provide large volumes of streaming media. If you are simply integrating a few FLV files, then Flash Media Server might not be an economically variable option when you consider the features that are not being used.

Any alternatives? Red5 (http://osflash.org/red5) is a fully featured open source alternative.

Flash Remoting

When developing rich Internet applications, you often need to retrieve data from a web application server—this is where Flash Remoting comes in, allowing you to integrate with ColdFusion, .NET, Java, and SOAP services on your server. It simplifies the development of XML-based messaging services and offers fairly decent performance; in addition, it offers the AMF protocol, which is a way of serializing data and transmitting it to clients, with significant performance advantages over straight XML.

In many ways, this is the little brother to LiveCycle Data Services—with a much smaller price tag and a feature set that reflects this.

When should you use it? When you are developing a data-driven rich Internet application but do not have the volumes of data or requirements to justify the added price tag.

Any alternatives? OpenAMF is a good J2EE-based solution. Libraries are also available for popular languages such as PHP, Ruby, Perl, Python, and .NET. You can find many alternatives on the open source Flash website (http://osflash.org).

Cairngorm

Cairngorm is an ActionScript 2.0 and 3.0 framework that can be used to build more complex Flash and Flex applications. It is based upon industry-standard programming design practices and provides a robust Model-View-Controller (MVC) architecture to build upon.

When should you use it? When you are tasked to build a fairly large application, Cairngorm can help you build something that is architecturally sound.

Any alternatives? Many open source pattern-based frameworks exist; however, few offer mature Flex support. Of particular note is PureMVC (http://puremvc.org), an ActionScript 3–based framework that is emerging as a serious competitor for Cairngorm. For ActionScript 2.0 development, it might be worth looking at ARP (http://osflash.org/arp), developed by Flash guru Aral Balkan.

Adobe Creative Suite

Adobe Creative Suite is a complete family of development tools including Flash, Photoshop, Dreamweaver, Illustrator, After Effects, and Acrobat. It's essentially all you will ever need, and then some, if you work in the field of creative design and web/print/video production!

Since Adobe acquired Macromedia, great advances have been made in terms of product integration—all of these applications come together to allow for streamlined workflows. For example, a designer could sketch something using Photoshop, convert it to a vector graphic using Illustrator, and then import it directly into Flash with any layers left intact.

When should you use it? All of the time!

Any alternatives? There are certainly a host of alternatives, from free software such as GIMP to more commercial offerings. The downside, especially compared to Creative Suite 3, is that they tend to lack the same level of product integration.

A plethora of other software can support Flash and Flex development, whether it is components, development tools, or server-side applications. Happily, there is a thriving open source movement within the Flash community that can be accessed at http://osflash.org.

Choosing a technology

So, you've seen the technology choices developers have when building web-based applications such as mashups. In the red corner, we have JavaScript, supported by a jubilant crowd of developers and designers. In the blue corner, we have Flash, supported by its brother, Flex, which is supported by a slightly smaller but similarly enthusiastic crowd composed of designers and developers, with a few artists thrown in for good measure. If this were a Harry Potter book, I'm sure Voldemort would also be lurking around somewhere, but the right choice really depends on what you want to do. If you are working with large volumes of data, complex visualizations, or video/audio content, then Flash/Flex might be the perfect solution for you. If you are consuming data feeds but not doing anything too complex with them, such as aggregating and presenting Flickr photos and other widgets in a blog sidebar, then JavaScript might be the answer. The same goes if accessibility is a concern.

Of course, there is also nothing wrong with using a combination of both. This has been done to great effect by companies such as Google with its Finance application (Figure 2-6). Table 2-1 compares the JavaScript and Flash-based solutions.

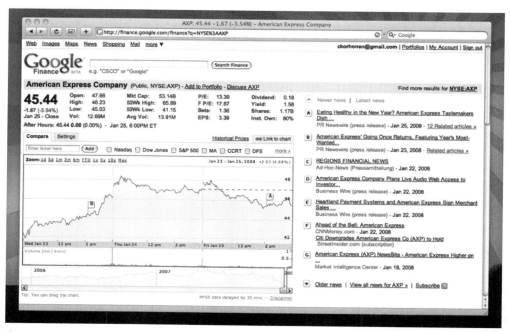

Figure 2-6. Google Finance, showing off JavaScript's power of DOM manipulation and Flash's rich data visualization capabilities

Table 2-1. Feature Comparison of JavaScript and Flash-Based Solutions

Feature	JavaScript/Ajax	Flash/Flex
Development tools	Text editor, dedicated IDEs available.	Flash CS3, Flex Builder. Third-party alternatives available.
Data formats	JSON, HTML, XML.	JSON, XML, AMF, and more.
Communication	HTTP.	HTTP, Binary (with Flex).
Security	Runs in browser sandbox.	Runs in browser sandbox; support for cross-domain communication.
Ubiquity	Supported in most desktop browsers and some mobile clients.	Flash Player has more than 95 percent desktop penetration.
Browser compatibility	Different browsers may require code workarounds and "hacks."	Flash content will behave consistently cross-platform.
Performance	Dependent on browser; generally lots of room to optimize download time, but client-side processing is often a bottleneck because of JavaScript performance.	Often larger initial download size but much greater performance when working with large data sets and processing-intensive operations.
Components	Dependent on framework being used.	Large selection of visual and nonvisual components.
Search engines	Data and semantic structure of a page is exposed to search engines.	Limited indexing takes place; for effective SEO, data should be exposed in the HTML of the page.
Accessibility	Yes.	Yes.
Video	No.	Flash is becoming the standard for delivering video content.
Audio	Limited.	Yes.

If you choose to develop a Flash-based application, another decision awaits you. Do you look toward Flash or Flex? The answer to this often depends on your user base, specifically on the versions of Flash Player they use. Flex and ActionScript 3.0 both require version 9 of Flash Player, which at the time of this writing has a penetration rate of about 80 percent. This means one in five visitors to your application wouldn't be able to use it properly.

> *It is often worth considering the user experience for those users without Flash when developing your application. Are you going to provide alternative content or a pointer to the Adobe website where they can download the player?*
>
> *Similarly, what kind of experience will you provide for users who do not have the latest version of the player? Using the ExpressInstall feature of Flash Player, it is possible to trigger an autoupdate of the user's player without taking them away from your site. This experience can even be customized to the look and feel of your site, making the upgrade painless and seamless!*
>
> *With AIR, Adobe's desktop platform, the process of installing an application can be just as painless, with Flash Player acting as a delivery platform for installing the runtime and applications from within the web browser. You'll learn more about this later in the book.*

Flex (or ActionScript 3.0–based applications) provides many advantages in terms of application performance, data integration, rich user interface components, and functionality. As a result, it can often be the preferred choice for a web application; however, it does add a significant file size overhead to your application (the Flex framework adds about 270KB to a SWF file).

For users, this will often mean a longer load time before they can begin interacting with an application. However, this can often be managed by providing preloader animations, which gives the user visual feedback that the application is loading, and other forms of smoke and mirrors.

Adobe is specifically aware of the file size overhead that the Flex framework presents, and as a remedy to this, the latest release of Flash Player 9 offers functionality that will automatically cache the core framework libraries following the initial download. These cached libraries can then be used with any other Flex application that the user views, meaning that only application-specific code and assets are downloaded—dramatically reducing load times.

Summary

In this chapter, you looked at each of the technology options at your disposal, comparing and contrasting them against various application requirements. Specifically, you saw when JavaScript might be preferable to Flash or Flex or when it simply does not provide the capabilities or flexibility to support more complex mashups. A key consideration when making these kinds of technology decisions should ultimately be the kind of user experience that each technology can offer, because this often makes or breaks an application.

You also looked at the wealth of complementary products available, both commercially and as open source. These can offer enhanced functionality for working with data in a more optimal manner, thus increasing the performance of your application; or they can offer prebuilt components that can be used to create more immersive and interactive user interfaces.

In the next chapter, you will get your hands dirty, creating your first Flex application mashup!

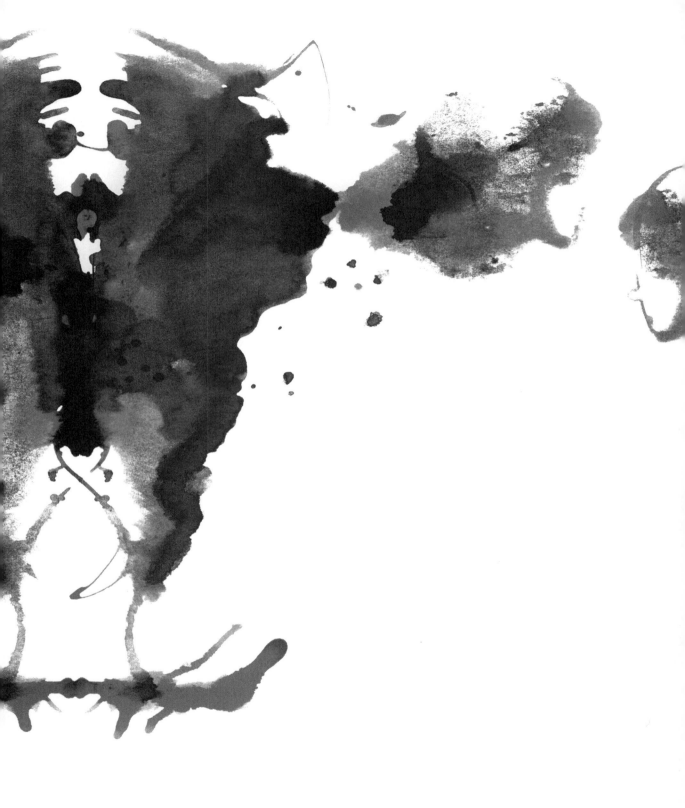

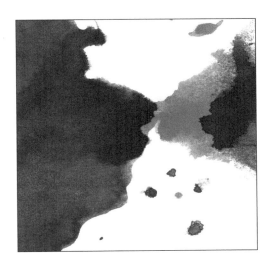

Chapter 3

AN INTRODUCTION TO FLEX

Before we begin talking about advanced concepts when building rich Flex-based mashups, we'll cover some of the functionality offered and the steps through which you can build a simple application using Flex 3, the latest release of the Flex framework and the Flex Builder integrated development environment (IDE). Since Flex 2, Adobe has focused on providing an environment for developing rich Internet applications that run inside Flash Player, even for developers who might not familiar with the animation and graphical metaphors used in Flash.

The Flex 3 framework, built around ActionScript 3.0, provides common components and functionality that can be used as a basis for developing applications. Although much of the framework functionality from previous versions remains the same, numerous evolutionary enhancements and additional features expand the toolset and make it possible to develop new types of applications.

Some of these enhancements include the following:

- **Support for building AIR applications**, which can run on the desktop, breaking free of the web browser. We will cover these later in the book.

- **Enhanced skinning and styling support**, giving the developer even greater control when visually customizing user interface components. Flex 3 adds CSS Design view, which helps streamline the customization workflow, as well as support for visual elements such as stateful component skins, which use the transitions available within the framework. The removes the need to create images or SWFs for each state.

- **More components**, especially for working with data. The DataGrid component has been enhanced, and there is a variant that supports OLAP queries, which are designed to make the slicing and dicing of data quick and straightforward for the end user. This in turn significantly enhances the built-in data analysis capabilities of Flex.

- **Developer tools**, including new performance and memory profilers that allow you to track the system resource utilization of your applications and discover opportunities for performance optimization.

- **Runtime localization**. Rather than creating multiple versions of an application or using external data files for different languages, you now can use the Resource Manager to manage your locales and ensure that data bindings remain linked to your content.

- **Performance enhancements**, which improve execution speed and reduce memory usage.

Building a Flex application

As a way of introducing Flex and many of the development concepts, we'll show you how to build a small application. As we go along, we will cover the relevant technologies and framework functionality, and in later chapters we will cover in more detail some of the specific features of Flex when it comes to building larger and more complex mashups.

This example uses Flex Builder to build the application. Adobe also provides the Flex SDK (http://labs.adobe.com/technologies/flex/sdk/) as a freely available download from its website; you can use the SDK in conjunction with any other IDE to compile your Flex applications should you not want to use Flex Builder. In addition, if you already use Eclipse as your IDE, Flex Builder is available as a stand-alone plug-in; you can install it using the Flex Builder installer.

For the example application, you'll learn how to build a simple front-end for Twitter, a web application whose API is fast becoming a form of "Hello World" for the web!

> *Twitter (http://www.twitter.com) is a social web application built around the premise of personal status (see Figure 3-1). It asks a simple question—"What are you doing?"—and provides an input box for a response. Updates are then shared with a user's friends via the website, by RSS feeds, or by text or instant messaging. Twitter allows groups of friends to keep track of what each other is doing and also provides a mechanism for social interaction where someone solicits information or asks a question and friends and followers respond.*

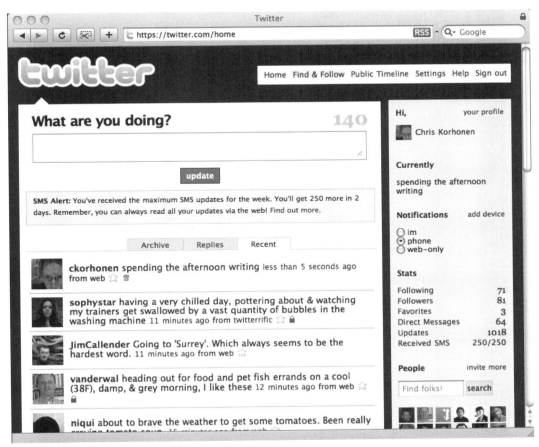

Figure 3-1. The Twitter home page, showing latest updates from friends

For the example application that you will build in this chapter, you'll want to display the list of updates from a set of friends. This data is provided as an RSS feed, which you will consume.

Creating a new Flex project

The first step is to create a new Flex project, so select File ➤ New ➤ Flex Project. When the New Flex Project Wizard appears, you need to give the project a name and a path (see Figure 3-2). Leave the other options alone for now.

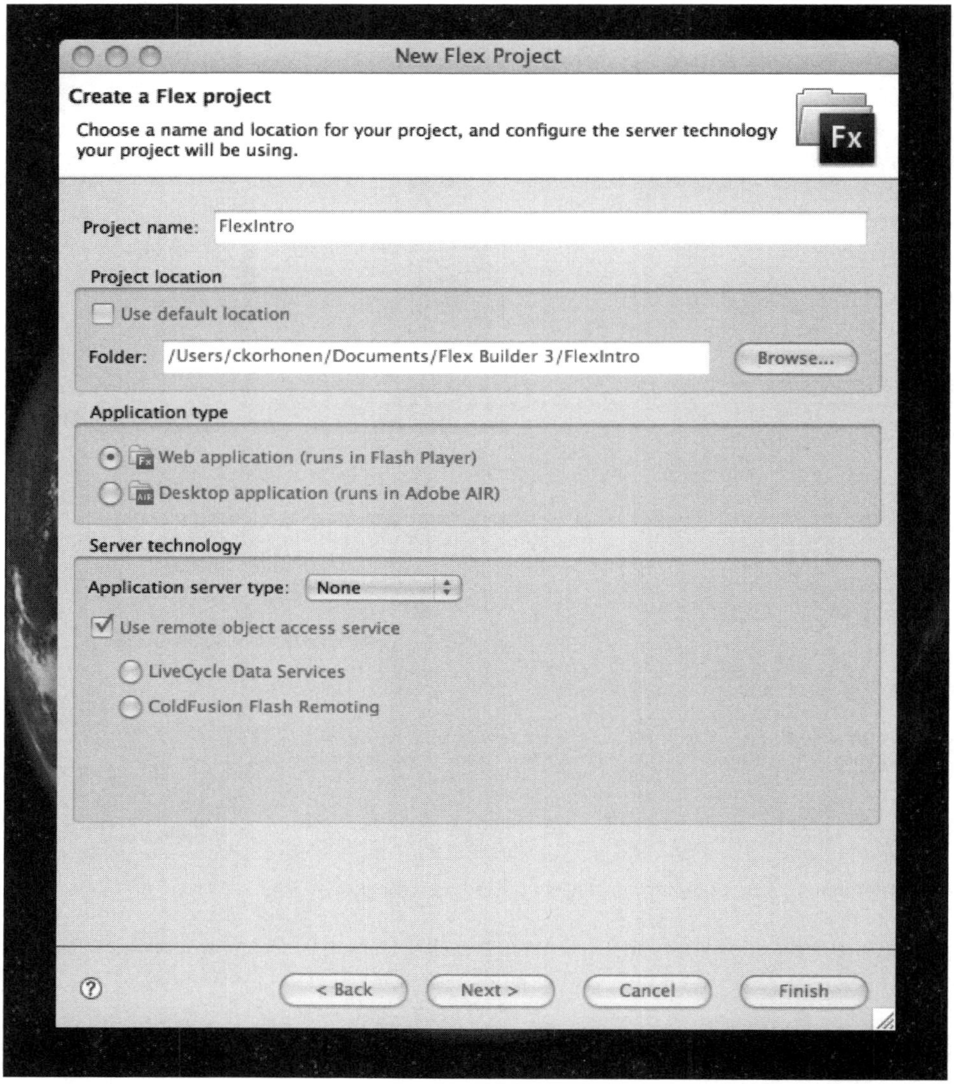

Figure 3-2. Creating a new Flex project

> It's worth noting that as of Flex 3, spaces in project names are no longer permitted as they were in Flex 2. This is worth keeping in mind if you are attempting to set up an existing Flex 2 project in version 3.

Click Finish, and Flex Builder will generate the directory structure for your application.

If you examine the directory structure, you will see several files and folders that have been created (see Figure 3-3):

- **bin**: This is the directory where the compiled version of your application is generated, including the SWF file and any HTML and JavaScript assets.

- **html-template**: Surprisingly enough, this is the HTML template for your application. You can customize this depending on your needs, or you can simply ignore this and incorporate the generated SWF file into your own pages.

- **libs**: This directory contains any code libraries specified during project creation.

- **src**: This directory contains your application source code, and you will be working from it as you proceed through this chapter.

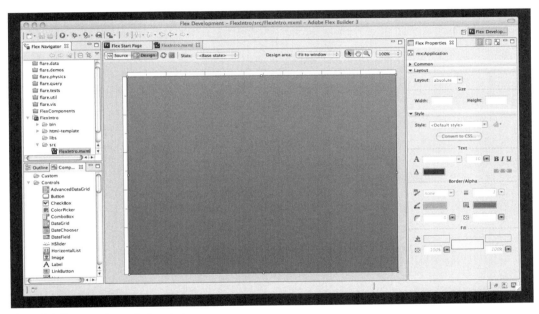

Figure 3-3. Your newly created project

Defining your application

In the src directory, you will see a file named `<project name>.mxml`. This is your application definition file. If you switch from Design view to Source view within Flex Builder, you should see this code:

```
<?xml version="1.0" encoding="utf-8"?>
<mx:Application xmlns:mx="http://www.adobe.com/2006/mxml"
                         layout="absolute">

</mx:Application>
```

> *MXML is an XML-based markup language used to define the user interface of Flex applications.*

In Design view, you can begin defining your application's user interface. From the Component panel, drag a Label component and a List component onto the canvas. The label is simply going to function as a title for your application. You can style it using the Property Inspector and then position it appropriately.

The list is going to be populated with Twitter updates when the application is initialized. So, make the list fairly large, and tweak the layout properties so that the component will always be a set distance from the sides of the application. This ensures that the layout does not break down visually as the application is scaled.

One final step before you are done with the initial layout is to give the list an id attribute in the Property Inspector. You do this simply by adding id="tweets" to the components' tag.

Assigning an id attribute to any object or component allows you to reference it later from your ActionScript code; otherwise, you have no easy way of referencing it. Generally, an identifier should be a unique string, similar to a variable name, and should not be used to identify any other component within the application.

You should now have something that looks like Figure 3-4, and if you switch to Source view, you can see your updated MXML:

```
<?xml version="1.0" encoding="utf-8"?>
<mx:Application xmlns:mx="http://www.adobe.com/2006/mxml"
                        layout="absolute">
    <mx:Label x="10" y="10" text="My Super Twitter Application!"
                    fontFamily="Arial" fontWeight="bold"
                    fontSize="15"/>
    <mx:List left="10" right="10" top="41" bottom="10" id="tweets">
    </mx:List>

</mx:Application>
```

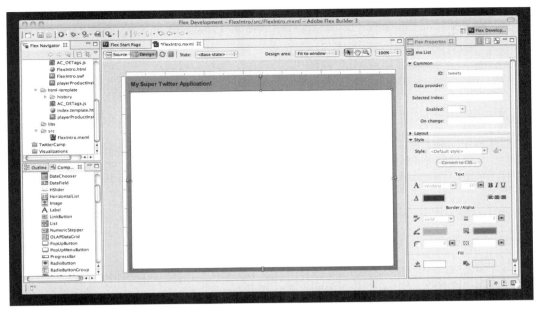

Figure 3-4. The initial user interface, displayed within the Flex Builder IDE in Design view

Integrating your data

Twitter conveniently provides an RSS feed with a user's latest updates together with their friends' updates. In addition, Twitter provides several API methods for interacting with Twitter services, which you will look at later in this chapter. Right now, let's look at how you bring an RSS feed into your application.

Flex provides an HTTPService component that allows for HTTP requests to be made and response data to be retrieved. To use it, switch to Source view, and define it in your MXML file within your <mx:Application> tags:

```
<mx:HTTPService id="twitterFeed"
    url="https://twitter.com/statuses/friends_timeline/25883.rss" />
```

As you can see, you are defining the HTTPService component with its own id attribute and also specifying the URL of the RSS feed to acquire. Before you can see any data, you need to take two steps. First, you need to trigger the HTTPService component and instruct it to attempt to load the URL of the RSS feed. Second, you need to take the data from the response and populate your list.

Logically, you want to attempt to load the RSS feed when the application is first loaded. You therefore modify the application definition to add an event, which is triggered once the creation of the user interface is completed:

```
<mx:Application xmlns:mx="http://www.adobe.com/2006/mxml"
                layout="absolute"
                creationComplete="twitterFeed.send()" >
```

Now that you have a way to load your RSS feed, the next step is to parse this XML document and update the content of the list.

Prior to ActionScript 3.0, XML document parsing involved lots of time writing code to traverse the node tree of a document, interrogating nodes and their children until you reached the area of the document in which you were interested. Now you have something much more powerful—E4X.

E4X allows the programmer to access an XML document in a more natural and intuitive way, at the same time offering better performance behind the scenes. For example, here is a compressed version of the RSS feed:

```
<?xml version="1.0" encoding="UTF-8"?>
<rss version="2.0">
    <channel id="tweets">
        <title>Twitter / ckorhonen with friends</title>
        <link>http://twitter.com/ckorhonen/with_friends</link>
        <description>
            Twitter updates from Chris Korhonen / ckorhonen and
            folks.
        </description>
        <language>en-us</language>
        <ttl>40</ttl>
        <item>
            <title>yezzer: battlestar galactica = tv crack</title>
            <description>
                yezzer: battlestar galactica = tv crack
            </description>
            <pubDate>Sat, 08 Dec 2007 15:29:02 +0000</pubDate>
            <guid>http://twitter.com/yezzer/statuses/481306382</guid>
            <link>http://twitter.com/yezzer/statuses/481306382</link>
        </item>
    </channel>
</rss>
```

If you wanted to access the value of the <title> node associated with the Twitter update, you would use the syntax rss.channel.item.title. It really is that simple. In the full RSS feed, where you have multiple <item> nodes, you access data in a similar way. However, this time you are dealing with an array of items:

```
rss.channel.item[0].title
```

You can also access the attributes of specific nodes using a similar syntax, but with the @ operator:

```
rss.channel.@id
```

To get this data into your List component, you can use something called a **data provider**. The component receives its data from a data provider, which conveniently takes the form of a collection of objects. This is just how the RSS feed is represented with E4X. All you need to do is tell the List component what its data provider is, using braces ({}) to denote the data binding:

```
<mx:List left="10" right="10" top="41" bottom="10" id="tweets"
        dataProvider="{twitterFeed.lastResult.rss.channel.item}" >
</mx:List>
```

Once you've downloaded the RSS feed, you will notice that numerous [object Object] elements are being rendered in the List component. This is data from your RSS feed; however, it exists as a complex object that your application does not know how to render as a simple string. Hence, you get the output [object Object].

If you compile your application and run it, you should see something like Figure 3-5.

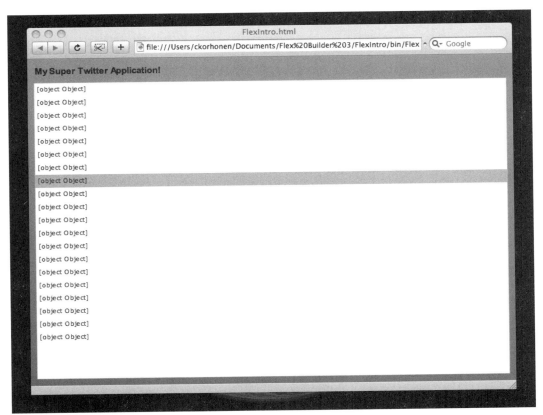

Figure 3-5. Your application, with dynamic data being loaded from an RSS feed

Each RSS item is actually a collection of subitems—the title, description, date, guide, and link. This means it cannot simply be rendered as a list item. One solution would be to use a DataGrid component rather than a standard List component, which will render subitems of objects within separate columns.

Instead, we'll show how to create an item renderer for the list. An item renderer offers a way of defining how a list item should be rendered and is usually built as a stand-alone MXML component. This gives you a great deal of control when it comes to both the look and feel and the functionality of your list.

If you select File ➤ New, you'll see an option to create an MXML component. Select this, and name the component Tweet. For the moment, you can continue with the default settings as defined in the wizard.

You can create an MXML component in the same way as your main application. Start by dragging several text fields onto the canvas in Design view. Arrange them however you want them to look. For the time being, let's expose the text of each Tweet component and the date posted.

Within your item renderer, data is passed in as a data object, with specific data items accessible as properties. Because you are binding data to your various components, here you also use braces to denote this data binding. In the following MXML example, you can see these data bindings in practice:

```
<?xml version="1.0" encoding="utf-8"?>
<mx:Canvas xmlns:mx="http://www.adobe.com/2006/mxml" width="100%"
           height="50">
    <mx:Text x="69" y="25" text="on {data.pubDate}" fontFamily="Arial"
             fontSize="12" fontWeight="bold" color="#969696"
             width="620"/>
    <mx:Text y="10" text="{data.title}" width="682" right="10"
             fontFamily="Arial"
             fontWeight="bold" fontSize="12"/>
</mx:Canvas>
```

Now if you link your newly created item renderer to the List component and recompile, you should see Twitter messages, or *Tweets* as they are affectionately known, rendered as in Figure 3-6:

```
<mx:List left="10" right="10" top="41" bottom="10" id="tweets"
         dataProvider="{twitterFeed.lastResult.rss.channel.item}"
         itemRenderer="Tweet">
</mx:List>
```

So, you have managed to grab a dynamic RSS feed, load its data, and render it within your application—all in less than about 20 lines of code, which shows you just how easy it is to work with and mash up data inside Flex.

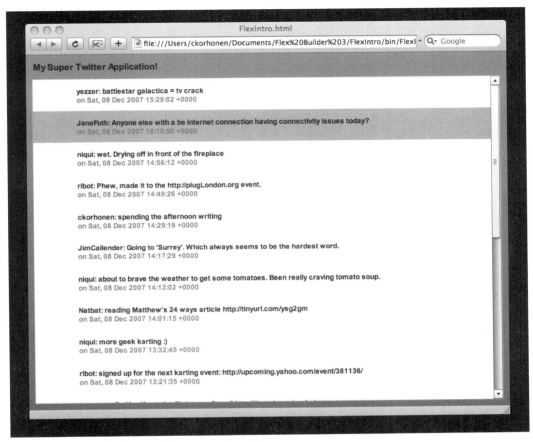

Figure 3-6. Your application, rendering a selection of Tweets

You are approaching the limits of what you can do with this RSS feed. We'll now cover what it takes to add functionality to your application using the Twitter API. Specifically, how do you transform this application from one-way interaction to two-way interaction, where a user can post Twitter updates back to the server?

Posting data to an API

Like many web applications, Twitter exposes a REST-based API that allows developers to access application functionality. Twitter also supports XML-based responses, which are perfect for using with the E4X parser.

> *You can view Twitter's API documentation at* http://groups.google.com/group/twitter-development-talk/web/api-documentation.

To post a status update, you will need to authenticate yourself. For Twitter, this is implemented using HTTP basic authentication, so you will need to include your Twitter username and password as part of the request headers. Here you are interested in the update method, which allows you to pass your new Twitter status as a parameter called status. This parameter should be no longer than 160 characters and, to make sure that certain characters do not break the URL, must be URL encoded.

So, now you have an idea of how you are going to update your status within the context of the Twitter API. Let's take a step back and figure out how you'll incorporate this into your application.

To capture user input, you'll need a text area within your user interface and also a button that will allow you to submit the request. In Design view, let's add these to your interface, and then you can go about making them work (see Figure 3-7).

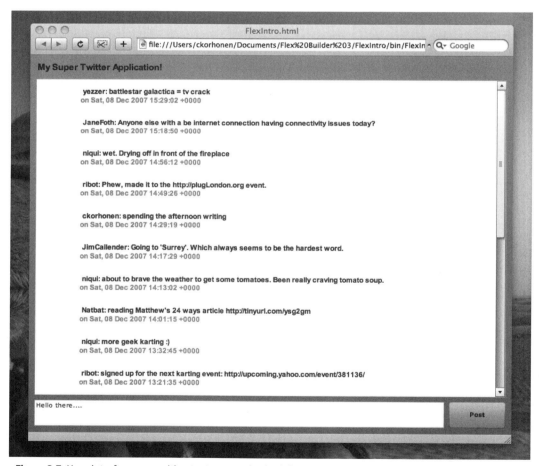

Figure 3-7. Your interface, now with a text area and submit button

You'll want to create these components with specific id attributes so that you can reference them later. It is also a good idea to set the maxChars attribute for the text field to 160 characters. This way, you don't need to worry about doing any additional validation at this time.

```
<mx:TextArea bottom="10" left="10" right="112" id="tweet_txt"
          maxChars="160"/>

<mx:Button label="Post" bottom="10" right="10" height="44"
          width="94" id="submit_btn"/>
```

You are now at the point where you will be getting your hands dirty with ActionScript. You need to create a function that will be triggered by a click of the submit button, which will take the contents of the text area and make a call to the Twitter API to post it. This function should also ensure that the appropriate headers are added to the request in order to authenticate the user. In addition, you should create a second function that is triggered when receiving a response from Twitter, which notifies the user of either success or failure.

When building Flex applications, ActionScript can be developed either as external .as classes or as functions contained in your MXML and encapsulated in <mx:script> tags. Because we are trying to create a simple example at the moment, we will show how to do it by keeping everything inside MXML. So, let's build the function to post data.

Because you are required to use HTTP authentication, you are forced to use the HTTPService object in order to send and receive your data. Previously in Flex 2, you could have achieved this using the standard URLLoader object, but Flex 3 does not allow authentication headers to be set.

```
public function postData():void{
    var request:HTTPService = new HTTPService();
```

You provide the URL of the REST API you are trying to access and set the HTTP method, which is in this case POST:

```
request.url = "http://twitter.com/statuses/update.xml";
request.method = "POST";
```

> *Within HTTP, you can access resources using either* GET *or* POST *requests. In practical terms, the key difference is that* POST *uses the HTTP request body in order to pass parameters or data, while with* GET*, the query string is used. Because of this,* POST *is often considered more secure because any parameters are obscured from casual logging utilities.*
>
> *Unfortunately, the disadvantage of* POST *requests is that they are not cached by the browser, often making them more suited to submitting data, while* GET *is often preferred for retrieving data.*

Now you need to handle the authentication with the API. As mentioned, you need to authenticate yourself in the HTTP header of the request. But before you can do this, you must encode your credentials as a Base64 string. This is to ensure that if your HTTP request is intercepted by a third party, your username and password are not easily compromised. There is no Base64 function within Flex 3, so you are able to use a third-party Base64 encoder/decoder ActionScript library written by Steve Webster (available at http://dynamicflash.com/goodies/base64/).

Obviously, it is bad practice to include login credentials within the source code of an application. You'll do it here only for the purposes of this example. A better approach is to present the user with a login box when they first load the application, requesting that they enter authentication details before proceeding.

```
var user:String = "myusername";
var pass:String = "mypassword";
var encodedCredentials:String = Base64.encode(user + ":" + pass);
```

Once you have encoded your credentials, you create a new array and then add the credentials to the array using the URLRequestHeader object:

```
var headerArray:Array = new Array(
    new URLRequestHeader("Authentication",
            "Basic " + encodedCredentials));
```

The headers of the request object are then set to the array:

```
request.headers = headerArray;
```

You must also add your parameters to the request. So, you create a simple object, and you pass in the text from your text field:

```
request.request = { status: tweet_txt.text };
```

You have to perform one final step before you can send your request. You need to set an event listener that will be triggered once a result has been received. You specify the event type that you want to listen to, in this case ResultEvent.RESULT, and you decide that you want to run the handleComplete method when this is triggered.

The HTTPService component also provides several other events that are triggered in the event of a failure or error. If you want to handle these, then you add event listeners in the same way.

Now with everything ready to go, you can send your request:

```
request.addEventListener(ResultEvent.RESULT,handleComplete);
request.send();
}
```

Within the handleComplete method, you'll do two things. First, you'll erase the text that was entered by the user. Second, you'll update the List component with the latest feed so that you can see the new post:

```
public function handleComplete(e:Event):void{
    tweet_txt.text = "";
    twitterFeed.send();
}
```

In its entirety, the MXML should now look something like this:

```
<?xml version="1.0" encoding="utf-8"?>
<mx:Application xmlns:mx="http://www.adobe.com/2006/mxml"
                        layout="absolute"
                        creationComplete="twitterFeed.send()">

    <mx:HTTPService id="twitterFeed"
        url="http://www.twitter.com/statuses/friends_timeline/25883.rss"
     />

    <mx:List left="10" right="10" top="41" bottom="62" id="tweets"
            dataProvider="{twitterFeed.lastResult.rss.channel.item}"
            itemRenderer="Tweet">
    </mx:List>

    <mx:Label x="10" y="10" text="My Super Twitter Application!"
            fontFamily="Arial" fontWeight="bold" fontSize="15"/>

    <mx:TextArea bottom="10" left="10" right="112" id="tweet_txt"
            maxChars="160"/>

    <mx:Button label="Post" bottom="10" right="10" height="44"
            width="94" id="submit_btn" click="postData()"/>

    <mx:Script>
        <![CDATA[

            import mx.rpc.events.ResultEvent;
            import com.dynamicflash.util.Base64;

            public function postData():void{
             var request:HTTPService = new HTTPService();
             request.url = "http://twitter.com/statuses/update.xml";
             request.method = "POST";
             request.addEventListener(ResultEvent.RESULT,
                                    handleComplete);

             var username:String = "username";
             var password:String = "password";
             var encodedCredentials:String =
                        Base64.encode(username + ":" + password);

             var headerArray = new Array(
                    new URLRequestHeader("Authentication",
                        "Basic " + encodedCredentials));
```

```
            request.headers = headerArray;
            request.request = { status: tweet_txt.text };

            request.send();
        }

        public function handleComplete(e:Event):void{
            tweet_txt.text = "";
            twitterFeed.send();
        }
    ]]>
  </mx:Script>
</mx:Application>
```

If you compile your application and run it, you should see your feed updated as expected (see Figure 3-8). Then when you update your status, you should see it at the top of the feed.

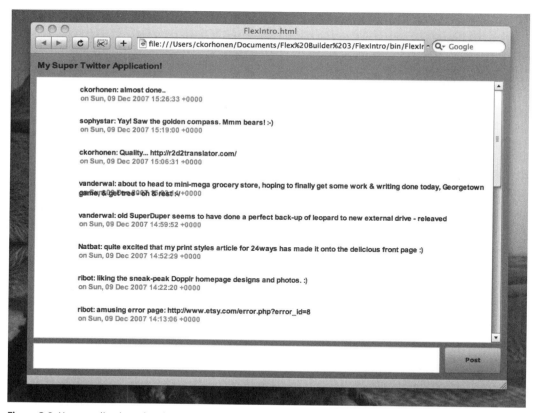

Figure 3-8. Your application, showing the posted Tweet

Next steps

You have successfully built a basic application within Flex that demonstrates the ease of interacting with data feeds and APIs. If you were to develop this application further, you could take it in a number of directions:

- **Leveraging the APIs**: You could see what other functionality is provided by the Twitter APIs. In particular, you could replace your RSS feed with a proper API call. This would give you access to more data, which you could use in your user interface, for example, to display images for individual contacts.

- **Enhancing the user interface**: At the moment, your application, using the default Flex look and feel, looks very rough. You could look at the components in much more detail and figure out how you could enhance them both visually and functionally (see Figure 3-9).

Figure 3-9. Examples of two Twitter clients, Twitterific and Snitter, each presenting a different look and feel

The great thing is that as more web-based applications expose their data using publicly available APIs in a similar way, many of the techniques demonstrated here are applicable to other applications. If you are interacting with data, then you will usually make requests using the HTTPService component, and then you will be parsing the response to populate your user interface components.

Many applications, as you will start to see in the next chapter, are much more complex in terms of user interface and interactions, but they all tend to function in a similar way. The main differences will show up in the overall architecture of the application. For one thing, as your application and its user interface become larger, it makes sense to switch from MXML code in favor of ActionScript classes.

You also see design patterns come into play, both for individual components and across entire applications. This helps make applications more maintainable by introducing a common language through which different developers can understand the composition of an application. It also helps promote programming best practices.

All these factors are arguably what makes a good application. By keeping your application internals simple, you can concentrate on the user experience by improving the look and feel and responsiveness, which can make all the difference when it comes to creating a successful application.

Summary

You should now have a clear understanding of how to build a simple Flex application and how the framework supports working with and manipulating data. You have also been introduced to some of the components available to developers.

Before moving on to the next chapter, we encourage you to spend additional time exploring your own creativity in the context of your example application, perhaps enhancing or refactoring its functionality.

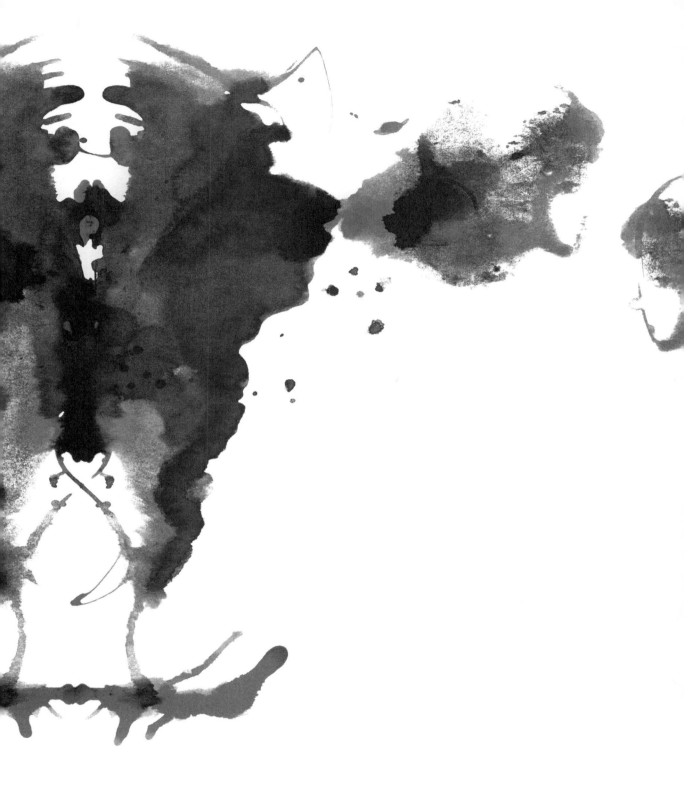

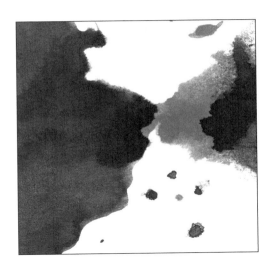

Chapter 4

FLEX COMPONENTS

Now that you've been introduced to the Flex framework, in this chapter you'll take a look at the components that you can utilize within your applications, as well as how they can be customized and extended.

Part of the power of the Flex framework comes in its diverse library of components—the building blocks of any application. These components come in many forms. Some are visual, perhaps providing the typical functionality that you might expect in a user interface, while others are nonvisual, providing useful functionality such as input validation, print formatting, and state management.

In many ways, the key benefit of utilizing these components is that, as a developer, you don't need to reinvent the wheel and instead can concentrate on the business logic behind your application without having to worry about having to program the functionality of a combo box or text field, for example. In addition, many nonfunctional requirements are also implemented within these components, such as data validation and formatting, tab ordering, and event broadcasting. These components will ease application development and enhance the experience of the end user.

In the past, many Flash developers have often avoided the Adobe user interface components that come with the Flash IDE mainly because of the immense file-size overhead they can add to the resulting application. This has been addressed to a certain extent in Flash CS3, though in some cases a third-party component may be preferable.

In the case of Flex, this is much less of a concern because these components are included in the weight of the framework itself; so, not using them will not reduce the size of your application. In addition, the Flex framework is cached by the latest version of Flash Player and made available to applications across domains, effectively giving your application zero file-size overhead once the user has viewed a single Flex application (whether it is yours or not!).

Before we get into the in-depth topic of customizing and extending these components, we'll cover exactly what is available.

Visual interface components

Components in Flex can mean one of two things. They can be classes that perform a specific task such as communicating with an HTTP web service, or they can be visual components that the user can interact with and that are used in constructing a user interface.

Building the user interface

On the visual side, we as Flex developers are really spoiled by a wealth of choices we have for supporting the development of applications with complex interactions.

In addition to the standard fare of check boxes, radio buttons, input fields, buttons, and combo boxes, there exists some very specific components such as the color picker and date pickers that are often much more intuitive ways to ask a user to provide complex data. See Figure 4-1 for a selection of the components provided by Flex.

Flex also offers components such as the progress bar, which is a prebuilt way of visualizing the loading progress to the user, and the horizontal and vertical sliders, which allow developers to start building user interfaces that are more akin to those found within desktop applications.

Not pictured in Figure 4-1 are standard components that handle tasks such as loading an image, video, or SWF file. These components make this process totally painless and also broadcast events as they display content or as the user interacts with content that can trigger interaction from other parts of the application. A good example of this is the VideoDisplay component, which broadcasts events at certain points as a video file is playing. This could trigger other components to refresh with data relevant to a particular scene; or when a video has finished playing, a feedback form could be displayed.

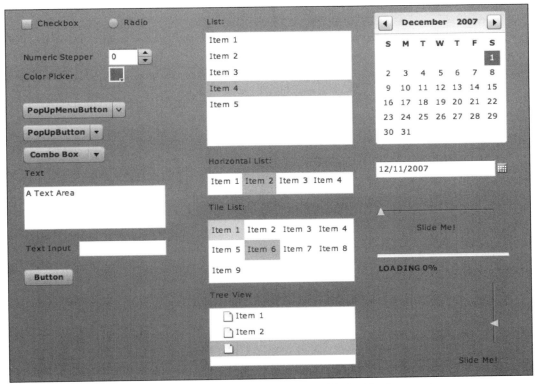

Figure 4-1. A selection of the user interface components available within the Flex framework

In addition, Flex offers many components that enable data to be represented easily and clearly. The list views, for example, do exactly what it says on the can; they take a data provider array and represent it in the form of a list. This is where you really start to see the power of the component framework—with data visualization and the ability to have data rendered as its own component that can be an item in another component such as a list.

In Flex 3, there have been an impressive number of improvements to these data-centric components, including the new AdvancedDataGrid component, which adds many new features to the standard DataGrid component, such as the ability to sort multiple columns at once and to group data in the form of a tree view. There is also functionality that enhances the overall experience of using the component. You can now copy and paste groups of individual cells, and with the nonvisual PrintAdvancedDataGrid component (see Figure 4-2), it is now possible to print this data in a usable form.

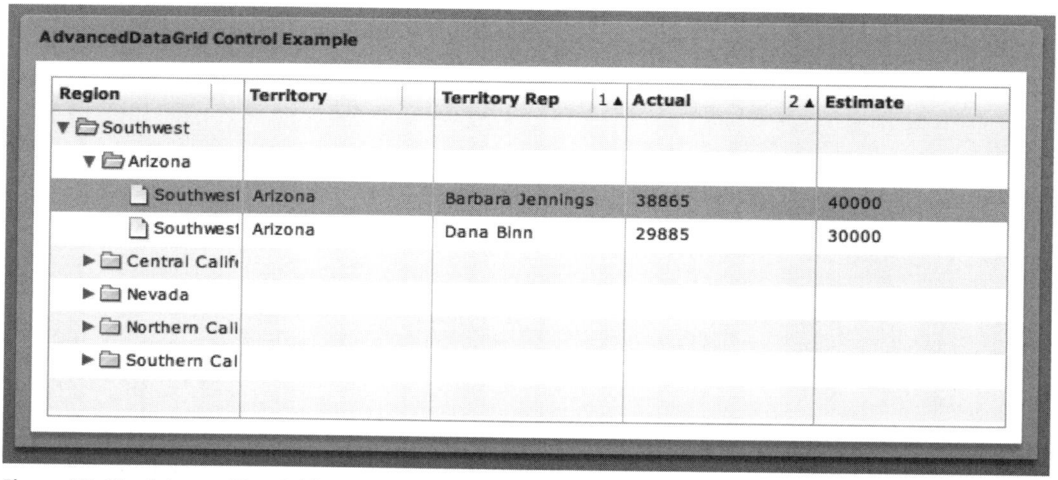

Figure 4-2. The AdvancedDataGrid component

> For heavier data analysis, you can use an OLAPDataGrid component, which allows you to look at data from different perspectives. This is often used when looking for hidden relationships and trends in data. For example, data miner will take a flat data set, define an OLAP cube based on the data, and then query this in a similar way that a developer might query a SQL database. The OLAPDataGrid component will then display the results of this query.
>
> Because you are mainly looking at Flex in the context of mashups and because a lot of data analysis has the unintentional side effect of making one go cross-eyed, we won't cover these topics here. If you are interested in learning more, please check out Abobe's component documentation available at http://livedocs. adobe.com/labs/flex3/.

The Flex Charting components are also available for data visualization; they allow you to throw a data set at a component that will then render the data as a graphical visualization (see Figure 4-3). These components are fully configurable and have a variety of rendering options available.

A final component of note is the new RichTextEditor component, which allows a user to apply styling and formatting to text while inputting it in much the same way that they would in a word-processing application. Similar interfaces exist that were built using JavaScript, such as the composer in Google Mail. However, in the past, browser compatibility issues have made this type of functionality problematic for developers.

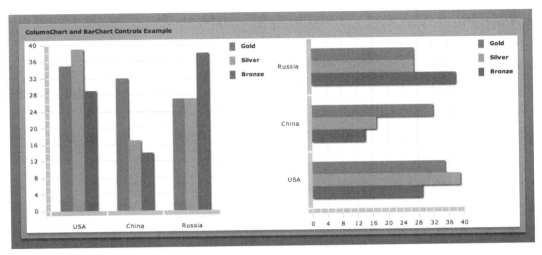

Figure 4-3. Flex Charting examples

The RichTextEditor component (Figure 4-4) does not suffer from any browser compatibility issues and can output content directly as HTML-formatted text, supporting a subset of HTML tags, with all the styles and formatting intact. This component is perfect for applications that interface directly with a blog or content publishing system.

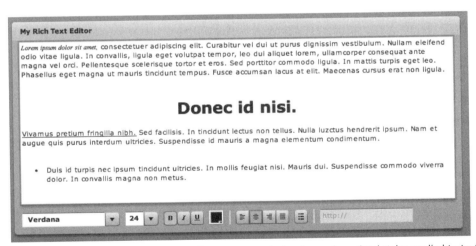

Figure 4-4. An example of the RichTextEditor component, showing various visual styles applied to text

Using effects and transitions to add shine

Once you have defined your user interface, it is usually a good time to add some eye candy to it! Luckily, Flex has specific components that can help you do this. These come in the form of effects and transitions.

An **effect** is a single visual or audio function. It can be a blur of an image, a rotation of a user interface element, or the playing of a sound clip. You can use effects on pretty much anything, and they can triggered by any event—a button, a mouse rollover, a timer, or something much more involved.

Effects are often best used to give feedback to a user interaction, such as rolling over an icon and having it glow or such as selecting an option on a form and having an additional field fade into view. You can customize and extend effects with ease, giving you control over the speed and playback of them.

For example, when a user hovers their mouse over an icon, it could expand to a specific size in a specific duration. When the user moves their mouse away, then this could simply trigger the reverse method of the event in order to restore the interface to normal.

You can use **transitions** when it is necessary to use multiple effects, such as when you want to switch between different states of an application using any form of animation. For example, old content can fade out, panels can resize, and the new content can fade in. You can achieve this functionality quite simply by creating a chain of individual effects that are executed sequentially or in parallel.

Validators, formatters, and other nonvisual components

In addition to the visual components, which can be used to create your user interfaces, you also have a variety of nonvisual components that perform useful tasks behind the scenes of your application. Many of these often work hand in hand with your visual components, such as the PrintDataGrid component, which adds print functionality to the DataGrid component.

Beyond this, probably the most used nonvisual components are the validators and data formatters. Validators make things easier when developing a form-based application, where you are concerned about the validity of user-entered data. Certain prebuilt classes can validate common data items such as phone numbers, credit card numbers, e-mail addresses, and more. In addition, you can simply extend the Validator class in order to develop your own custom validation routines.

Let's look at an example. Say you are creating your own custom validator component that will check whether the first character of the input string is the letter *A*.

The validation is performed in the doValidation method, where you use a regular expression to validate your string. This method returns an array containing the results of the validation, which you can use if you want to return a helpful error message.

```
package
{
    import mx.validators.ValidationResult;
    import mx.validators.Validator;

    public class SampleValidator extends Validator{
        private var results:Array;
```

```
    public function SampleValidator(){
        super();
    }

    override protected function doValidation(value:Object):Array{
        results = [];
        results = super.doValidation(value);

        // check we have a value and not an empty string
        if(results.length > 0){
            return results;
        }
        if(String(value).length == 0){
            return results;
        }

        // define regular expression and run it on our string
        var pattern:RegExp = /^Ae/;
        var resultArray = pattern.exec(String(value));

        if(resultArray==null){
            results.push(new ValidationResult(true,null,null,
                                "String must begin with A"));
            return results;
        }
        return results;
    }
  }
}
```

Formatters work in a similar way. In conjunction with visual components, they format a user's input in a specific way so that it appears how you want it. They are especially useful when capturing telephone numbers, addresses, and dates, all of which are often displayed in a specific format.

Component customization and skinning

Flex components come with their own look and feel right out of the box, which in many ways is good because it is one less thing to worry about. It is also a curse and often leads to the general criticism that all Flex applications look the same! In fact, the better Flex applications are often those that have taken the trouble to define their own look and feel consistent with the brand they are trying to represent.

In addition to enhancing the look and feel of the finished application, **skinning** can also be useful when prototyping in order to give an early concept an almost wireframe look and feel. You can use this technique to great effect when getting clients to spend time considering the core functionality of an application rather than getting wrapped up in visual details.

Styling components with CSS

With Flex 3, you can use several levels of styling and skinning components depending on how deeply you want to go. We'll present an example of a simple button to see what you can do with it! Figure 4-5 shows the button.

Figure 4-5. A simple Button component

First examine the button's properties and then make basic changes to many of its visual attributes (see Figure 4-6).

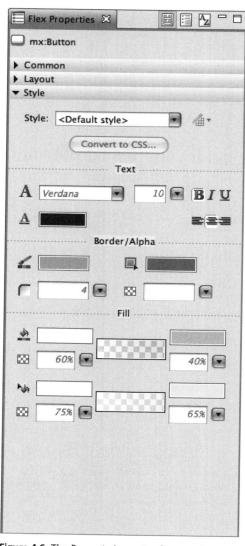

Figure 4-6. The Property Inspector for your button

As you can see, you have some control over the fonts used, the border, the roundness of the corners, the color, and the transparency. It's not exactly awe-inspiring, and it's also a bit annoying if you want to reuse this style, because your MXML code ends up looking something like this:

```
<mx:Button x="38"
           y="30"
           label="A Simple Button. Click Me!"
           width="183"
           height="22"
           fontFamily="Arial"
           fontWeight="normal"
           fontSize="12"
           color="#000000"
           borderColor="#505050"
           cornerRadius="0"
           fillAlphas="[0.21, 0.9, 0.9, 0.9]"/>
```

As you build more complex interfaces (or if you are building pure ActionScript 3.0 applications), then this approach can become tedious to the point where user interfaces became unmaintainable because you are repeating lots of code while you build your interface and often end up with large amounts of MXML describing every aspect of your application's look and feel.

Thankfully, HTML developers solved this problem for you almost a decade ago. Rather than embedding visual styles within the HTML pages that made up a website, Cascading Style Sheets (CSS) emerged as a standard for separating content and presentation. Within Flex, you can use CSS to do the same thing.

Within the Property Inspector, if you click Convert to CSS, then you will be prompted to create a style sheet for your application. Once you do this, your MXML is tidy again:

```
<mx:Button x="38" y="30" label="A Simple Button. Click Me!"
           width="18" height="22">
<mx:Style source="app.css"/>
```

Within your newly created app.css file, you can see that the visual properties you have assigned to the Button component are now represented here:

```
Button
{
        borderColor: #505050;
        color: #000000;
        cornerRadius: 0;
        fillAlphas: 0.21, 0.9, 0.9, 0.9;
        fontFamily: Arial;
        fontSize: 12;
        fontWeight: normal;
}
```

Within the Flex IDE, if you switch to Design view, you can also see styled component previews, which should give you some idea of how your button will look in its various states (see Figure 4-7). In addition, you have several additional options in the Property Inspector.

Figure 4-7. Previewing your CSS styles

With the new live preview of your CSS styles applied to a button, it takes only a few minutes to come up with a slightly tacky-looking big red button (see Figure 4-8).

Figure 4-8. An example of your styled button

The beauty of using CSS is that because you have now defined your button's look and feel separately from where you are defining your button, you can now use this button style across the entire application, without having to specifically set the properties of each button. You can also use this style across many projects in order to create visual consistency.

For many applications, this level of visual customization may be entirely sufficient—allowing you to break free of the default Flex look and feel. However, one of the traditional benefits of Flash is that it can offer a rich visual experience. Surely you can make your buttons look better than this? Yes, you can.

Applying graphical skins

We have been looking at component styling; the other method of changing the visual look and feel of a component is **skinning**. This allows you to use your own graphical assets (flat images or SWFs) to visually define what a component looks like.

To activate skinning mode, open your CSS file in the Property Inspector, and click the Skin drop-down list at the top (see Figure 4-9).

Figure 4-9. Choosing an image skin from the Property Inspector

Here you can select image files to import as your skin for each of the button states.

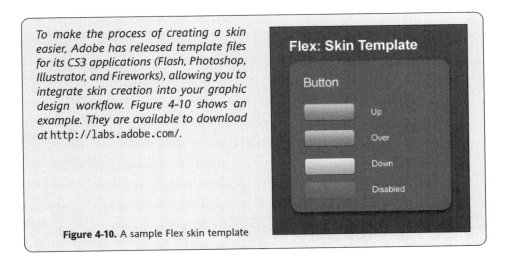

To make the process of creating a skin easier, Adobe has released template files for its CS3 applications (Flash, Photoshop, Illustrator, and Fireworks), allowing you to integrate skin creation into your graphic design workflow. Figure 4-10 shows an example. They are available to download at http://labs.adobe.com/.

Figure 4-10. A sample Flex skin template

If you select a set of image files that you prepared earlier (Figure 14-11), then they will appear in the component preview. Adjust the component padding and fonts, and you are almost finished. Only a single task remains, and that is to set the scale grids.

75

Here you use a technique known as *scale nine* in order to make your button graphic scalable, meaning that you can resize it, and graphical details such as corners and edges will remain in proportion. Figure 14-12 shows the image with the scale-nine grids in place.

If you click Edit Scale Grid, then you will bring up scaling grids for your skin. These let you specify that parts of the image should be stretched horizontally and vertically and that parts of the image should not be scaled, such as fine details.

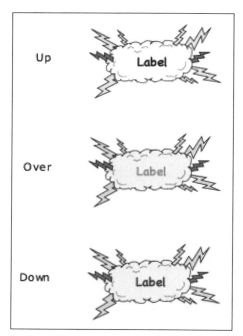

Figure 4-11. Your new button skins after importing with subtle graphical differences for mouseover and mousedown states.

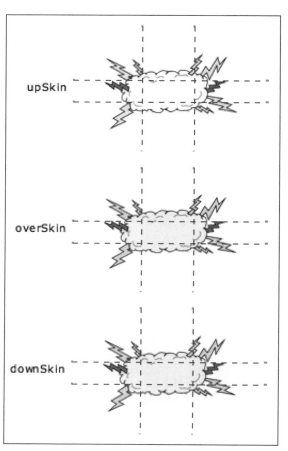

Figure 4-12. The scale-nine grids aligned with your texture. It's worth noting that in this example things won't stretch optimally in the vertical direction.

If you take a look at the CSS style, then you can see how the skins have been applied to the component:

```
Button
{
        fontFamily: Chalkboard;
        fontSize: 12;
        fontWeight: bold;
        paddingLeft: 8;
        paddingRight: 15;
        paddingTop: 15;
        paddingBottom: 10;
        textAlign: center;
        upSkin: Embed(source="../img/Button_Up.png",
                            scaleGridTop="37",
                            scaleGridLeft="49",
                            scaleGridRight="98",
                            scaleGridBottom="58");
        overSkin: Embed(source="../img/Button_Over.png",
                            scaleGridTop="37",
                            scaleGridLeft="49",
                            scaleGridRight="98",
                            scaleGridBottom="58");
        downSkin: Embed(source="../img/Button_Down.png",
                            scaleGridTop="37",
                            scaleGridLeft="49",
                            scaleGridRight="98",
                            scaleGridBottom="58");
}
```

Figure 4-13 shows the finished button.

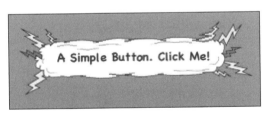

Figure 4-13. The skinned button

This section has demonstrated how easy it can be to break away from the default look and feel in your Flex applications.

Extending components

When you consider the range of components available within the Flex framework, in most cases it has everything a developer would need in order to build an application. However, occasionally it is necessary to create a totally new component or extend an existing one to add functionality.

In the following sections, you will learn how to create a custom numeric dial component in Flex 3.

Selecting a superclass

When creating a custom component, it is important to have your goal in mind. Often this may be as simple as adding functionality to an existing component—for example, extending the ComboBox component so that items are autoselected as you type.

In other cases, you may need to create something totally different. And perhaps it's something without an existing component that visually or conceptually represents what you are trying to achieve. Here you will need to build a new component from scratch.

When building new components, you should consider extending two classes. If you are creating a user interface control, then you will want to extend UIComponent. And if you are creating a custom container, which will contain other UIComponent classes, then you will want to extend the Container class.

The UIComponent class is an abstract class, containing methods but no specific implementation, that all other controls and containers inherit from. By extending it, you get three core benefits:

- You will be able to use your component in the various Flex containers since they require components to be subclasses of the UIComponent class.
- Your component will be more intuitive to developers because it follows the same blueprint as the other Flex components.
- You inherit various constructs that make your life as a developer easier and that rapidly allow you to build a robust component. These include sizing, skinning, event handling, styling, validation, rendering, automation, and accessibility.

The Container class is a subclass of the UIComponent class and should be used if your custom component will need to manage children with built-in scrolling and clipping support.

Follow the framework

By following the technical implementation blueprint that comes with extending one of these core classes, you will benefit from the abstract classes that have been designed to make development tasks easier. This will help you save time when implementing functionality that is not native to Flash Player such as component styling and accessibility.

It also ensures that you use a standard set of APIs that define the structure of a Flex component, providing more predictable behavior to other developers who might utilize your component.

Use the component life cycle

All components that inherit from the UIComponent class should follow the predefined life cycle that is common across components and optimized for the way a Flex application functions.

The component life cycle has three phases: initialization, update, and destruction (see Figure 4-14).

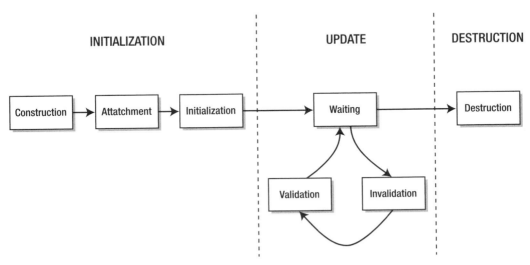

Figure 4-14. The Flex component life cycle

Initialization

During this phase, the component is constructed, attached to the display list, and initialized. During the construction part of the initialization phase, the class constructor is called. This is the only method called before a component is added to the display list, and to ensure optimal performance, it should be kept light.

```
public function NumericDial(p_minValue:Number=0,
                           p_maxValue:Number=360,
                           p_currentValue:Number=0){
    super();

    minValue = p_minValue;
    maxValue = p_maxValue;
    currentValue = p_currentValue;
}
```

In the constructor, you should call super() to initialize inherited properties and also take the opportunity to initialize and configure variables that are needed even if the component is never added to the display list. This usually includes initializing properties and adding listeners for application-level events.

79

At this point, you don't need to spend time creating and positioning child elements.

> *In ActionScript 3.0,* super() *will be called automatically if it is not called explicitly. However, calling it explicitly allows you to call it at any point in the constructor, meaning that you can place it before or after other statements.*

During the attachment part of the initialization phase, the component is added to the display list, either using the addChild() or addChildAt() method or being defined in MXML.

Once this happens, the component's initialize() function will be invoked.

During the initialization part of the initialization phase, the following actions take place:

- The preinitialize event is dispatched.
- The createChildren() method is called. In this case, it is overridden in order for you to add child components.

Here you initialize the various components in the component and register events:

```
protected override function createChildren():void{
    super.createChildren();

    if(_dialTrack == null) {
        _dialTrack = new _dialTrackImage();
    }
    addChild(_dialTrack);

    if(_dial == null) {
        _dial = new _dialImage();
        _dial.addEventListener(MouseEvent.MOUSE_DOWN
                            onMouseEventDown ,false ,0 ,true);
        _dial.addEventListener(MouseEvent.MOUSE_MOVE,
                            onMouseEventMove ,false ,0 ,true);
        _dial.addEventListener(MouseEvent.MOUSE_UP ,
                            onMouseEventUp ,false ,0 ,true);
    }
    addChild(_dial);

    if(_rotationCanvas == null) {
        _rotationCanvas = new Shape();
    }
    addChild(_rotationCanvas);
}
```

Generally, you should use `createChildren()` to create the following:

- Children that are persistent throughout the component's life cycle
- Children created in a superclass that will be overridden

Children do not need to be of any particular type, provided that at the lowest level they are extending the `DisplayObject` class.

You will notice that in this example you are not bothering to size and position any of the child objects. This is because at this point you do not know the dimensions of your component. However, if children need any additional initialization, then you should do this.

In terms of the execution sequence, the following happens:

1. The initialize event is dispatched.
2. A round of invalidation/validation happens.
3. The `creationComplete` event is dispatched.

Update

The update phase encapsulates everything that happens between component initialization and destruction. Here the component can potentially cycle repeatedly through waiting, invalidation, and validation steps. This is of course based on whether the component is interacted with. If it is never interacted with, then it will remain in the waiting state until the destruction phase.

During the waiting part of the update phase, the component listens for update requests. Any kind of user interaction, such as a user entering data or selecting an item that changes the value of the component, will take it out of this state.

During the invalidation part of the update phase, certain methods are called to mark certain aspects of the component as *dirty*. This is done in order to help optimize the rendering performance of the custom components. It is designed with the idea that even though something has been updated, it may not be necessary to redraw the whole component.

A component can be marked as dirty in three ways:

- If you want to mark properties dirty, then use the `invalidateProperties()` method. This causes the `commitProperties()` method to be invoked on the next frame.
- If the component has been resized, then mark the sizing as dirty using the `invalidateSize()` method. This causes `measure()` to be invoked on the next frame.
- If you want to mark the drawing and layout as dirty, then use the `invalidateDisplayList()` method. This causes `updateDisplayList()` to be called on the next frame.

Invalidation is much more efficient than calling the validation methods directly, because properties can change many times during a single frame of rendering. Because only the last value is used on the next frame, it becomes beneficial to queue changes for the next frame rather than processing them straightaway.

Validation allows a developer to queue component changes for the reason just mentioned. Without it, application performance would be significantly degraded by unnecessary processing and activity.

Different methods will be called during the validation part of the update phase, depending on whether properties, sizing, or drawing have been changed and marked as dirty.

If the properties have been changed, then you use the commitProperties() method:

```
protected override function commitProperties():void {
    super.commitProperties();

    if(_rotationValueChanged) {
        _rotationValueChanged = false;
        _rotationCanvas.rotation = _rotationValue;
    }
}
```

During this method, you would usually work with properties that are public and set through setters. Any properties that can affect rendering should be handled here.

If the sizing of a component has changed, then you should use the measure() method:

```
protected override function measure():void {
    super.measure();

    measuredHeight = measuredMinHeight = _dialTrack.height;
    measuredWidth = measuredMinWidth = _dialTrack.width;
}
```

This method is used to perform measurement and sizing calculations, leaving the actual sizing to be determined by the layout management system. It will be called when the size of a component is not specified or when constraint-based layout is in use.

It is important to take into account the sizes of any chrome, padding, or child components when implementing this method. To this end, when you are measuring child components that are a subclass of UIComponent, then you should use the methods getExplicitOrMeasuredWidth() and getExplicitOrMeasuredHeight() rather than the child's own width and height properties in order to obtain accurate values.

If the drawing or layout has changed, then use the updateDisplayList() method:

```
protected override function updateDisplayList(unscaledWidth:Number,
unscaledHeight:Number):void {
    super.updateDisplayList(unscaledWidth,unscaledHeight);

    _dialTrack.x = (unscaledWidth - _dialTrack.width) / 2;
    _dialTrack.y = (unscaledHeight - _dialTrack.height) / 2;

    _dial.x = (unscaledWidth - _dial.width) / 2;
    _dial.y = (unscaledHeight - _dial.height) / 2;
```

```
        _dialOriginX = _dial.x + (_dial.width / 2);
        _dialOriginY = _dial.y + (_dial.height / 2);

        _rotationCanvas.x = _dialOriginX;
        _rotationCanvas.y = _dialOriginY;

        drawDialCircle(_rotationCanvas.graphics, _dial.height / 2 - 2);
    }
```

This method handles the layout and drawing of the component and is where most of the component's implementation is performed.

It receives two parameters that represent the actual amount of real estate that the component has been given.

In general, when you are coding the validation steps, you should optimize them as much as possible, bearing in mind that any of these three methods may be called many times during an application's execution.

Destruction

The destruction phase occurs whenever a component is removed from the display list and is no longer participating in layout events. This usually occurs when a component's parent is removed from the display list or removeChild() is explicitly called on the component.

You should be careful to remove any references to the component that may be held by other components so that the component can be garbage collected by Flash Player so that memory and resources can be released.

Create custom properties

When you build components, you are most likely going to need to create custom properties that define the component and its state. When you do this, you should try to use getter/setters wherever possible and, if necessary, properties.

If a component has properties that take a set of string values, then it is often worth creating static constants for those string values in order to increase the overall maintainability of the component.

Use metadata

You can use metadata to allow the compiler and Flex Builder to understand the inner workings of your component. These are some key metadata tags to keep in mind when developing custom components:

- Bindable defines properties that can be watched for changes.
- Event defines what custom events a component will dispatch.
- Style defines visual styles.
- Inspectable defines information on properties and their potential values.
- IconFile specifies an icon that will display for a component in Flex Builder.

Create custom events

You can use custom events or a custom component to dispatch data to the rest of the application.

If you want to implement custom events within a component, you will need to create a custom event class:

```
package {
    import flash.events.Event;

    public class RotationChangeEvent extends Event{

        public var result:String;

        public function RotationChangeEvent(p_type:String,
                                            p_result:String,
                                            p_bubbles:Boolean=false,
                                            p_cancelable:Boolean=false){
            super(p_type, p_bubbles, p_cancelable);
            result = p_result;
        }


    }
}

package {
    import flash.events.Event;

    public class RotationChangeEvent extends Event{

        public var rotation:Number;

        public function RotationChangeEvent(p_rotation:Number,
                                            p_bubbles:Boolean=false,
                                            p_cancelable:Boolean=false){
            super("rotationChange", p_bubbles, p_cancelable);
            rotation = p_rotation;
        }


    }
}
```

Next, set up the event metadata on your custom component:

```
[Event(name="rotationChange",type="RotationChangeEvent")]
```

And finally, dispatch the custom event within your component:

```
override public function set rotation(value:Number):void {
    _rotationValue = value;
    _rotationValueChanged = true;

    invalidateProperties();

    dispatchEvent(new RotationChangeEvent(value));
}
```

Add styling support

Inheriting from UIComponent means you can use the built-in styling support, which makes it easier to give your components a custom look and feel. To do this, you need to set up style metadata tags outside the class declaration. These tell the compiler that custom styles are supported by the component.

```
[Style(name="dialMarkerColor", type="uint", format="Color",
    inherit="no")]
```

Now you override the styleChanged() method. This is used to monitor when custom styles are changed so that they can be handled within the component. Custom styles are called automatically whenever a style is changed.

```
public override function styleChanged(styleProp:String):void {
    super.styleChanged(styleProp);

    if(styleProp == "dialMarkerColor") {
        invalidateDisplayList();
    }
}
```

Now that you have invalidated the display list, the updateDisplayList() method will be called, which in turn calls your drawDialCircle() method:

```
private function drawDialCircle(p_graphics:Graphics,
                               p_circleY:Number):void {
    p_graphics.clear();
    p_graphics.beginFill(getStyle("dialMarkerColor"));
    p_graphics.drawCircle(0,-p_circleY,3);
}
```

This method uses getStyle() in order to retrieve the value for the dialMarkerColor style. If there is no value for the style, then this method will return undefined. It is important to handle this potential point of failure. Once good option is to wrap the calls to the getStyle() method in a private getter, which will allow you to define a default value in the case of undefined.

A complete component

You've learned about the various parts of the component life cycle and the sequence in which important methods are called, so now you can take a look at how they are applied to construct a complete component.

In this example, say you are building a numerical dial component that can be rotated by events dispatched by other components (see Figure 4-15). It can be used to represent a value between 0 and 360.

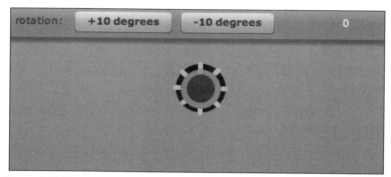

Figure 4-15. Your numerical dial

The component is built in pure ActionScript, with no MXML used to define its interface.

Within your .as file, you begin by importing the external classes that you will be using. Most are standard Flash classes, used by most components you will run across, with the exception of the RotationChangeEvent class, which is specific to this project and is an event that is fired if the control is located.

RotationChangeEvent simply extends the standard Event object, allowing a parameter named rotation to be passed. This is the current rotation angle of your dial.

```
package com.realeyesmedia.V1.core.controls{

    import com.realeyesmedia.V1.core.events.RotationChangeEvent;

    import flash.display.DisplayObject;
    import flash.display.Graphics;
    import flash.display.Shape;
    import flash.events.EventDispatcher;
    import flash.events.MouseEvent;

    import mx.core.UIComponent;
    import mx.styles.CSSStyleDeclaration;
    import mx.styles.StyleManager;
```

You can also take this opportunity to define your own metadata; this code defines a custom RotationChangeEvent and also defines a CSS style that you will be using to define the color of your dial:

```
[Event(name="rotationChange",
    type="com.realeyesmedia.V1.core.events.RotationChangeEvent")]

[Style(name="dialMarkerColor", type="uint", format="Color",
        inherit="no")]
```

Now you can define your NumericDial class and its constructor. Here you perform a check to see whether any CSS styles exist for your component. If not, you can set default values.

```
public class NumericDial extends UIComponent{

    private static var classConstructed:Boolean =
                                    ClassConstruct();

    private static function classConstruct():Boolean {
        if (!StyleManager.getStyleDeclaration("NumericDial")){
            var newStyleDeclaration:CSSStyleDeclaration =
                                    new CSSStyleDeclaration();
          //Default styles
            newStyleDeclaration.setStyle("dialMarkerColor",
                                            0xFF0000);
            StyleManager.setStyleDeclaration("NumericDial",
                                    newStyleDeclaration, true);
        }
        return true;
    }
```

In addition to your constructor, within your class you also declare a number of static variables that you use to represent various items, such as the minimum numeric value supported by your dial:

```
private var _minValue:Number;
```

The following is an indicator used to denote whether the minimum value has changed, which is used when you decide whether your component is dirty and should be redrawn:

```
private var _minValueChanged:Boolean;
```

The following is the maximum numeric value of the dial:

```
private var _maxValue:Number;
```

The following is an additional dirty flag for the maximum value:

```
private var _maxValueChanged:Boolean;
```

The following is the current value of the component:

```
private var _currentValue:Number;
```

The following is its dirty flag:

```
private var _currentValueChanged:Boolean;
```

The following is the current rotation value, in degrees:

```
private var _rotationValue:Number;
```

The following is its dirty flag:

```
private var _rotationValueChanged:Boolean;
```

The example also embeds external assets that represent the look and feel of the dial and its dial track that themselves are display objects. By using external assets here, it becomes straightforward to perform skinning:

```
[Embed(source="/assets/images/dial.png")]
private var _dialImage:Class;

[Embed(source="/assets/images/dialTrack.png")]
private var _dialTrackImage:Class;

private var _dial:DisplayObject;
private var _dialTrack:DisplayObject;
```

Because the appearance of the dial will change as it is rotated, create a Shape that you will use to represent the rotating dial. You also have X and Y coordinates that are used as the origin point for rotation.

```
private var _rotationCanvas:Shape;
private var _dialOriginX:Number;
private var _dialOriginY:Number;
```

A boolean flag is also set that tracks whether the component is in a state where it can be interacted with. This is useful if you want to disable the component or prevent its value from being modified by multiple inputs at the same time.

```
private var _movable:Boolean;
```

The constructor is straightforward, creating a new dial instance covering a given range of values, and super() is also called in order to initialize inherited properties:

```
public function NumericDial(p_minValue:Number=0,
                            p_maxValue:Number=360,
                            p_currentValue:Number=0){
        super();

        minValue = p_minValue;
        maxValue = p_maxValue;
        currentValue = p_currentValue;
}
```

Once the constructor has been executed, the component is attached to the display list and initialized.

You use the createChildren method to add child components. In this case, it is where you set up the objects corresponding to your dial. So, create new instances of your dialTrack, dial, and rotationCanvas, adding event listeners where necessary:

```
protected override function createChildren():void{
    super.createChildren();

    if(_dialTrack == null){
        _dialTrack = new _dialTrackImage();
    }
    addChild(_dialTrack);

    if(_dial == null){
        _dial = new _dialImage();
        _dial.addEventListener(MouseEvent.MOUSE_DOWN,
                        onMouseEventDown ,false ,0 ,true);
        _dial.addEventListener(MouseEvent.MOUSE_MOVE,
                        onMouseEventMove ,false ,0 ,true);
        _dial.addEventListener(MouseEvent.MOUSE_UP ,
                        onMouseEventUp ,false ,0 ,true);
    }
    addChild(_dial);

    if(_rotationCanvas == null){
        _rotationCanvas = new Shape();
    }
    addChild(_rotationCanvas);
}
```

Referring to the component life cycle, this represents the end of the Initialization phase, meaning that your component is now fully initialized and in a state where you are waiting for interaction.

To change the value and properties of the component, you can define several getters and setters:

```
public function get minValue():Number{
    return _minValue;
}

public function set minValue(p_value:Number):void{
    _minValue = p_value;
}

public function get maxValue():Number{
    return _maxValue;
}

public function set maxValue(p_value:Number):void{
    _maxValue = p_value;
    _maxValueChanged = true;

    invalidateProperties();
}
```

```
public function get currentValue():Number{
    return _currentValue;
}

public function set currentValue(p_value:Number):void{
    _currentValue = p_value;
    _currentValueChanged = true;

    invalidateProperties();
}
```

Where you change properties that have an impact on the state of your component, you call the invalidateProperties method, which will call the commitProperties method and ultimately lead to the redrawing of the component.

You can also have getters and setters for the rotation value of your dial. It's worth noting that you are visually rotating the _rotationCanvas shape and not the component itself. Again, you are invalidating the properties and also broadcasting a RotationChangeEvent, in case you are interested in doing this elsewhere.

```
override public function get rotation():Number{
    return _rotationCanvas.rotation;
}

override public function set rotation(value:Number):void{
    _rotationValue = value;
    _rotationValueChanged = true;

    invalidateProperties();

    dispatchEvent(new RotationChangeEvent(value));
}
```

When you commit your properties, you check whether the rotation value has been changed. If this is the case, you update the rotation property of _rotationCanvas accordingly:

```
protected override function commitProperties():void{
    super.commitProperties();

    if(_rotationValueChanged){
        _rotationValueChanged = false;
        _rotationCanvas.rotation = _rotationValue;
    }
}
```

Following the life cycle, the next step is to update the display list, redrawing the visual aspects of the component where necessary.

Here you position your various visual components: the dial track, the dial itself, and your rotation canvas. You also draw a circle using the graphics APIs to represent your dial.

```
protected override function updateDisplayList(
                        unscaledWidth:Number,
                        unscaledHeight:Number):void{
    super.updateDisplayList(unscaledWidth,unscaledHeight);

    _dialTrack.x = (unscaledWidth - _dialTrack.width) / 2;
    _dialTrack.y = (unscaledHeight - _dialTrack.height) / 2;

    _dial.x = (unscaledWidth - _dial.width) / 2;
    _dial.y = (unscaledHeight - _dial.height) / 2;

    _dialOriginX = _dial.x + (_dial.width / 2);
    _dialOriginY = _dial.y + (_dial.height / 2);


    _rotationCanvas.x = _dialOriginX;
    _rotationCanvas.y = _dialOriginY;

    drawDialCircle(_rotationCanvas.graphics, _
                        dial.height/2 -2);

}
private function drawDialCircle(p_graphics:Graphics,
                        p_circleY:Number):void{
    p_graphics.clear();
    p_graphics.beginFill(getStyle("dialMarkerColor"));
    p_graphics.drawCircle(0,-p_circleY,3);
}
```

When creating the component, you need to override other methods that exist outside the component life cycle. One of these is the measure function, which is called by the Flex framework when it does not know how large a component should be. If an explicit width and height is supplied as a property, then measure will never be called. This is worth keeping in mind and ensuring that this does not contain anything critical, because there is no guarantee that it will be called.

```
protected override function measure():void{
    super.measure();

    measuredHeight = measuredMinHeight = _dialTrack.height;
    measuredWidth = measuredMinWidth = _dialTrack.width;
}
```

The styleChanged method is used to monitor when custom styles are changed and is called automatically. This allows you to handle this event within your component.

In the case of the example, you need to ensure that your custom style for dialMarkerColor is handled. If this is changed, you invalidate the display list, triggering your component to redraw.

```
public override function styleChanged(styleProp:String):void{
        super.styleChanged(styleProp);

        if(styleProp == "dialMarkerColor"){
                        // your displayList is no longer valid
                invalidateDisplayList();
        }
}
```

You also need to add mouse event holders if you want to allow your component to be interacted with:

```
private function onMouseEventDown(p_evt:MouseEvent):void{
    _movable = true;
}

private function onMouseEventMove(p_evt:MouseEvent):void{
    if(_movable == true){
            // Here we would rotate the dial, updating the
            // component's value as we go
    }
}

private function onMouseEventUp(p_evt:MouseEvent):void{
    _movable = false;
}

    }
}
```

Summary

You should now have an understanding of the variety of components available within the Flex framework and how they can be customized in order to meet the visual requirements of your applications. You should also have a grounding in the steps and considerations that are important when it comes to both extending the functionality of preexisting components and developing entirely new components.

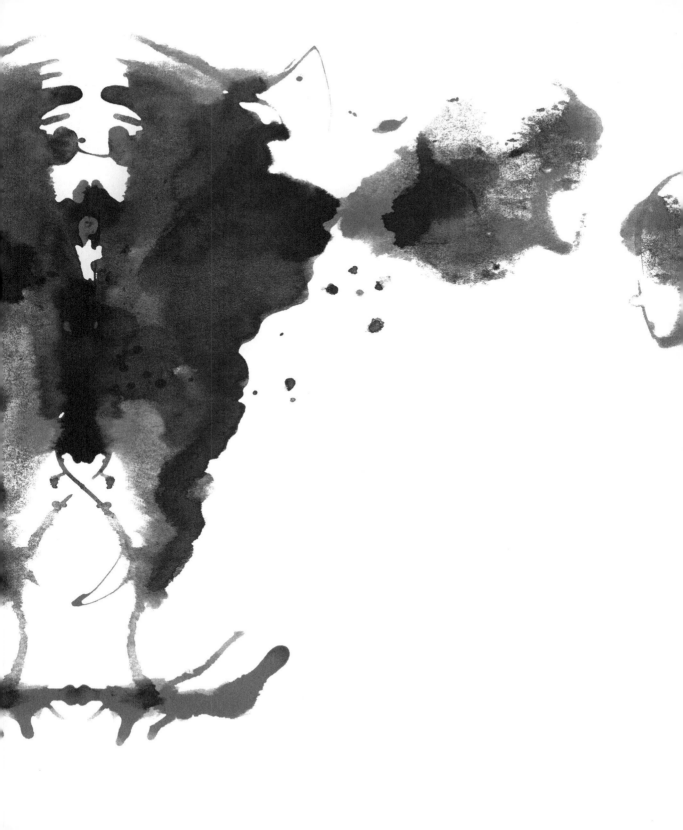

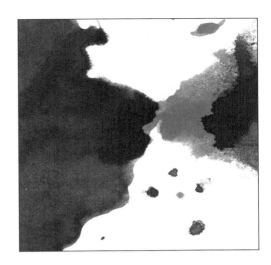

Chapter 5

FLEXING YOUR MUSCLES

In this chapter, you'll apply what you have learned about the Flex framework to building a larger application that interacts with various Internet services. Along the way, you'll explore core concepts of architecting applications to make them more manageable and reusable.

The concept of a mashup is quite straightforward. It is essentially an application that consumes one or more data sources. You have seen how this can vary from small widgets, often built to give web applications a more portable presence across the Web, to larger applications, which often perform more useful tasks.

As applications evolve from widgets to something larger, it becomes necessary to spend more time considering the components and functions that make up an application and how they link together and communicate. This allows you to build applications that are more robust, easier to maintain, and facilitate component reuse.

Architectural considerations when developing Flex applications

Within the Flash world, architecture is often ignored. Flash's roots in animation tend to make this less of a surprise, because designers often don't have a background in software engineering and their main concern is often how the finished product looks. Although this approach is fine for those creating movies, advertising banners, and even widgets to some degree, as you begin to develop larger, richer applications for both the Web and the desktop, it often helps to think about the architecture of your application.

For both Flash and Flex, a handful of different application frameworks allow developers to leverage architectural patterns within their applications. Previously we mentioned Cairngorm and PureMVC as two of the more popular ActionScript 3 frameworks available.

> *Flex is a component framework, but here we are referring to different application frameworks. The distinction is that the Flex framework provides developers with the building blocks for their applications, and application frameworks such as Cairngorm and PureMVC provide the cement that binds the building blocks together.*

Many of the popular frameworks seek to implement design patterns, which are defined and repeatable solutions for common programming problems, often specifying the relationships and interactions between different classes within an application.

Using the Model View Controller pattern

The main design pattern concept you can take from frameworks such as Cairngorm and PureMVC is the Model View Controller (MVC) pattern. MVC is a software architecture pattern developed at Xerox in 1979 and is popular amongst developers. With implementations available in many different programming languages, MVC encourages developers to separate an application into three distinct layers labeled *model*, *view*, and *controller* (Figure 5-1).

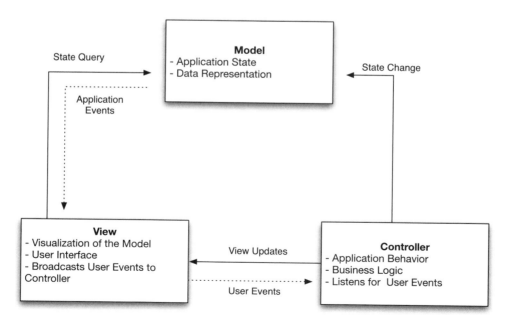

Figure 5-1. A common representation of the Model View Controller pattern

The model encompasses any domain-specific attributes of the application. For example, if you look at your Twitter application from Chapter 3, its **model** would consist of the logic and interpretation of data retrieved from the Twitter APIs.

The **view** would be your user interface, which is often based on the model and provides some form of visualization of the data within.

Finally, the **controller** is the brain behind the application. It processes and responds to events, such as when a user clicks a button in the user interface. In response to these events, the controller may change items in the model, which in turn can result in updates to your view.

The clear advantage of the MVC pattern is that it leads to application components being decoupled from each other, reducing complexity and promoting reuse.

In the following section, you'll begin to implement the MVC pattern within the application you will be creating in this chapter, and along the way, you'll learn about the advantages it provides you.

Your application

In this section, you'll build a more involved mashup application that allows users to search for data from multiple sources. This will allow your users to quickly discover information about a topic from data sources that are more specific than a general-purpose search engine such as Google.

As the data sources in this example, you will be using the following:

- Technorati (www.technorati.com/), an online aggregator of content from millions of blogs. Technorati is useful when searching for information that may not be found on your typical news website; it can also be invaluable when trying to gauge widespread sentiment about a particular topic, event, or product.

- Upcoming (http://upcoming.yahoo.com/), an online event database that allows users to post new events and to sign up to attend events. Its community aspect allows you to view other attendees and create event groups about specific topics. In addition, events can be searched and viewed by specific geographic locations.

- Flickr (www.flickr.com/), the photo-sharing website.

A user will be expected to enter a search term, and the various components of the application will be populated with data, retrieved from the APIs of the individual services. Once data has been loaded, the user should be able to navigate through the search results and click through to access websites containing further information. Figure 5-2 shows the interface.

Figure 5-2. The interface of the example application, showing data being pulled from multiple sources

Application architecture

As we show how to build this application, we will be building an MVC architecture to reduce complexity and to demonstrate many of the concepts behind MVC.

In terms of our application model, a user's global search term is the only item you need to track with regard to the application's state. You'll use this search term to query the various APIs and web services that your application will be interacting with.

For the view, the main user interface will be static, containing Flex panel components that house individual views for the different data sources.

The data views will contain a mini-MVC architecture responsible for managing and orchestrating data service interactions. To map the model data to the view, we will show how to use the Item Renderer pattern, which is provided in the Flex framework.

The main application class will serve as the controller, setting up events that listen for user interaction and orchestrating the calls to Technorati, Upcoming, and Flickr.

This approach gives you **scope** to reuse components in other applications. So if you want to build a Flickr photo browser, you can simply reuse the individual application component, spending minimal effort separating the logic from the current application.

This decoupled approach can also be useful if you want to reuse components across various website areas. You can package the components as individual SWF files and load them into larger applications.

The application shell

Before we get into how you go about interacting with services, we'll explain the shell of the application so you can understand how the user interface is built and how it connects to the various ActionScript classes that provide much of the application's functionality.

MXML

You'll define the application using MXML, where you utilize the Flex framework components in order to construct the user interface:

```
<?xml version="1.0" encoding="utf-8"?>
<mx:WindowedApplication
    xmlns:view="com.realeyesmedia.mainapp.view.*"
    xmlns:mx="http://www.adobe.com/2006/mxml"
    layout="absolute"
    minWidth="875" minHeight="650"
    width="875" height="650"
    creationComplete="onCreationComplete()">

        <mx:VDividedBox left="5" top="5" bottom="5" right="5">
```

The application control bar contains the search box that will be used for the user to input search terms, which in turn drives the content of the application. When the search term is changed, you update the value that is stored in the model:

```
<mx:ApplicationControlBar id="main_acb" width="100%"
                                            top="0">
    <mx:TextInput id="searchTerm_ti"
                width="250"
                text="{model.searchTerm}"
                change="model.searchTerm =
                event.target.text" />
    <mx:Button id="searchAll_btn" label="Search All"
                click="onSearchAll(event)" />
</mx:ApplicationControlBar>

<mx:HDividedBox id="top_hb"
                x="93" y="0" width="100%"
                height="100%">
```

Within the main area of the interface, you'll have three Panel components that represent the views associated with each of the data sources (Technorati, Upcoming, and Flickr). These each contain the logic to orchestrate service requests, passing specific items such as search parameters, user credentials, and API keys as part of the request:

```
<mx:Panel id="technorati_pnl"
          title="Technorati Search"
          width="100%" height="100%"
          layout="absolute">
    <view:Technorati id="technorati_vw"
                     left="0" top="0"
                     bottom="0" right="0"
                     apiKey="xxxxxxxxxxxxxxxx"
                     model="{model}" />
</mx:Panel>

<mx:Panel id="upcoming_pnl"
          title="Upcoming Search"
          width="100%" height="100%">
    <view:Upcoming id="upcoming_vw"
                   left="0" top="0"
                   bottom="0" right="0"
                   apiKey="xxxxxxxxxxxxxxx"
                   model="{model}" />
</mx:Panel>

</mx:HDividedBox>

<mx:Panel id="flickr_pnl"
          title="Photos from Flickr"
          width="100%" height="100%">
    <view:Flickr id="flickr_vw"
                 left="0" top="0" bottom="0" right="0"
                 apiKey="xxxxxxxxxxxxxxxxxxxx"
                 secret="xxxxxxxxxxxxxxxxxxxx"
                 model="{model}" />
</mx:Panel>

</mx:VDividedBox>
```

Finally, you have the ActionScript code, which imports several of the classes you will be using and also provides you with two distinct methods that are triggered at various points during the application life cycle:

- onCreationComplete is called when the user interface has been created. Its primary function is to get an instance of your application model, which will keep track of application state.

- onSearchAll is triggered when a user enters a search term and clicks the Search All button. Its purpose is to execute the onSearch method in each of the data source views. This causes them to query their data sources and retrieve data corresponding to the new search term.

Here's the ActionScript:

```
<mx:Script>
    <![CDATA[
        import com.realeyesmedia.mainapp.model.ModelLocator;
        import mx.core.Application;
        import mx.utils.ObjectUtil;
        import mx.rpc.events.ResultEvent;

        [Bindable]private var model:ModelLocator;

        private function onCreationComplete(
                                   p_event:Event=null):void{
            // Create our model references
            model = ModelLocator.getInstance();
        }

        private function onSearchAll(p_event:MouseEvent=null):void{
            // Fire the search for all views
            technorati_vw.onSearch();
            upcoming_vw.onSearch();
            flickr_vw.onSearch();
        }

    ]]>
</mx:Script>

</mx:WindowedApplication>
```

The model

In this case, the model is a singleton class, of which only a single instance exists within a single instance of the application. Its purpose is to hold data that is used globally within the application and can be used to keep track of application state in larger, more complex applications.

For this application, the model is used only to keep track of the global search term. This allows you to make it available to each of the data source view objects without explicitly passing it back and forth as a parameter. It also guarantees that the same value is used across the entire application.

```
package com.realeyesmedia.mainapp.model{
    import flash.events.EventDispatcher;
    import flash.events.Event;

    [Event("searchTermChanged", "flash.events.Event")]

    [Bindable]

    public class ModelLocator extends EventDispatcher{
```

Within the ModelLocator class, you create an instance of ModelLocator. This is part of the Singleton design pattern and is used in conjunction with the following getInstance method.

By using the getInstance method to retrieve an instance of a singleton class, you can ensure that only a single instance of the class is ever instantiated.

```
static private var _instance:ModelLocator;
```

You are also defining static strings, which are used for the names of custom events. This makes them easier to reference and, combined with the Event metadata shown earlier, also allows for the Flex Builder IDE to utilize event names in its code completion:

```
static public var SEARCH_TERM_CHANGED:String =
                                      "searchTermChanged";
```

The search string is also represented as a variable within the model:

```
private var _searchTerm:String = "";

public function ModelLocator(){

}

static public function getInstance():ModelLocator{
    if(!_instance){
        _instance = new ModelLocator();
    }
    return _instance;
}
```

Within the application, the individual components will use the getter method to retrieve the search string prior to any data calls. The setter method will be used as the user types a value into the main search box.

When the search term changes, you broadcast an event. The individual data source view components will listen to this in order to allow them to update their user interfaces as the user types:

```
public function get searchTerm():String{
    return _searchTerm;
}
public function set searchTerm(p_value:String):void{
    _searchTerm = p_value;
    dispatchEvent(new Event(SEARCH_TERM_CHANGED));
}

    }
}
```

Accessing web services

Within the example application, each of the data sources has its own view. And each of these views manages and choreographs the data service instantiation, requests, and responses. All the data services, although they are constructed in a similar manner, have minor differences because of the variation between the APIs with which they are interacting.

The data services are all singleton classes that extend the HTTPService class, adding functionality beyond what is provided as standard. For consistency, everything is funneled through a method named makeAPICall. Once a service returns a result, you can use asynchronous tokens to determine what to do with the individual responses.

Technorati

Of the three data sources used in this chapter, Technorati's interface is by far the most straightforward to interact with. Beyond the API key, no additional method of authentication or authorization is required in order to retrieve data.

The TechnoratiService class extends the HTTPService class, adding various helper methods that allow you to interact with the Technorati API and interpret responses:

```
package com.realeyesmedia.webapi.technorati{

    import com.realeyesmedia.webapi.util.NameValuePair;

    import mx.rpc.AsyncToken;
    import mx.rpc.events.FaultEvent;
    import mx.rpc.events.ResultEvent;
    import mx.rpc.http.HTTPService;
    import com.realeyesmedia.webapi.technorati.events.TechnoratiEvent;

    public class TechnoratiService extends HTTPService{
```

Because the class is a singleton, you define the standard instance variable and the getInstance method:

```
        static private var _instance:TechnoratiService;
        static public function getInstance():TechnoratiService{
            if(!_instance){
                _instance = new TechnoratiService();
            }
            return _instance;
        }
```

You also define static string variables and the base URL, which you'll be using later to construct the Technorati service URL. Although you could just go ahead and specify the URL within the method itself, this approach makes it simpler to make updates should the URL scheme change at any point.

You also define a variable for the API key; this is already specified in the MXML and will be assigned once the service is instantiated:

```
static public var SEARCH_KEY_WORDS:String = "search";
static public var SEARCH_TAGS:String = "tag";

static public var baseURL:String = "http://api.technorati.com/";
static public var apiKey:String;
```

In the constructor for the service, you call the super constructor for the class you are extending (HTTPService). You also call the init method, which checks that an API key has been supplied, sets several parameters on the service, and registers event listeners for any service responses or errors:

```
public function TechnoratiService(){
      super();
      init();
}

private function init():void{
      if(apiKey == ""){
            throw new Error("You must provide an API key!");
      }

      method = "GET";
      resultFormat = RESULT_FORMAT_E4X;

      addEventListener(ResultEvent.RESULT, onResult);
      addEventListener(FaultEvent.FAULT, onFault);
}
```

All the service interactions are funneled through the makeAPICall method, which is responsible for constructing the request URLs based on the application state and for making the API call. You pass the method, a string value, denoting the remote API to call, along with an array containing any associated parameters that should be included with the API call. This method name should be one of the static string parameters defined earlier in your class.

As part of the process of constructing the URL, you use a utility function named NameValuePair, which simply takes a name and a value and formats them as they would appear in a URL's query string.

Once you have constructed the URL, you create the AsyncToken and make the actual API call:

```
private function makeAPICall(p_method:String,
                             p_request:Array=null):void{
      url = baseURL + p_method + "?";

      if(p_request == null) {
            p_request = new Array();
      }

      p_request.sortOn("name");
```

```
        p_request.push(new NameValuePair("key", apiKey));

        var len:Number = p_request.length;
        for(var i:Number = 0; i<len; i++){
            var nv:NameValuePair = p_request[i];
            url += i == 0 ? nv.toURLString() : "&" +
                    nv.toURLString();
        }

        var token:AsyncToken = send();
        token.method = p_method;
    }
```

When you query the TechnoratiService, you should not be using the makeAPICall directly. Instead, you should be using either the searchKeywords method or the searchTags method in order to call the data service.

Because you have the option of searching the articles in Technorati either by keyword or by tag, you need some way of distinguishing this when you make the API call, which is why you have the two following methods. They format search strings into name-value pairs, which are passed to makeAPICall, which then calls the appropriate method name.

```
        public function searchKeyword(p_keyWord:String):void{
            var params:Array = [new NameValuePair("query",
                                                p_keyWord)];
            makeAPICall(SEARCH_KEY_WORDS, params);
        }

        public function searchTags(p_tags:String):void{
            var params:Array = [new NameValuePair(p_tags)];
            makeAPICall(SEARCH_TAGS, params);
        }
```

Finally, for the service you define two event handlers. One is used when a result is received, and another is for when something goes wrong. When a result is returned, you first ensure that the API has not returned an error, perhaps because of an invalid URL or call parameters. If this is the case, then you broadcast a specific event to denote this.

Assuming everything is in order, you now need to identify which API method was called so that you can alert the appropriate event handler in your view. You do this by retrieving the AsyncToken and accessing its method property. From there, you can use a case statement to select the appropriate course of action:

```
        private function onResult(p_result:ResultEvent):void{
            var xResult:XML = p_result.result as XML;
            var method:String = p_result.token.method;
```

```
                if(xResult.document.result.error){
                    dispatchEvent(new TechnoratiEvent(
                                        TechnoratiEvent.FAULT, xResult));
                }

                switch(method){
                    case SEARCH_KEY_WORDS:
                    {
                        dispatchEvent(new TechnoratiEvent(
                                        TechnoratiEvent.SEARCH_RESULT,
                                        xResult));
                    }
                    case SEARCH_TAGS:
                    {
                        dispatchEvent(new TechnoratiEvent(
                                        TechnoratiEvent.TAG_RESULT,
                                        xResult));
                    }
                }
            }
```

In the case of an error, you simply broadcast the FaultEvent error. If you wanted to display this error to the user, you would have another component in your view or controller listening for these events and use them to trigger an error dialog box.

```
                private function onFault(p_fault:FaultEvent):void{
                    dispatchEvent(p_fault);
                }
            }
        }
```

The onResult method dispatches custom TechnoratiEvents that contain the resultant XML response from the API call. TechnoratiEvent is a simple extension of the Event object within ActionScript, and it contains an additional result parameter, which is the XML response:

```
    package com.realeyesmedia.webapi.technorati.events{

        import flash.events.Event;
        import mx.utils.ObjectUtil;

        public class TechnoratiEvent extends Event{

            static public var SEARCH_RESULT:String = "SEARCH_RESULT";
            static public var TAG_RESULT:String = "TAG_RESULT";
            static public var FAULT:String = "FAULT";

            public var result:XML;
```

```
        public function TechnoratiEvent(p_type:String, p_result:XML,
                                        p_bubbles:Boolean=false,
                                        p_cancelable:Boolean=false){
            super(p_type, p_bubbles, p_cancelable);
            result = new XML(p_result);
        }
    }
}
```

The NameValuePair *class is designed to make constructing a URL string slightly easier. Taking data values and offering an option to return them as formatted strings is not complicated and is useful because it saves you repeating the same code in various places.*

```
        package com.realeyesmedia.webapi.util{

            public class NameValuePair{
                public var name:String;
                public var value:String;

                public function NameValuePair(p_name:String="",
                                              p_value:String=""){
                    name = p_name;
                    value = p_value;
                }

                public function toURLString():String{
                    return name + "=" + value;
                }

                public function toString():String{
                    return name + value;
                }
            }
        }
```

Especially in larger applications, these utility functions can become useful in ensuring that "simple" and repeated operations are done consistently across the entire application. They also become a useful source of code snippets, which can be transferred between projects, saving time and effort.

Upcoming

The Upcoming API requires an additional layer of authentication before you can access its functionality. Upcoming uses token-based authentication on its API methods. Before a third-party site or application can access a user's data, it must first redirect the user to a special URL on the Upcoming website. A user must log in and authenticate themselves before a website or application can access data on Upcoming.

Once approved, the user is given an access code, known as a FROB (see Figure 5-3). This contains the user's identify and can be used to make API requests. This method adds a bit of complication for the developer but adds security for the user. It means that the user's username and password do not need to be stored and are not transmitted over the wire as part of each API call.

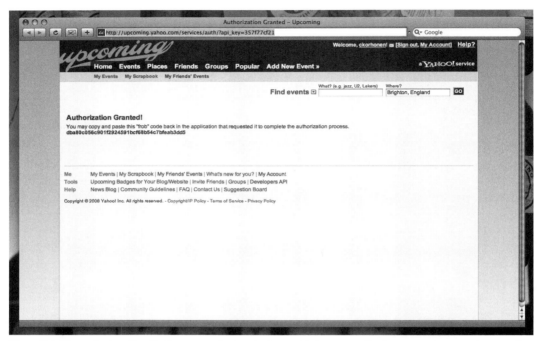

Figure 5-3. Upcoming's authentication page, displayed when a third-party application requests access to a user's data

One of the downsides of using token-based authentication for APIs is the impact it has on the user experience, since the user must be redirected to a special page in order to give permission for an application to proceed. This can be confusing for the average user and can cause concern over the security of the transaction. We know of no industry best practices for designing these authentication steps, but it is worth looking at the messaging used by both Flickr and Facebook, which we consider good models.

With the Upcoming service, you follow the same structure as your Technorati service. The key difference comes with how you handle authentication with the web service in order to accommodate the token-based authentication method:

```
package com.realeyesmedia.webapi.upcoming{

    import mx.rpc.http.HTTPService;
    import mx.rpc.events.ResultEvent;
    import mx.rpc.events.FaultEvent;
    import mx.rpc.Fault;
    import mx.rpc.AsyncToken;
```

```
import com.realeyesmedia.webapi.util.NameValuePair;
import mx.utils.ObjectUtil;
import flash.events.Event;
import com.realeyesmedia.webapi.upcoming.events.UpcomingEvent;

public class UpcomingService extends HTTPService{

    static private var _instance:UpcomingService;

    // Method names
    static public var GET_TOKEN:String = "auth.getToken";
    static public var SEARCH:String = "event.search";

    // Application Events
    static public var TOKEN_LOADED:String = "TOKEN_LOADED";
    static public var SEARCH_RESULT:String = "SEARCH_RESULT";
```

In addition to the base URL and API key, you are also defining a URL for authentication. This is the page you will redirect the user to in order to authenticate with Upcoming and obtain a FROB:

```
    static public var API_KEY:String;
    static public var BASE_URL:String =
        "http://upcoming.yahooapis.com/services/rest/?";
    static public var AUTH_URL:String =
        "http://upcoming.yahoo.com/services/auth/?api_key=";
    static public var FROB:String;

    public var authData:Object;

    public function UpcomingService(rootURL:String=null){
        super(rootURL);

        init();
    }

    static public function getInstance():UpcomingService{
        if(!_instance){
            _instance = new UpcomingService();
        }
        return _instance;
    }
```

Assuming an API key is present, it will be appended to the authentication URL. This is required in order for Upcoming to associate the FROB token with a specific third-party application:

```
    private function init():void{
        if(API_KEY == ""){
            throw new Error("You must provide an API key!");
        }
```

109

```
        AUTH_URL += API_KEY;

        method = "GET";
        resultFormat = RESULT_FORMAT_E4X;

        addEventListener(ResultEvent.RESULT, onResult);
        addEventListener(FaultEvent.FAULT, onFault);
}
```

In this case, the makeAPICall method remains largely unchanged, with only minor differences in how the request is constructed. This is because of how parameters are handled by the different APIs:

```
private function makeAPICall(p_method:String,
                            p_request:Array=null):void{
    url = BASE_URL;

    if(p_request == null) {
        p_request = new Array();
    }

    p_request.sortOn("name");
    p_request.push(new NameValuePair("api_key", API_KEY));
    p_request.push(new NameValuePair("method", p_method));
    request = new Object();

    var len:Number = p_request.length;
    for(var i:Number = 0; i<len; i++){
        var nv:NameValuePair = p_request[i];
        request[p_request[i].name] = p_request[i].value;
    }

    var token:AsyncToken = send();
    token.method = p_method;
}
```

You'll make an additional call to retrieve your authentication token for the service. When this call is made, you must pass the FROB as a parameter to verify your authenticity.

The getToken method will be called from the Upcoming controller, outside of this service, when the application is initialized:

```
public function getToken():void{
    var params:Array = new Array();
    params.push(new NameValuePair("frob", FROB));

    makeAPICall(GET_TOKEN, params);
}
```

To search for an event, you call the eventSearch method, which constructs a parameter's object and calls the makeAPICall method. Upcoming offers many options for searching events. However, for this application, you will be using only the first parameter, a search keyword:

```
public function eventSearch(p_searchText:String="",
                            p_location:String=null,
                            p_radius:Number=50,
                            p_countryID:String="",
                            p_stateID:String="",
                            p_metroID:String="",
                            p_venueID:String="",
                            p_categoryID:String="",
                            p_minDate:Date=null,
                            p_maxDate:Date=null,
                            p_tags:String="",
                            p_perPage:Number=100,
                            p_page:Number=1,
                            p_sort:String="start-date-desc",
                            isAuth:Boolean=false):void{
    var params:Array = new Array();
    params.push(new NameValuePair("search_text",
                                    p_searchText));

    if(p_location){
        params.push(new NameValuePair("location",
                                        p_location));
    }

    if(p_location){
        params.push(new NameValuePair("radius",
                                        p_radius.toString()));
    }

    if(p_countryID != ""){
        params.push(new NameValuePair("country_id",
                                        p_countryID));
    }

    if(p_stateID != ""){
        params.push(new NameValuePair("state_id",
                                        p_stateID));
    }

    if(p_metroID != ""){
        params.push(new NameValuePair("metro_id",
                                        p_metroID));
    }
```

```
          if(p_venueID != ""){
              params.push(new NameValuePair("venue_id",
                                              p_venueID));
          }

          if(p_categoryID != ""){
              params.push(new NameValuePair("category_id",
                                              p_categoryID));
          }

          if(p_minDate){
              var minDate:String =
                  p_minDate.getFullYear().toString() + "-" +
                  p_minDate.getMonth().toString() + "-" +
                  p_minDate.getDay().toString();
              params.push(new NameValuePair("min_date", minDate));
          }

          if(p_maxDate){
              var maxDate:String =
                  p_maxDate.getFullYear().toString() + "-" +
                  p_maxDate.getMonth().toString() + "-" +
                  p_maxDate.getDay().toString();
              params.push(new NameValuePair("max_date",maxDate));
          }

          params.push(new NameValuePair("tags", p_tags));
          params.push(new NameValuePair("per_page",
                              p_perPage.toString()));
          params.push(new NameValuePair("page", p_page.toString()));
          params.push(new NameValuePair("sort", p_sort));

          if(isAuth){
              params.push(new NameValuePair("token",
                                              authData.token));
          }

          makeAPICall(SEARCH, params);
      }
```

As with the Technorati service, results are passed using event handlers. You have also defined a custom event type, which contains the XML response. First, you check for errors. Then, using the asynchronous token, you determine the method that was called and perform the appropriate action. If a token has been returned, then you set the authData object of the service before dispatching the TOKEN_LOADED event:

```
      private function onResult(p_result:ResultEvent):void{
              var xResult:XML = p_result.result as XML;
              var method:String = p_result.token.method;
```

```
if(xResult.document.result.error){
    var fault:Fault = new Fault("" ,"");
    dispatchEvent(new FaultEvent(FaultEvent.FAULT,
                                false, true,
                                fault, p_result.token));
}

switch(method){
    case GET_TOKEN:
    {
        authData = new Object();
        authData.frob = FROB;
        authData.token =
            String(xResult.token.@token);
        authData.userID =
            String(xResult.token.@user_id);
        authData.userName =
            String(xResult.token.@user_username);
        authData.name =
            String(xResult.token.@user_name);

        dispatchEvent(new Event(TOKEN_LOADED));
    }
    case SEARCH:
    {
        dispatchEvent(new UpcomingEvent(SEARCH_RESULT,
            xResult));
    }
}
}
}
}
}
```

Flickr

Like Upcoming, Flickr uses a token-based authentication mechanism. However, this time you have additional steps to perform. First, you need to obtain an API key for the application from the Flickr site. Then, you need to configure your API key, and in the process you'll receive a secret API key.

> *This step allows you to specify your application's name and description and (option-ally) upload an image that will represent your application. The user will be redirected to Flickr for authentication, and your application will display its identity.*

Within your application, you construct a login URL containing your API key and API signature. The API signature is used to tell the Flickr API that the request is being made from a legitimate instance of your application and is created from your secret API key.

Once the user has logged in, they receive a FROB.

Before you can make calls to the API, you need to convert the FROB to a token by passing it and the API key to an API method. Once this step is complete, you can begin interaction with the API.

If you take a look at the code, you can see what Flickr is doing differently:

```
package com.realeyesmedia.webapi.flickr{
     import com.adobe.crypto.MD5;
     import com.realeyesmedia.webapi.flickr.events.FlickrFaultEvent;
     import com.realeyesmedia.webapi.flickr.events.FlickrResultEvent;
     import com.realeyesmedia.webapi.util.NameValuePair;

     import flash.events.Event;

     import mx.rpc.AsyncToken;
     import mx.rpc.Fault;
     import mx.rpc.events.FaultEvent;
     import mx.rpc.events.ResultEvent;
     import mx.rpc.http.HTTPService;
     import mx.utils.ObjectUtil;

     public class FlickrService extends HTTPService{

     static public const BASE_URL:String =
                         "http://api.flickr.com/services/rest/?";
     static public const AUTH_URL:String =
                         "http://www.flickr.com/services/auth/?";

     static private var _instance:FlickrService;
```

You are defining a large number of static constants for this service, which is because of the large number of parameters you can use and the responses you receive from the Flickr API:

```
// HTTP Methods
static public const GET:String = "GET";
static public const POST:String = "POST";

// Permissions
static public const READ:String = "read";
static public const WRITE:String = "write";
static public const DELETE:String = "delete";

// API Settings
static public var _apiKey:String;
static public var _secret:String;
static public var _method:String = GET;
static public var _perms:String = READ;
```

```
// Event Names
static public const FAIL:String = "fail";
static public const OK:String = "ok";
static public const FROB_LOADED:String = "FROB_LOADED";
static public const AUTHORIZED:String = "AUTHORIZED";
static public const SEARCH_RESULT:String = "SEARCH_RESULT";
static public const SEARCH_FAULT:String = "SEARCH_FAULT";
static public const LOCATION_RESULT:String = "LOCATION_RESULT";
static public const LOCATION_FAULT:String = "LOCATION_FAULT";

// API Method Names
static public const GET_FROB:String = "flickr.auth.getFrob";
static public const GET_TOKEN:String = "flickr.auth.getToken";
static public const SEARCH:String = "flickr.photos.search";
static public const GET_WITH_GEODATA:String =
                        "flickr.photos.getWithGeoData";

// Internal data for the API call management
private var _frob:String;
private var _token:String;
private var _loginURL:String;

public var authData:Object;
```

As before, you are checking the API key, and you are also looking for the secret API key. If either is missing, you must throw an error:

```
public function FlickrService(rootURL:String=null){
    super(rootURL);

    if(!_apiKey) {
        throw new Error("You must specify an API key!");
    }
    if(!_secret){
        throw new Error("You must specify your API secret!");
    }

    init();
}

static public function getInstance():FlickrService{
    if(!_instance){
        _instance = new FlickrService();
    }
    return _instance;
}

private function init():void{
    resultFormat = RESULT_FORMAT_E4X; // For simplicity's sake
```

```
        addEventListener(ResultEvent.RESULT, onResult);
        addEventListener(FaultEvent.FAULT, onFault);

        url = BASE_URL;
        method = _method;
    }
```

The makeAPICall method does not differ significantly from the previous service methods, except in the specifics of constructing the service URLs and added parameters:

```
private function makeAPICall(p_method:String, p_request:Array=null,
                            p_isAuthCall:Boolean=false):void{
    if(p_request == null){
        p_request = new Array();
    }

    p_request.push(new NameValuePair("api_key", _apiKey));
    p_request.push(new NameValuePair("method", p_method));
    if(p_isAuthCall){
        if(!authData.token){
            throw new Error("No authentication data exists!");
        }
        p_request.push(new NameValuePair("token",
                    authData.token));
    }

    p_request.push(new NameValuePair("api_sig",
                        getSignature(p_request)));
    request = new Object();

    var len:Number = p_request.length;
    for(var i:Number = 0; i < len; i++){
        request[p_request[i].name] = p_request[i].value;
    }

    var token:AsyncToken = send();
    token.method = p_method;
}
```

You have a method that is used to request a FROB from the API. This is one of the first steps of authentication.

```
public function getFROB():void{
    makeAPICall(GET_FROB);
}
```

You also have a helper method that will build the login URL containing the API key, FROB, and other required values:

```
public function getLoginURL():String{
    var params:Array = new Array();
    params.push(new NameValuePair("api_key", _apiKey));
    params.push(new NameValuePair("frob", _frob));
    params.push(new NameValuePair("perms", _perms));
    params.push(new NameValuePair("api_sig",
                        getSignature(params)));

    var loginURL:String = AUTH_URL;

    var len:Number = params.length;
    for(var i:Number = 0; i < len; i++){
        var nv:NameValuePair = params[i] as NameValuePair;
        loginURL += i == 0 ? nv.toURLString() : "&" +
                        nv.toURLString();
    }

    return loginURL;
}
```

The getSignature method is used when you are constructing the Flickr login URL for your application. Rather than transmitting your secret API key, which could be intercepted, you use an MD5 hash constructed using it. For the MD5 function, you are using the AS3CoreLib package, which is available at http://code.google.com/p/as3corelib/. This provides a variety of useful utility functions and saves you from having to reinvent the wheel.

```
private function getSignature(p_request:Array):String{
    p_request.sortOn("name");
    var args:String = p_request.join("");
    return MD5.hash(_secret + args);
}
```

The final step in authentication is to exchange your FROB for a token that you can use to call specific API methods. This is achieved by a simple API call with the FROB as a parameter.

```
public function getToken():void{
    var params:Array = [new NameValuePair("frob", _frob)];
    makeAPICall(GET_TOKEN, params);
}
```

In addition to authentication, you use the API search method to construct an API request around your keyword. Like Upcoming, Flickr offers a comprehensive set of search parameters that you can use to filter the search results, so for example, you may want to restrict results to photos taken within the past seven days. You can find more details in the API documentation at www.flickr.com/services/api/.

```
public function search(p_nsid:String="", p_tags:String="",
                       p_tagMode:String="any",
                       p_text:String="",
                       p_minUploadDate:Date=null,
                       p_maxUploadDate:Date=null,
                       p_minTakenDate:Date=null,
                       p_maxTakenDate:Date=null,
                       p_license:Number=-1,
                       p_extras:String="",
                       p_perPage:Number=100,
                       p_page:Number=1,
                       p_sort:String="date-posted-desc"):void{

    var params:Array = new Array();

    if(p_nsid != ''){
        params.push(new NameValuePair("user_id", p_nsid));
    }

    if(p_tags != ""){
        params.push(new NameValuePair("tags", p_tags));
    }

    params.push(new NameValuePair("tag_mode", p_tagMode));

    if(p_text != ""){
        params.push(new NameValuePair("text", p_text));
    }

    if(p_minUploadDate){
        params.push(new NameValuePair("min_upload_date",
                        p_minUploadDate.toDateString()));
    }

    if(p_maxUploadDate){
        params.push(new NameValuePair("max_upload_date",
                        p_maxUploadDate.toDateString()));
    }

    if(p_minTakenDate){
        params.push(new NameValuePair("min_taken_date",
                        p_minTakenDate.toDateString()));
    }

    if(p_maxTakenDate){
        params.push(new NameValuePair("max_taken_date",
                        p_maxTakenDate.toDateString()));
    }
```

```
            params.push(new NameValuePair("licence",
                            p_license.toString()));
            params.push(new NameValuePair("extras", p_extras));
            params.push(new NameValuePair("per_page",
                            p_perPage.toString()));
            params.push(new NameValuePair("page", p_page.toString()));
            params.push(new NameValuePair("sort", p_sort));

            makeAPICall(SEARCH, params);
        }
```

Finally, you have event handlers, which function in a similar manner to the previous services:

```
            private function onResult(p_result:ResultEvent):void{
                var method:String = p_result.token.method;
                var xResult:XML = p_result.result as XML;

                if(xResult.rsp.@stat == FlickrFaultEvent.FAIL){
                    var fault:Fault = new Fault(xResult.err.@code,
                            xResult.err.@msg, xResult.err.@msg);
                    dispatchEvent(new FlickrFaultEvent(
                            FlickrFaultEvent.FAIL,
                            false, true, fault, p_result.token));
                } else {
                    switch(method){
                        case GET_FROB:
                        {
                            _frob = String( xResult.frob );
                            dispatchEvent( new Event( FROB_LOADED ) );
                        }
                        case GET_TOKEN:
                        {
                            authData = new Object();
                            authData.token = String(
                                xResult.auth.token);
                            authData.read = String(
                                xResult.auth.perms);
                            authData.nsid = String(
                                xResult.auth.user.@nsid);
                            authData.userName = String(
                                xResult.auth.user.@username);
                            authData.fullName = String(
                                xResult.auth.user.@fullname);

                            dispatchEvent( new Event( AUTHORIZED ) );
                        }
                        case SEARCH:
```

```
                                {
                                        dispatchEvent(new FlickrResultEvent(
                                                SEARCH_RESULT,
                                                false, true, p_result.result,
                                                p_result.token));
                                }
                        }
                }
        }

                private function onFault(p_fault:FaultEvent):void{
                        dispatchEvent(p_fault);
                }
        }
}
```

Building the views

The views of each service are defined as MXML components. These contain user interface components to be displayed in the final interface, as well as various ActionScript classes and snippets that provide the controller layer for these services.

Viewing your Technorati data

Because you do not need to worry about service authentication, Technorati is once again the simpler example (see Figure 5-4).

Figure 5-4. The view of the Technorati services. Note the data bindings to the model.

The interface is defined using MXML, with an application control bar allowing the user to enter a keyword, specify a search type, and perform the actual search.

A list view forms the bulk of the interface and is populated by the search results. When a list item is selected, information around the selected item will be displayed on the right of the interface, along with LinkButtons, which will take the user to specific URLs where they can learn more.

It is worth noting the instances where you are binding data directly to your interface using the { } notation.

Within your layout, you are using nested horizontal and vertical boxes in order to simplify the positioning and alignment of your user interface elements:

```xml
<?xml version="1.0" encoding="utf-8"?>
<mx:Canvas xmlns:mx="http://www.adobe.com/2006/mxml"
        creationComplete="onCreationComplete()">

    <mx:ApplicationControlBar id="technorati_acb"
                    right="0" left="0" top="0" height="33">
        <mx:TextInput id="search_txt"
                width="250"
                text="{model.searchTerm}" />
        <mx:Button label="Search"
                click="onSearch(event)"/>
        <mx:RadioButtonGroup id="searchType_rbg"/>
            <mx:RadioButton label="Key Word"
                        selected="true"
                        groupName="searchType_rbg"/>
            <mx:RadioButton label="Tag"
                        groupName="searchType_rbg"/>
    </mx:ApplicationControlBar>

    <mx:List id="result_list"
            dataProvider="{techData}"
            labelField="title"
            top="41" left="0"
            selectedIndex="0"
            bottom="0" width="260"/>
    <mx:VBox id="technoratiItem_cvs" bottom="0" top="41"
            left="268" right="0">
        <mx:VBox width="100%">
            <mx:VBox>
                <mx:Label id="title_lbl"
                    fontWeight="bold"
                    text="{result_list.selectedItem.title}"/>
                <mx:Label id="blogName_lbl"
                    text="{'By: ' +
result_list.selectedItem.weblog.name}"/>
                <mx:Label id="created_lbl"
                    text="{result_list.selectedItem.created}"/>
            </mx:VBox>
        </mx:VBox>
```

```
<mx:VBox width="100%">
    <mx:HBox>
        <mx:LinkButton id="blogURL_lnk"
                       label="Blog URL"
                       click=" ➥
navigateToURL( new URLRequest(result_list.selectedItem.weblog.url),
                       '_blank')" />

        <mx:LinkButton id="rssURL_lnk"
                       label="RSS URL"
                       click=" ➥
navigateToURL(new URLRequest(result_list.selectedItem.weblog.rssurl),
                       '_blank')" />
    </mx:HBox>
    <mx:HBox>
        <mx:LinkButton id="atomURL_lnk"
                       label="ATOM URL"
                       click=" ➥
navigateToURL(new URLRequest(result_list.selectedItem.weblog.atomurl),
                       '_blank')" />
        <mx:LinkButton id="created_lnk"
                       label="Perma Link"
                       click=" ➥
navigateToURL(new URLRequest(result_list.selectedItem.permalink),
                       '_blank')" />
    </mx:HBox>
</mx:VBox>
<mx:Text id="expert_txt"
         htmlText="{result_list.selectedItem.excerpt}"
         width="100%" height="100%"/>
</mx:VBox>
```

The ActionScript behind this component is relatively straightforward:

```
<mx:Script>
    <![CDATA[


        import mx.utils.ObjectUtil;
        import mx.events.ListEvent;
        import com.realeyesmedia.mainapp.model.ModelLocator;
        import flash.net.navigateToURL;
        import com.realeyesmedia.webapi.technorati.events.
TechnoratiEvent;
        import com.realeyesmedia.webapi.technorati.
TechnoratiService;
```

You are registering properties for the API key, the model, and the data feed as bindable in order to allow Flex to update this property within your view should it be updated:

```
[Bindable]public var apiKey:String;
[Bindable]public var model:ModelLocator;
[Bindable]public var techData:XMLList;

private var _techSvc:TechnoratiService;
```

Once the interface has been initialized, you pass the Technorati service your API key, retrieve an instance, and bind your listeners that will be triggered upon a response from an API request:

```
public function onCreationComplete():void{
    TechnoratiService.apiKey = apiKey;

    _techSvc = TechnoratiService.getInstance();
    _techSvc.addEventListener(
        TechnoratiEvent.SEARCH_RESULT,
        onSearchResult);
    _techSvc.addEventListener(
        TechnoratiEvent.TAG_RESULT,
        onSearchResult);
}
```

The event listener will retrieve the result object from a TechnoratiEvent object, assigning its value to that of the internal techData object. Because this is bound as the data provider to your user interface, this will feed your user interface controls with content.

When you have search results to display, you need to reset your list control. By broadcasting a ListEvent.CHANGE event, you can invalidate the component and trigger a redraw:

```
private function onSearchResult(
        p_event:TechnoratiEvent):void{
    techData = p_event.result.document.item as XMLList;
    result_list.selectedIndex = 0;

    if(model.searchTerm != ""){
        result_list.dispatchEvent(new ListEvent(
            ListEvent.CHANGE));
    }
}
```

The onSearch method is triggered when the user clicks the search button. It calls the appropriate method within Technorati:

```
public function onSearch(p_event:MouseEvent=null):void{
    if(searchType_rbg.selectedValue == "Key Word"){
        _techSvc.searchKeyword(search_txt.text);
    } else if(searchType_rbg.selectedValue == "Tag"){
        _techSvc.searchTags(search_txt.text);
    }
}
```

```
            ]]>
        </mx:Script>
    </mx:Canvas>
```

Viewing Flickr data

To render data from Flickr, you again need to define the interface using MXML, tying it to the controller (Figure 5-5).

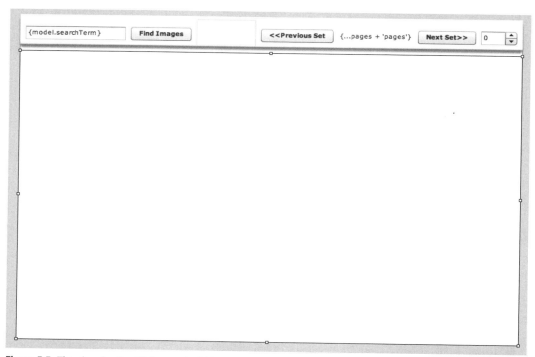

Figure 5-5. The view for the Flickr panel within the application, with an application toolbar and large area used when displaying thumbnails

The MXML file defines the interface or the application. For Flickr you are creating two canvas elements, one that will contain your application bar with search and navigation controls and a second that you will be using to hold your search results, arranged within a TileList component.

For image rendering, you have developed a custom item rendering component called FlickrImageRenderer within your mode. You have also created a Photo object that encapsulates a Flickr Photo ID and provides utility methods to retrieve the image, sized to various dimensions.

In your item renderer, you are defining an Image component, which will be the thumbnail of your image. Then you are using the Photo object to retrieve the thumbnail URL and the target URL of your image. These are used by the Image component.

```xml
<?xml version="1.0" encoding="utf-8"?>
<mx:VBox xmlns:mx="http://www.adobe.com/2006/mxml"
         width="75" height="75"
         horizontalScrollPolicy="off"
         verticalScrollPolicy="off">

    <mx:Script>
        <![CDATA[
            import flash.net.navigateToURL;
            import com.realeyesmedia.webapi.flickr.model.Photo;

            private var _data:Object;

            [Bindable]public var photo:Photo;
            [Bindable]public var imageURL:String;
            [Bindable]public var linkURL:String;

            override public function get data():Object{
                return _data;
            }

            override public function set data( p_value:Object ):void{
                super.data = p_value;
                _data = p_value;

                photo = Photo( p_value );

                imageURL = photo.getImageURL( Photo.SMALL_SQUARE );
                linkURL = photo.viewableURL;

            }

        ]]>
    </mx:Script>

    <mx:Image id="img" source="{imageURL}"
              width="75" height="75"
              doubleClickEnabled="true"
              doubleClick="navigateToURL(
              new URLRequest( linkURL ) );"/>

</mx:VBox>
```

If you return to the main MXML file, you can see the user interface you have defined for your Flickr component.

You'll place the ActionScript code for this example in an external file, which will be referenced by the <mx:Script> tag. This is recommended practice when dealing with complex functions and helps to keep the MXML tidy and comprehensible.

125

```xml
<?xml version="1.0" encoding="utf-8"?>
<mx:Canvas
    xmlns:mx="http://www.adobe.com/2006/mxml"
    width="100%" height="100%"
    verticalScrollPolicy="off"
    creationComplete="onCreationComplete()">

    <mx:Script>
        <![CDATA[
            import com.realeyesmedia.mainapp.view.itemrenderer.
FlickerImageRenderer;
        ]]>
    </mx:Script>

    <mx:Script source="_asincludes/_Flickr.as" />

    <mx:Canvas id="images_cvs"
                width="100%" top="60" bottom="0">

    <mx:TileList id="images_tile"  top="0" bottom="0"
                left="0" right="0"
                itemRenderer="com.realeyesmedia.mainapp.
view.itemrenderer.FlickerImageRenderer"/>

</mx:Canvas>

<mx:Canvas id="control_cvs" width="100%" height="50">
        <mx:ApplicationControlBar id="flickrControl_acb" width="100%"
                                    height="50">
            <mx:TextInput id="search_txt"
                        text="{model.searchTerm}"/>
            <mx:Button id="search_btn"
                    label="Find Images"
                    click="onSearch(event)"/>
            <mx:Spacer width="100%" height="50" />
            <mx:Button id="previous_btn"
                    label="&lt;&lt;Previous Set"
                    click="onPreviousSet(event)" />
            <mx:Label id="total_lbl"
                    text="{'Current page ' + page +
                                    ' of ' + photoList.pages +
                                    'pages'}" />
            <mx:Button id="next_btn"
                    label="Next Set&gt;&gt;"
                    click="onNextSet(event)" />
```

```
            <mx:NumericStepper id="newPage_ns"
                        minimum="0"
                        maximum="{photoList.total}"
                        value="{page}"
                        change="onPageChange(event)" />
        </mx:ApplicationControlBar>
    </mx:Canvas>
```

The MXML code goes beyond simple instantiation of the Flickr service and event assignment. It must support additional items, such as pagination, and also facilitate the process of authentication within your user interface.

First, import the classes you'll be using:

```
import com.realeyesmedia.mainapp.model.ModelLocator;
import com.realeyesmedia.webapi.flickr.FlickrService;
import com.realeyesmedia.webapi.flickr.events.FlickrResultEvent;
import com.realeyesmedia.webapi.flickr.model.Photo;
import com.realeyesmedia.webapi.flickr.model.PhotoList;

import flash.events.Event;
import flash.events.MouseEvent;
import flash.filesystem.File;
import flash.filesystem.FileMode;
import flash.filesystem.FileStream;
import flash.net.navigateToURL;

import mx.accessibility.AlertAccImpl;
import mx.controls.Alert;
import mx.utils.ObjectUtil;
```

Next, it is important to declare your variables as bindable because of the reasons we have already outlined. In addition to specifying the API keys, you must define variables for use by other user interface components to display the API call results:

```
[Bindable]public var apiKey:String;
[Bindable]public var secret:String;
[Bindable]public var model:ModelLocator;
[Bindable]public var picsPerPage:Number = 90;
[Bindable]public var page:Number = 0;
[Bindable]public var photoList:PhotoList;
[Bindable]public var imageSize:String = Photo.SMALL_SQUARE;

private var _flickrSvc:FlickrService;
```

For access to the local filesystem, you'll use several Adobe AIR APIs. This will allow you to store authentication tokens for use in future sessions and negate the need for authentication on every run of the application.

If you are developing a web application and don't have access to the filesystem for storage, then an alternate approach would be to store the token within a SharedObject:

```
private function checkForTokenFile():Boolean{
    var tokenFile:File = File.applicationStorageDirectory;
    tokenFile = tokenFile.resolvePath( "ApplicationToken.txt" );
    if(tokenFile.exists) {
        var tokenFileStream:FileStream = new FileStream();

        tokenFileStream.open( tokenFile, FileMode.READ );
        _flickrSvc.authData = tokenFileStream.readObject();

        tokenFileStream.close();
        return true;
    }

    return false;
}
```

Once your interface has been initialized, you perform the usual tasks of assigning variables and creating event listeners.

In addition, you check to see whether the user already has an authentication token stored locally. If this is not the case, then you begin the process of obtaining one by instructing the Flickr Service to get a FROB:

```
private function onCreationComplete():void{
    FlickrService._apiKey = apiKey;
    FlickrService._secret = secret;

    _flickrSvc = FlickrService.getInstance();

    _flickrSvc.addEventListener(FlickrService.FROB_LOADED,
                                        onFrobLoaded);
    _flickrSvc.addEventListener(FlickrService.AUTHORIZED,
                                        onAppliationAuthorized);
    _flickrSvc.addEventListener(FlickrService.SEARCH_RESULT,
                                        onSearchResult);

    var tokenFileExists:Boolean = checkForTokenFile();


    if(!tokenFileExists){
        // If not start the authorization process by getting the FROB
        _flickrSvc.getFROB();
    } else {

    }
}
```

Once your service has received a FROB, you need to open a web browser window and redirect the user to the login URL provided by your service (Figure 5-6).

Upon completion, the user should return to the application and close the alert box displayed (Figure 5-7). This will initiate a callback to the onAuthWindowClose method.

```
private function onFrobLoaded(p_event:Event):void{
    navigateToURL( new URLRequest( _flickrSvc.getLoginURL() ) );
    Alert.show( "Click 'OK' once you have authorized this application.",
                "Flickr Authorization", 4, this,
                onAuthWindowClose );
}
```

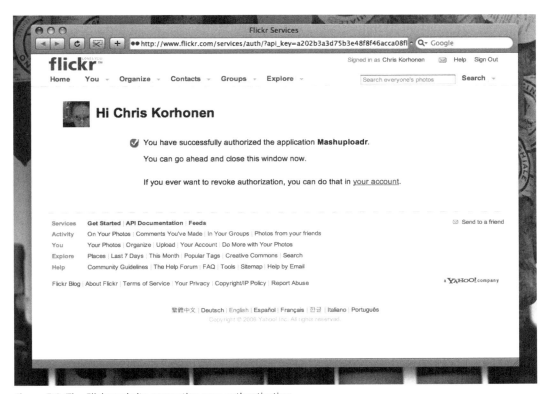

Figure 5-6. The Flickr website requesting user authentication

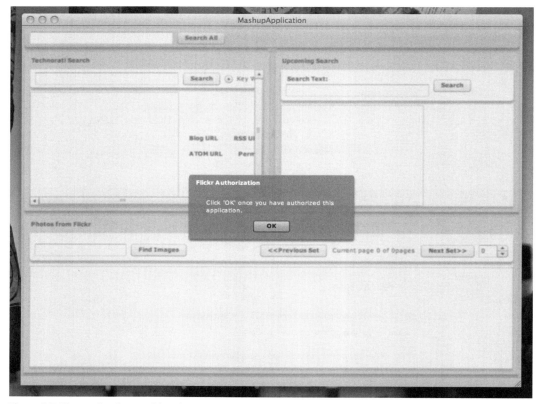

Figure 5-7. The application awaiting the user to authenticate on the Flickr website

Once the user has authenticated and returned to the application, you instruct the Flickr Service to fetch the authentication token and make the service calls:

```
private function onAuthWindowClose(p_event:Event):void{
        _flickrSvc.getToken();
}
```

onApplicationAuthorized is called once the AUTHORIZED event is broadcast upon the token being granted.

In this example, you are writing your token to the local filesystem, but for web applications, you may want to store it within a shared object:

```
private function onAppliationAuthorized(p_authorize:Event):void{
     trace( "Save the token data" );
     trace( ObjectUtil.toString( _flickrSvc.authData ) );

     var tokenFile:File = File.applicationStorageDirectory;
     tokenFile = tokenFile.resolvePath( "ApplicationToken.txt" );
```

```
var tokenFileStream:FileStream = new FileStream();

// Write the token data to our file
tokenFileStream.open(tokenFile, FileMode.WRITE);
tokenFileStream.writeObject( _flickrSvc.authData );

// Clean up our FileStream
tokenFileStream.close();
}
```

Within the code, you also have the handler for search results. You simply take the list of photos returned by your service call and assign them as the data provider for the TileList component:

```
private function onSearchResult(p_result:FlickrResultEvent):void{
    photoList = new PhotoList(p_result.result as XML);
    images_tile.dataProvider = photoList.photos;
}
```

Similarly, you have a handler for the search event that invokes the appropriate method within the Flickr service.

As part of this request, you are adding the picsPerPage parameter, which specifies the number of pictures to return in the request, and you are also adding the page parameter, which specifies the current page to retrieve. These allow you to paginate your resulting TileList component:

```
public function onSearch(p_event:MouseEvent=null):void{
    _flickrSvc.search('', '', 'any', search_txt.text, null, null,
                      null, null, -1, '', picsPerPage, page)
}
```

When a user requests the next page of results, you increment the page number and request a new set of results:

```
private function onNextSet(p_event:MouseEvent=null):void{
    if(page < photoList.total){
        page = page + 1;
    }
    onSearch();
}
```

To view the previous page, you decrement the page number and request a new set of results:

```
private function onPreviousSet(p_event:MouseEvent=null):void{
    if(page >= 0){
        page = page - 1;
    }
    onSearch();
}
```

131

Navigation is also possible by changing the value in the NumericStepper, either by using the arrow controls (incrementing or decrementing) or by typing in a value. Once again, you change the page number and request a new set of results.

To handle a case where the requested page exceeds the number of pages available, you check the next page against the number of photos to ensure that the requested page actually exists. You can further decide to display a notification to the user.

```
private function onPageChange(p_event:Event):void{
    var newPage:Number = p_event.target.value;
    if(newPage > 0 && newPage < photoList.total){
        page = newPage
        onSearch();
    } else {
        // Out of Bounds
    }
}
```

Summary

In this chapter, you learned how you might go about building a larger application, specifically how architectural patterns can simplify development and facilitate component reuse. In addition, they create a common language between developers that aids in the understandability of applications, something that is important in larger teams.

Using a Model View Controller architecture, we have demonstrated how to achieve a separation of the various layers of an application, how you can manage data effectively and efficiently, and how you can develop visual components in a way that they encapsulate internal logic and can easily be reused.

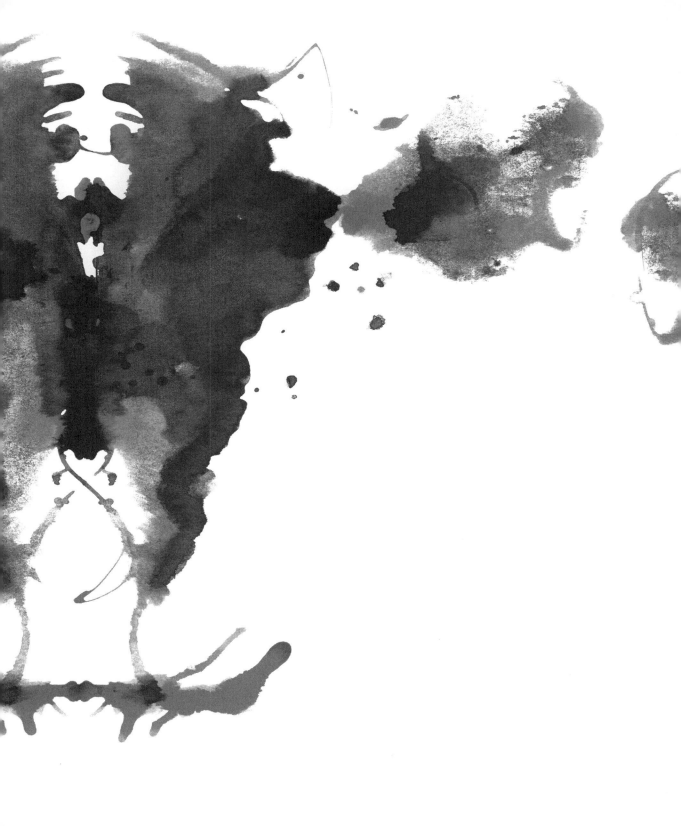

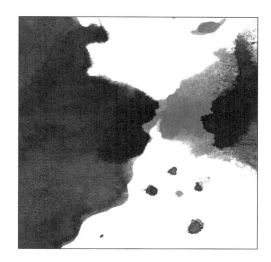

Chapter 6

PERFORMANCE MANAGEMENT IN FLEX APPLICATIONS

Performance can make or break your application. Its impact can ruin the most carefully designed user interface and bring data processing to a crawl. In this chapter, you'll learn how to optimize your applications and streamline your workflow.

Let's face it. No one likes an application to run slowly. It's frustrating to work with an application that is peppered with annoying delays whenever you interact with it. In the same way, using an application whose interface moves in jerks and spasms or frequently loses part of the display is also a frustrating experience. It's even more frustrating when the application just plain doesn't work and continually pops up with errors.

Don't let your application be one of those applications.

These problems often arise when either there wasn't sufficient debugging or the application is asking too much of the client machine and the processor or graphics card can't keep pace with the demands the application is putting on it. One way you can combat this sort of problem is by optimizing the application's memory and processor usage levels. So, this chapter covers how you can optimize your application's performance to keep it running smoothly and provide a problem-free experience for your user.

First, you'll gain some context by looking at how Flash Player and ActionScript work. Then you'll learn about the pitfalls of premature optimization and the best practices of good optimization. Finally, you'll see some optimization methods and tools that can help make your optimization efforts more effective.

How Flash Player and ActionScript work

Before we get into the business of optimizing performance and debugging, we'll explain how Flash Player and ActionScript work.

When a SWF is generated, its code is turned into ActionScript byte code in an .abc file. That byte code is passed to the .abc parser and then verified by—what else?—the byte code verifier. From there, code is passed to the interpreter, which then passes it to the runtime system.

The byte code verifier also passes byte code to the just-in-time (JIT) compiler. This compiler handles translating ActionScript byte code into machine language, which will execute faster. This machine language also gets passed to the runtime system.

The runtime system then uses the memory manager and garbage collector to allocate memory for objects it creates and to remove objects from memory. While the application is running, player and network events are processed, ActionScript is executed, and visual assets are rendered in response to the events and ActionScript.

You can see that a lot of computation is going on in the background of a Flash application. The way you create your application can affect how intensely the computer has to work and how much memory it consumes while running these processes. This work is reflected in the performance of your application on the client's machine.

Not surprisingly, optimization can make your application faster and more efficient. Code optimization is primarily a matter of using memory efficiently, releasing memory once it is free, and minimizing the amount of processing the system needs to do.

The dangers of premature optimization

Optimization is not without its pitfalls. One thing you should avoid is premature optimization. Simply put, premature optimization is taking care of optimization problems before you even know whether they exist. Conventional wisdom advises that an ounce of prevention is worth a pound of cure, but that doesn't necessarily hold true in the world of Flex optimization, or code optimization in general.

In the push to optimize everything before you have your application working, you can make your code more complex than it needs to be, which ironically will increase the number of lines of code. It may save a bit of performance, but it also adds to your app's file size. Beyond that, it can make your code less readable, which means you're going to spend more time working with your code for the sake of a possible small savings in performance. All of this is also assuming you can accurately predict where the bottlenecks will be.

Until you have done performance profiling, you will be primarily guessing at where you need to use optimization techniques. If you guess wrong, you'll be wasting time and effort and creating extra work for yourself.

Don't forget that part of optimization is also optimizing your workflow, as well as your application's performance. Your clients may be less than thrilled if you're adding on extra billable time to shave off bytes of memory usage, rather than making the application more functional.

This is not to say that you shouldn't plan for optimization. There are times for optimizing before development, during development, and at the end of development.

In the beginning, when you're designing your application with wireframes and flow diagrams, by all means keep the performance goals for your application in mind. Flag the areas of the application that are potential bottlenecks. For instance, maybe loading the entire code framework and an animated gallery of photographs at the same time isn't the best use of the client machine's processing power.

During development, following best practices in coding will help you optimize your application without having to go to elaborate lengths. We'll be looking at some of the practices such as strong data typing that can optimize both your application and your development. Part of being a good developer is knowing which measures to take during normal application development to optimize code, and if you're not already familiar with those measures, by the end of this chapter, you will be.

At the end of an application's development process is the traditional time to do optimization. This is when you can break out the hard-core optimization techniques and less standard tricks and tools. When your app is essentially complete and near its final form, then you can profile its performance.

Enough changes in your application occur during development that doing this sort of stuff earlier in the development process would be premature and not an efficient use of your time. After the application has gelled, you can more confidently assess the bottlenecks and memory leaks that have somehow wormed their way into your masterpiece of code. You can then compare the performance with the requirements that were set out in the design phase.

Once you've profiled what the problems are and where they are lurking, you can break out the heavy optimization artillery to eradicate those problems, leaving your app a gleaming paragon of digital efficiency. We'll introduce some profiling methods and tools later in this chapter to help you in your optimization efforts.

Achieving optimization

So, how can you achieve optimization for your applications? Let's take a look at the best practices to make your code slim and trim and to run efficiently.

The main considerations we'll look at are giving variables strong data types, using data binding, using local variables, managing Number data types, and working with arrays. We'll also talk about some of the ways you can monitor the performance of your applications.

Best practices

One way to improve application efficiency is to use **strongly typed** variables. This means that when you declare your variables, you specify a data type for the variable, such as Number or Array. This tells the compiler that the variable will be only that particular data type. Strong data typing looks like this:

```
public var myNumber:Number = 0;
```

The colon lets the compiler know you're specifying a data type, and what follows the colon is the name of the specific data type. You can use data typing only when you are declaring a variable with the var keyword.

Even before we get to how strong data typing optimizes your code, we'll review the ways it can optimize your development process.

Since the compiler knows what data type a variable should be, it will throw errors if your code is inadvertently returning data of a different type. For instance, if you have a variable with a numeric data type and you attempt to set it to a value you think is a number but is actually a string, you will receive an error. This lets you know up front that your code is not returning the value you thought and saves you the time it would take to discover that your code is returning "42" rather than 42.

In this way, strong data typing simplifies the debugging process. You can be more certain that your code is using the right data.

Strong typing also helps when writing the code. The code hinting system in Flex Builder is based on strong data typing. If you are writing custom classes in Flex and provide data types for its properties, Flex Builder will be able to give you code hinting for those properties. For example, if you have a class with a property that has its data type specified as an Array, Flex will then supply Array code hints when you access that property (Figure 6-1).

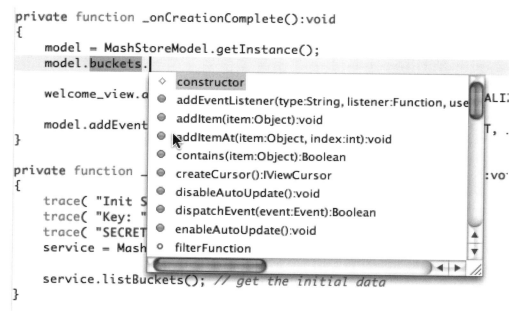

Figure 6-1. Code hinting in action within Flex Builder. Note the array specific methods that are displayed.

Strong data typing and code optimization

Now we'll talk about how strong data typing optimizes your code. First, **data typing** will help optimize your byte code. Because the compiler knows what type of data you'll be storing in the variable, it knows how much memory to allocate for that variable. This allows it to write the byte code used to build the application more efficiently. Otherwise, it assigns the data as a less efficient hash table, which has a negative effect on both performance and memory consumption.

It also affects the way Flash Player accesses the members of classes and objects. When the compiler has already allocated the bytes for the data, it can access them more quickly. If it hasn't, it has to retrieve them as a hash table, which takes more time to look up specific data items.

When referring to a variable, you should also use **strong references**. This means you must use the dot operator to access the member, not square bracket (or hash) notation. Hash notation is a weak reference. However, even if you use dot notation for the reference, if the data type is weak, it will still be accessed as a hash notation. So for strong references, you need a strong data type and dot notation:

```
class Example extends Object{
     var foo:String;
}

function a(o:Object){   //weak
    return o.foo;       //weak
}

function b(o:Object):String{   //weak
    return o.foo;              //weak
}

function c(o:Example){   //strong
    return o.foo;         //weak
}
function d(o:Example):String{   //strong
    return o.foo;               //strong
}
```

Why does this matter? Well, based on performance benchmarks by the Flash Player team at Adobe, weak references are about ten times slower than a strong reference. When you think of all the times in a Flash application that you reference a variable, you can imagine how this will quickly add up.

So, the bottom line is that you should data type your variables. Which variables? All of them.

If it is a member of a class or a local variable, type it.

If it is the return value of a function, even if it is void, type it.

If it is a parameter, type it.

If it is a loop counter, type it.

Anywhere it is feasible, type it.

If there is a var in the statement, there had better be a colon and a data type there too!

Even if you're building a dynamic class that can accept dynamically declared properties, you can create precompiled slots for variables that the virtual machine can take advantage of. New properties are going to require the hash lookup, and this means a weak reference and less efficient execution.

You can further make your application efficient through data typing by **casting**, or **coercing**, unknown data types into a specific data type. Casting is generally done by passing the data you want to coerce into the class constructor for the data type you want the data to cast as. If you will be receiving numeric data from an external data source, you might not know whether it will be coming in as a text string of numbers or an actual numeric data type.

By passing the data into the Number class's constructor method, you can ensure that it will be a numeric data type when you work with it in your application:

```
var localData:Number = Number(externalData);
```

You can also cast data as a specific data type by using the as operator. When you assign data to a variable, use the as operator followed by the data type for which you want to cast the data as.

```
var localData:Number = externalData as Number;
```

Not only does the coercion of data types help you know what type of data you'll be working with, but it also speeds up performance.

A virtual machine (VM) error can be ten times slower than the time it takes for a coercion to execute. Making your coercion explicit by using the as operator or a class constructor rather than leaving it as implicit coercion also speeds things up. If you did not cast the external data coming in, the virtual machine would still coerce it (if possible) to be a Number because of the strong data typing. This is known as **implicit coercion**, and it slows down performance.

Again, the bottom line is that you should data type everything you can.

Typing with numeric data types

In ActionScript 2.0, we had only the Number data type when working with numeric data. Now, with ActionScript 3.0, we have three different numeric data types: uint, int, and Number.

The uint data type is an unsigned integer data type, which means it is for positive whole numbers only. It can take any positive number between 0 and 4,294,967,295.

The int data type can be a whole number that is either positive or negative but is limited between positive and negative 2,147,483,647.

The Number data type doesn't have those restrictions and can handle any number.

Now, the uint and int types are going to use less memory than the Number data type, so it's preferred to use them performance-wise. You'd also think that uint would be more efficient to use than int, but actually it turns out that the int data type provides a performance savings over both uint and Number when used as a loop counter. The int data type also tends to outperform uint when used for other mathematical operations; however, Number often yields the best performance, making it a classic choice between whether you want to optimize your code for memory usage or for performance.

Data binding considerations

Another place to get some performance savings is in the area of data binding. Data bindings are nice and handy for setting up applications quickly, because you don't have to explicitly make all the assignments of values and properties, instead using the {} notation in order to link components to data providers. For example:

```
<mx:Label id="title_lbl"
          fontWeight="bold"
          text="{result_list.selectedItem.title}" />
```

Unfortunately, the convenience of data bindings comes with a cost. Binding expressions takes up memory and can slow down the start-up of an application when they are initialized within Flash Player.

In addition, bindings are general cases, so they can't have optimized execution paths. To put this another way, if your data binding uses dot notation to access a property, the first part of the reference isn't going to change, but the data binding doesn't know that it won't change. Every time it is checking the binding, it has to look up the path of the complex reference, which slows down performance.

When it comes to optimizing the performance of the code, take a close look at the data bindings you are using. If you're going to use the data just once and it won't change after that, it may be more efficient to do an assignment in ActionScript rather than create a binding for it. If you don't really need to do the binding, reconsider whether to use it. Binding may make your development faster, but it can make your application run slower.

Leverage local variables

So, we just mentioned the downside of using complex references in data bindings. When you have an extended reference path, the application has to look up each segment in the reference path. So, a reference to alien_mc.head_mc.antennae[0].color has to first look up alien_mc, then look up the head_mc member of alien_mc, then look up the antennae property, and so on. This isn't a big deal if it is happening only once, but if it is happening many times, such as with a data binding, the added processing will slow things down.

For a solution, you can take the value of a long reference path and store it as a local variable. Then you can just reference that variable and have to look up only one item, rather than the five in the previous example.

This is OK:

```
var fruit:Fruit;
if(fruit.type == "apple" || fruit.type == "orange" ||
   fruit.type == "banana")
```

But this is better:

```
var fType:String = fruit.type;
if (fType == "apple" || fType == "orange" || fType == "banana")
```

If a complex reference is in a loop, every dot represents a lookup, and the lookup happens on every loop iteration, which means the repeated use of processing power. Replacing multiple complex references with local variables also makes your code more readable, less verbose, and smaller in file size. Sure, the file size difference may be tiny, but it is there, and the code is much easier for humans to read.

Array member access

Using arrays in Flex and AIR is another opportunity to optimize your application. In general, arrays in Flash-based applications are fast. They have what is called **fast path** for accessing array members. This form of member access is as fast as C++; however, fast path applies only in dense portions of arrays.

A **dense** portion of an array is where all the indices of the array are contiguous and contain values. The reference to an array member becomes **slow path** when there is a gap between the array's indices and you are referencing a value on the far side of that gap:

```
var numbers_arr:Array = [4,8,15,16,23,42];
numbers_arr[900] = 900;
numbers_arr[3];     //This is fast
numbers_arr[900];   //This is slow
```

So, the solution is easy: don't have gaps in your array. It is best practice to keep your indices contiguous, and it speeds up your application's performance.

Also, if you have gaps in your array, the chance of referencing an empty index and "missing" is higher. Misses in array lookup will also slow down your application.

Optimizing application instantiation

If your application starts up and **instantiates**, or creates, all the assets it needs at the beginning, it's going to take a performance hit while it is creating all those assets. You can improve the performance of your application by using **delayed instantiation**.

If you try to eat a steak all at once, you're going to choke on it. If you eat it in bite-sized bits, you'll be able to eat your steak without being introduced to Mr. Heimlich's maneuver. It's the same with your application. If it tries to process all its assets simultaneously, it's going to choke, especially if the user's processor is of an older, more leisurely processor generation. So, by delaying the instantiation of classes and assets your application uses until it needs them or until it is at a lull in its activities, you can keep performance at a good level.

In most cases, you would do this in your application controller class through proper sequencing and design. For instance, you would often create only certain elements of your user interface when they are required for user interaction, rather than up front where they would delay the initial load of the application.

Performance monitoring

How can you tell whether your app is performing like a champ or shuffling along like it has the gout? Let's take a look at some ActionScript methods, Flex tools, and third-party applications that can help you evaluate your application's performance.

First on the list is the most basic: getTimer(). A call to this function returns the number of milliseconds that have elapsed since your application started running. By tracing this, you can see how long individual processes are taking in your app and see where your application's bottlenecks are.

When you are tracing the time, you can trace out the totalMemory property of the System class as well. This property returns the total amount of memory allocated to Flash Player. This isn't all the memory being used by the objects in Flash Player, or just your own application, but rather the amount that the system has allocated Flash Player. This does change over time, so you can get a basic picture of how frugal your application is with the memory.

A more complicated and robust tool is the Flex Profiler. In Flex, click the little icon that shows a stopwatch behind the run icon; this opens the Flex Profiler (Figure 6-2).

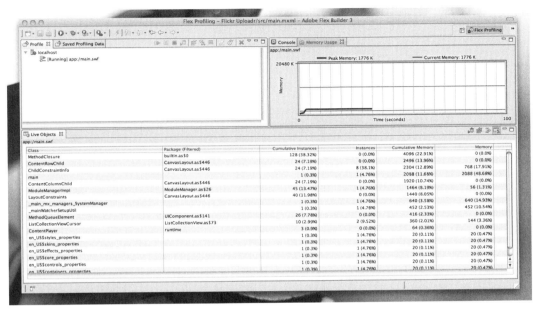

Figure 6-2. The Flex Profiler displaying information about an AIR application

The profiler has options for tracing memory usage, profiling performance, watching live memory data, and even generating stack traces for object allocation. Much like the debugger in Flex, you can move through the application using controls in the profiler; only here you can grab snapshots of memory usage and performance while you move through the application.

The memory profiling feature allows you to collect information about memory usage every time an object is created and garbage collected. If you find objects that aren't getting garbage collected or are sticking around longer than they should (called **loitering** objects), you can identify memory leaks in the application.

> *Garbage collection occurs when Flash Player attempts to reclaim the memory used by objects that no longer exist within the application. This may include components that have been removed from the display list or variables that have been reset.*

The Flex Profiler even has a tool that allows you to look for memory leaks between two memory snapshots of the application. You can access it in Flex Builder by selecting the Run ➤ Profile [Application Name] menu. It consists of several panels.

The Live Objects panel (Figure 6-3) of the profiler breaks down memory usage by the classes used in the application, including those classes and objects used internally by the Flex framework. The Allocation Trace panel allows you to see which functions are using the most memory in your application. In general, the profiler allows you to drill down deeply into the objects and methods of your application to see which ones are using the most memory and processor time.

Class	Package (Filtered)	Cumulative Instances	Instances	Cumulative Memory	Memory
MethodClosure	builtin.as$0	128 (38.32%)	0 (0.0%)	4096 (22.91%)	0 (0.0%)
ContentRowChild	CanvasLayout.as$446	24 (7.19%)	0 (0.0%)	2496 (13.96%)	0 (0.0%)
ChildConstraintInfo	CanvasLayout.as$446	24 (7.19%)	8 (38.1%)	2304 (12.89%)	768 (17.91%)
main		1 (0.3%)	1 (4.76%)	2088 (11.68%)	2088 (48.69%)
ContentColumnChild	CanvasLayout.as$446	24 (7.19%)	0 (0.0%)	1920 (10.74%)	0 (0.0%)
ModuleManagerImpl	ModuleManager.as$26	45 (13.47%)	1 (4.76%)	1464 (8.19%)	56 (1.31%)
LayoutConstraints	CanvasLayout.as$446	40 (11.98%)	0 (0.0%)	1440 (8.05%)	0 (0.0%)
_main_mx_managers_SystemManager		1 (0.3%)	1 (4.76%)	640 (3.58%)	640 (14.93%)
_mainWatcherSetupUtil		1 (0.3%)	1 (4.76%)	452 (2.53%)	452 (10.54%)
MethodQueueElement	UIComponent.as$141	26 (7.78%)	0 (0.0%)	416 (2.33%)	0 (0.0%)
ListCollectionViewCursor	ListCollectionView.as$73	10 (2.99%)	2 (9.52%)	360 (2.01%)	144 (3.36%)
ContentPlayer	runtime	3 (0.9%)	0 (0.0%)	64 (0.36%)	0 (0.0%)
en_US$styles_properties		1 (0.3%)	1 (4.76%)	20 (0.11%)	20 (0.47%)
en_US$skins_properties		1 (0.3%)	1 (4.76%)	20 (0.11%)	20 (0.47%)
en_US$effects_properties		1 (0.3%)	1 (4.76%)	20 (0.11%)	20 (0.47%)
en_US$core_properties		1 (0.3%)	1 (4.76%)	20 (0.11%)	20 (0.47%)
en_US$controls_properties		1 (0.3%)	1 (4.76%)	20 (0.11%)	20 (0.47%)
en_US$containers_properties		1 (0.3%)	1 (4.76%)	20 (0.11%)	20 (0.47%)

Figure 6-3. The Live Objects panel

In addition, third-party tools can help you analyze the performance of your application. RealEyes Media (www.realeyes.com) offers a tool called the RED|bug Console, which allows you to track the performance of your application. The current release features the RED Logger, RED Capabilities, and RED Memory modules that enable you to collect stats on memory usage, performance, and system capabilities. We'll talk more about RED|bug and other debugging consoles in the next chapter.

Summary

Optimizing the performance of your application is not too difficult to do. You can achieve good optimization simply by following coding best practices such as using strong data typing, using data binding only where necessary, avoiding overuse of complex references, and keeping your arrays dense and contiguous.

You don't have to perform voodoo or black magic. The tools we talked about for monitoring your application's performance are easy to use and will tell you where to focus your efforts.

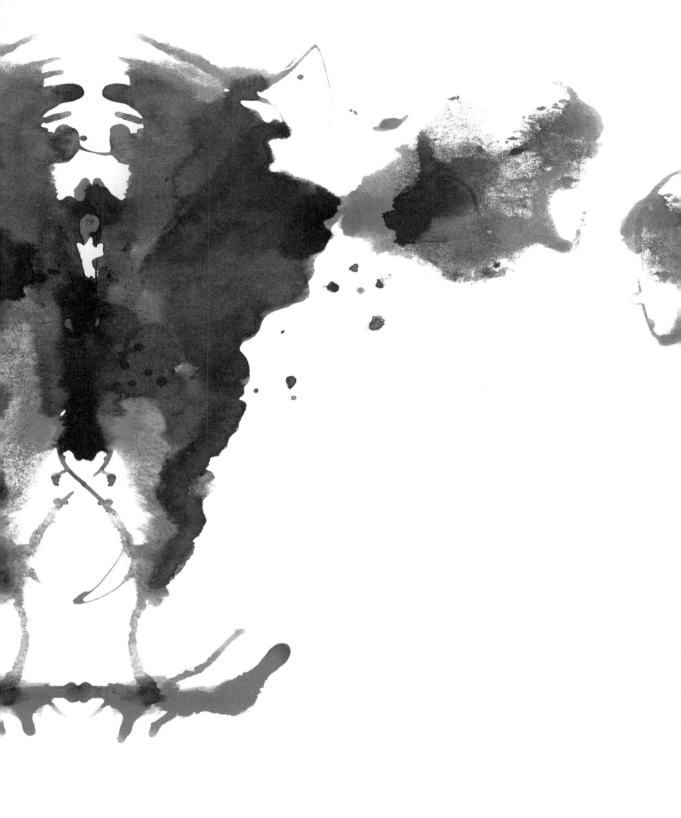

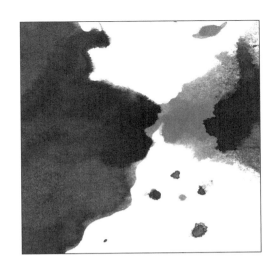

Chapter 7

DEBUGGING FLEX 3: THE TRIED-AND-TRUE, PLUS THE NEW

Debugging applications can turn into a nightmare, especially if the application is an unknown code set or is poorly designed. But if you have a plan of attack and use the tools provided by Flex 3 and ActionScript 3.0, then the process of debugging an application can be much less of a nightmare.

In this chapter, you'll look at the processes and tools that have been used to debug Flash Platform applications with great success. Next, we will discuss some of the tools that are provided with Flex Builder, as well as tools that have been created with Flex and ActionScript 3.0.

Debugging an application

One of the most important things to consider when debugging an application is where to start, especially when you are dealing with larger applications. The first thing you should do when debugging any application is to review the errors or bugs that are known, make note of them, and create a structured plan based on those bugs. Once you have the list of bugs, ask a few questions:

- Is this bug part of a particular system?
- Is this bug part of the actual code or caused by an outside interaction?
- Are any of the bugs related?

These questions begin to group bugs, not just together in groups of similar bugs but into manageable sets specific to areas or systems that are part of your application. Something to keep in mind while debugging an application is that you probably will run into or create additional bugs. Don't let these new bugs distract you. Make note of them, add them to your list, and continue on with the current bug.

Letting new bugs distract you can turn into a wild goose chase and waste more of your valuable time. Once you have your list of areas and systems that need to be debugged, you can begin to debug the application.

The Flex Debug Player

Before you get started debugging your Flash Platform application, there is one primary tool you'll need to make sure you have: the Flash Debug Player.

The Flash Debug Player is a version of the Flash Player that allows you to use the Debugger tool in Flex, as well as to display output such as trace statements and error messages in the Console view of Flex Builder. Flex requires the Flash Debug Player version 7.0.14 or higher to work.

This debugger is not the default version of the player that you may have installed in your browser. This is a separate player that has extra functionality in it, so you must acquire it either from the Adobe website or from the files included with the Flex SDK.

You can find an installer for the Flash Debug Player included with Flex by going to your root directory for Flex and then navigating to the /player/debug directory. It is a good idea to uninstall your current version of the Flash Player before you install the new version of the player. You can remove previous versions with the uninstaller that is freely available on the Adobe website (www.adobe.com/support/flashplayer/downloads.html).

One thing to note about the Flash Debug Player is that anyone with the debug version of the player will be able to view your application's trace statement output. For optimization's sake alone, you should remove all trace statements from your application before you distribute it, but luckily, you can also choose to omit trace statements within the compiler when you are creating your release build.

Debugging tools

You can debug your applications in many ways.

The trace() function

The trace() function is one of the most basic, but quite powerful, debugging tools. A call to the trace() method logs output to the Console view in Flex Builder.

The trace() function is useful for looking at the state of an object and/or its properties at a specific location in the application that you are debugging. Let's take a look at the default functionality of the trace() function:

```
trace("Hello World!");   // Traces: "Hello World!"

var myObj:Object= {item:'item 1', desc:'This is item 1'};
trace(myObj);    // Traces [object Object]
```

As you can see in the previous code sample, the trace() function doesn't help much when it comes to complex objects. That is because messages that are logged using the trace() function should be strings. There are a few solutions for this problem:

- Cast the message to a string using the String() conversion function. This will usually work only if the object contains text attributes.
- Create a for loop in order to loop through each property in the object, and then call the trace() function to output each of those properties and its value.

Each of these solutions has their limitations, and the for loop is great for quick-and-dirty object introspection. The for loop is also a holdover from ActionScript 2.0 and can get messy if you have more complex objects and other nested data types.

> When creating custom classes, it is often a good idea to implement a toString method that outputs information as to the state of the object. This helps by providing you with meaningful trace messages from anonymous objects.

Flex now has the ObjectUtil (mx.utils.ObjectUtil) class. This class has quite a few utilities for dealing with and managing objects. The method that you are interested in is the toString() method. This method recursively outputs all object properties and their values and all nested object properties and their values.

```
var myArray:Array = new Array(
    {item:'item 1', desc:'This is item 1'},
    {item:'item 2', desc:'This is item 2'}
);

trace(ObjectUtil.toString(myArray));
```

Now you have the trace() function in your toolbox. The trace() function is a simple tool that can help debug some complex issues.

Create complex trace() calls

Sometimes those trace calls can get a bit overwhelming. If you have a large application to debug and have trace statements pouring out of your application like a rushing river, you may find it hard to locate the trace statement you need. It also may be difficult to pick out where sections of codes start and leave off.

If you want to see where in the application flow a certain method or loop is ending, it can be a daunting task when you have pages and pages of trace statements to sift through. This is when it's useful to use some more complex trace() calls.

One trick you can use is to break up long trace statements onto multiple lines to make it easier to pick out the individual parts of the statement. You can put line breaks into your trace statements by using the new line escape code. The escape code is simply a backslash and the letter *n*, and it can go in the string literal with the rest of your text:

```
trace("I am on this line,\n but I am on the next line");
```

Even more useful is adding dividers to your trace statements. Dividers can separate blocks of trace statements from the rest of the application's output. This is as simple as adding another trace statement before and after the block of code you want to separate. Usually, you can create a visual divider by repeating a character such as an equal sign or an asterisk.

```
var len:uint = myArray.length;
trace("==========================================");
for(var i:uint = 0; i < len; i++){
    trace(i + " in myArray is " + myArray[i]);
}
trace("==========================================");
```

Timing execution getTimer() and duration

If using dividers is not accurate enough to tell you when certain blocks of your code are executing, there is always the getTimer function mentioned earlier. Not only will it tell you how fast your application is executing, but it can also tell you precisely when certain operations are occurring. By using getTimer to capture the amount of milliseconds since the application started, you can get a more precise means to tell when things are happening.

You can also use getTimer to measure how long animations such as transitions take and see whether that meets your design requirements. A more precise method, however, is to set durations for your transitions and effects. When you use the transition classes such as WipeLeft or Fade, you can specify a duration in milliseconds for them. This simplifies the process of trying to time transitions. Happily, this is not just limited to transitions and effects. The Tween class in Flex also has a duration property, so if you are animating elements using this class, you can also use the duration property to precisely set the amount of time your animations take to complete.

Builder: Flex Debugging perspective

In Flex, the easiest way to do some debugging of your application is to click the Debug button in the Flex SDK. This will start running your application in the Flash Debug Player. This will be a debug version of the SWF, which is larger in file size than normal. It will allow you to receive output messages, pause the application, step through its processes line by line, and log your application's activity to an external text file or application. Of course, remember that you need the Flash Debug Player for this.

When you are debugging your application, you're probably going to be spending time in the Flex Debugging perspective. By default, you are prompted to automatically enter the Debugging perspective whenever your application experiences a runtime error, but it does not open by default when you start a debug session. The perspective is a collection of views or panels that are useful when debugging applications. It contains the Navigator, Debug, Variables, Breakpoints, Expressions, Console, and Problems views (Figure 7-1).

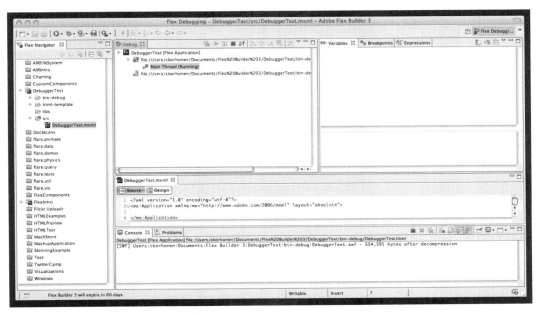

Figure 7-1. The Flex Debugging perspective

The Navigator view shows your project's file structure, and the Debug view shows the various stack frames for each thread that is running and the processes that are running in those threads. Stack frames are essentially the subroutines of the application that are waiting to be executed. Essentially, the Variables view allows you to track what values are in your variables as the application runs. Above this view are controls that allow you to suspend the application and step through it line by line and trace the values of variables as the application runs.

The Variables, Breakpoints, and Expressions views are all lumped together by default. The Variables view contains information about those variables in the currently selected stack frame in the Debug view. The Breakpoints view shows the various breakpoints you have set in the application and allows you to manage them. We'll talk about them more in just a minute. The Expressions view allows you to create expressions using variables from your application and track their values as the application runs.

The Console and Problems views are the bread and butter of debugging in Flex. The Problems view is where all the potential compile errors and warnings of potential problems get displayed. By double-clicking a problem, Flex will route you to the file and line where the error is taking place. The Console view is where the output from your application shows up. This is where trace statements and runtime errors get displayed, making it the main line of communication between you and your app. The communication can also be two-way. When you are debugging an application, you can provide input where needed using the console.

Through the Preferences dialog box, accessible by selecting the Window ➤ Preferences menu item, you can configure the console to have different appearances as well as toggle whether the console shows errors or standard trace output. The console options are under the Run/Debug node in the dialog box's topic tree.

Setting run/debug preferences

The Preferences dialog box also allows you to set a few more preferences for running and debugging your project in Flex Builder. Here you can set preferences about which perspectives and views are opened and when they are opened. For instance, you can make it so the Debugging perspective automatically opens whenever you start a debug session in Flex. You can also turn off any default perspective or view changes. In addition, you can set the styling for the Debugging perspective's views to help you identify things such as changed values.

Managing the debug session

Now that you're familiarize with the Debugging perspective, it's time to go over how you actually use the debugger. Again, to start a debug session, all you need to do is click the Debug button in the Flex toolbar to start debugging the default application. Your application will run as normal, but now any trace statements or errors will show up in the Console view.

Switch to the Debugging perspective, and notice the buttons above the Debug view. These are the controls used to navigate through your application.

The first button is the Remove All Terminated Launches, which cleans up old debug sessions from your Debug view.

Next is the Resume button, which starts running your application again after you have paused it either by using a breakpoint or by clicking the Suspend button, which is the next button.

Next to the Suspend button is the Terminate button, which ends your debug session.

To the right of that is the Disconnect button, which breaks the connection between your machine and a remote machine where you are debugging.

Remote debugging is a bit beyond the scope of this book, so we'll move on to the important stuff, namely, the controls that allow you to move through the application. There are four of them, and they are the next group of buttons in the Debug view: Step Into, Step Over, Step Return, and Drop to Frame.

You use these four controls when the application is suspended to move incrementally through the flow of the application. When the application is suspended, you will see in the code editor the code the application is currently on; the current line is highlighted and indicated by a pointer in the editor's left margin. As the application works, you will see the highlighted line change.

Clicking Step Into moves you line by line through the code. This includes going into the code of individual methods. If you come to a method call, such as `myComponent.myMethod();`, in the application flow and use the Step Into command, Flex will open the code for `myComponent` in the code editor and step line by line through the `myMethod` method. When the method call is complete, you will return to the line of the method call and continue through the application.

Step Into takes you to every line of code as it is executed. Of course, that can be a bit tedious. That is why there is the Step Over command.

Clicking Step Over will jump over blocks of code such as method calls. That way you don't have to go line by line through all the constructors in your application if you don't want. However, it won't step over things like loops.

To move even faster through your application, you can click the Step Return button. Step Return allows you to step to the end of a function or method that is currently executing and return to the main application flow. If you want to end your line-by-line examination and have the application continue running, you can click the Resume button, and the application will continue running until it suspends again.

The last command, Drop to Frame, allows you to run your application backward to a certain extent. You can select a stack frame in the Debug view and then use this command to return to that stack frame. The interesting thing is that global variables will still have the same values when you do this, so you are taking your current global variable values and returning to a previous point in the application with them. This command is enabled only if the underlying virtual machine supports this command, though.

One final button on the Debug view is the Use Step Filters button. Clicking Use Step Filters allows you to skip parts of your application that you have no interest in seeing. For instance, if you have a third-party debugging framework that does not affect the application flow at all, you could filter it out so that your stepping through the application would always move over those lines without stepping into them. The Use Step Filters button is just a toggle switch that determines whether you want to use those filters.

Setting Flex breakpoints

Now the Step Into and Step Over controls are very nice and all, but not many people are going to want to step through their application from line 1 to get to the area they want to debug. This is where breakpoints come into play.

Breakpoints are incredibly useful tools when debugging an application. Setting a breakpoint in your application tells the Flex Debugger to pause the application at that particular point. That way you don't have to go through the whole app line by line, but rather you can start stepping through code from any point you choose. Then from that point, you use the Debug view's controls to step through the application line by line or chunk by chunk.

This allows you to more quickly follow the application flow to make sure it is executing in the order you expect and to make sure the values in the variables are the same as you expect. You can also tell the application to resume, and it will continue until the next breakpoint. This way you can see what the values of variables are at certain points in the application by looking in the Variables view. Breakpoints just allow you to stop at a certain point in the application rather than wading through the application incrementally just to get to the portion of the application in which you are interested.

Setting a breakpoint is easy. Just right-click in the margin of the code editor next to the line numbers, and then select Toggle Breakpoint from the context menu. This will display a little magnifying glass icon in the margin letting you know that there is a breakpoint there. Then just debug the application, and the application will automatically suspend at the first breakpoint it encounters. Then you can use the Step Into, Step Over, and Step Return controls of the Debug view to move through the application.

The Logging API

If you want to get a bit more creative in your logging efforts, you can tap into Flex's Logging API to do some custom logging. The Logging API is a collection of classes that allows you to grab data and messages from your application. The API consists of a logger, a log target, and a destination. We'll take a look at each of these components of the API and then go over some of the considerations of making a custom logger.

As you might guess, the **logger** is the central part of the Logging API. It can be a custom class that you write that interacts with the Log class by calling its methods. Logger classes must also implement the ILogger interface.

The logger classifies data by two factors: category and level.

Category is just an arbitrary designation for a logger used to group log targets together. For instance, all data sent through a logger with the category of "fruit" will be sent to log targets in the same category. It is convention, however, to set the category to the fully qualified class name of the object that is the focus of the logging.

Level is determined by the importance of the message. The LogEventLevel supports five different levels of increasing importance: Debug, Info, Warn, Error, and Fatal. It also has one catchall level called All that includes all messages of every type of level. However, each of the other levels also reports all messages of higher importance. So, setting your logger's level to Warn means you will log messages of the Warn, Error, and Fatal levels.

The **log target** of the API is usually a TraceTarget instance but can also be a MiniDebugTarget.

The TraceTarget class is simply an object that uses the global trace method to output messages from the application.

The MiniDebugTarget allows you to send log messages to a LocalConnection object. The receiver of those messages is the Destination. It is simply where the log message is written, either a file, such as the flashlog.txt, or a LocalConnection object, which allows you to work with that data in other applications, such as debugging consoles.

So, that is nice in theory, but how does it actually come together to work and do some logging? Well, you need a logger, a log target, and a destination, so let's start with the logger. You can create a logger by getting a logger instance from the Log class. It helpfully has a getLogger method that takes a category name as a parameter. This will return a logger instance, which is of the ILogger data type. If a logger has already been defined for that category, it will return that logger, but if there is not one for that category, it will create one.

Using the logger, you can then output messages through the log target using the logger's debug, info, warn, error, and fatal methods. Observant readers will note that these are the same names as the different levels of log events. You pass in the message you want to log as the parameter for these methods. ILogger throws in one bonus method on top of those: log. The log method allows you to pass in the log event's level and message as parameters. The level should be sent as an integer, but because it's much easier to remember a name than a number, you can use the constants of the LogEventLevel class instead. Again, they have the same name as the different log event levels.

```
myLogger.log(LogEventLevel.WARN, "I'm warning you!");
```

One useful aspect of the methods of the ILogger interface is that you can pass in extra parameters that can then be dynamically inserted into the message that is being output. You can dynamically insert those parameters into your message using curly braces and the index of the additional parameters. This can make code a bit more readable.

```
myLogger.log(LogEventLevel.WARN, "I'm warning you! {0} is of the type
        {1}!", "Fruit", "durian");
//Outputs: I'm warning you! Fruit is of the type durian!
```

The next component of the process is to specify a log target. It is easiest to just use the TraceTarget class in Flex for this purpose. You can create your TraceTarget in MXML if you like. In your TraceTarget, you'll specify a level. This is the level of the events the target is to log. Again, it is intended to be an integer, but the LogEventLevel class's constants are much easier to remember. When a TraceTarget has a level set, the logger can detect whether the target is handling events of a particular level: isDebug, isInfo, isWarn, isError, and isFatal. They return a boolean value, so these are useful for determining whether your logger should take care of a particular event.

You may also configure what information gets output by the target through the use of its includeCategory, includeLevel, includeDate, and includeTime properties. These are just boolean values that, if true, will include their particular information in the logged message.

The addLogger and removeLogger methods allow you to manually manage from which loggers the target is receiving events. You can also specify a filter to limit what categories, classes, or packages will be served by this TraceTarget. These filters allow wildcarding through the use of asterisks, but the asterisk has to be at the end of each expression. So, there's no wildcarding in the middle of package names. But if you want your TraceTarget to work for everything, just use a single asterisk as its filter. When you put this all together in the MXML, it would look something like this:

```
<mx:TraceTarget level="{LogEventLevel.ALL}" includeDate="true"
                includeTime="true" includeCategory="false"
                includeLevel="true">
    <mx:filters>
        <mx:Array>
            <mx:String>myPackage.controls.*</mx:String>
            <mx:String>myPackage.views.*</mx:String>
        </mx:Array>
    </mx:filters>
</mx:TraceTarget>
```

Now, the TraceTarget outputs messages to wherever your trace messages are being logged. That's the Destination part of the API. But what if you want to output your messages to an object rather than to an external text file? In that case, you would want to substitute a MiniDebugTarget for your TraceTarget. It works the same as the TraceTarget, except that the Destination is changed to a LocalConnection object. When you instantiate the MiniDebugTarget, you need to pass in the name of the connection specified when you created the LocalConnection object that will receive log messages. You can also specify which method will be called on the remote connection when the log message is received. This defaults to trace.

Essentially, the MiniDebugTarget is designed with external debugging consoles in mind. The LocalConnection allows your Flash application to communicate with other Flash Platform applications, as long as they initialize the connection.

```
private var myLC:LocalConnection;
private var myMDT:MiniDebugTarget;

private function initCustomDebug():void{
    myLC = new LocalConnection();
    myMDT = new MiniDebugTarget("_myConnection");
}
```

Using other debugging applications

If you're not in the mood to create your own debugging console, there are a few out there such as Luminic Box and RED | bug already waiting to make you more efficient in your debugging. First we'll take an in-depth look at one of these: RED | bug. Then we'll show an example debugging scenario using the RED | bug console. Then we'll cover some of the other third-party debugging consoles available on the Web.

RED | bug

The RED | bug console is an AIR application put out by RealEyes Media and is available for download at www.realeyesmedia.com/redbug. The console allows you to choose which of its modules you want to include in your application and also leaves the door open for extensibility through more consoles.

Currently, RED | bug has a logger module for receiving messages and objects output by the application, a memory module that tracks your application's use of the system's memory, and a capabilities module that allows testers to view and save data about their system's capabilities to enable easy comparison of the different settings between testers. You can choose which modules are included by whether you import the individual classes for those modules.

You also need to import the core REDbug class from the RED | bug client library, which is also available for download from the RealEyes Media site. The RED | bug classes communicate messages from your application to the console, but all you need to do is to import the RED | bug class. RED | bug even allows you to create custom log levels and custom-named functions for sending debug messages. You can also use multiple loggers in your application and have individual functions for each of the loggers.

So, let's look at how you can use RED | bug to debug an application.

Assuming you have the RED | bug console and client library downloaded, you need to bring in the client library to your Flex or AIR project. To do this, you create a directory called `lib` and extract the SWC files in the client library to this location.

Within Flex Builder, if you right-click your project and select Properties, the Properties panel will open.

If you select Flex Build Path and within this view the Library Path tab, you are presented with an option to add a SWF folder. If you navigate to the folder you have just created, then you can add it here.

Now you can open the component, class, or application that you want to debug and import your ActionScript classes:

```
import com.realeyesmedia.debug.redbug.REDAppTypes;
import com.realeyesmedia.debug.redbug.REDbug;
import com.realeyesmedia.debug.redbug.modules.RED_Capabilities;
import com.realeyesmedia.debug.redbug.modules.RED_Logger;
import com.realeyesmedia.debug.redbug.modules.RED_MemUtil;
import com.realeyesmedia.debug.redbug.modules.RED_MemUtilTimer;
import com.realeyesmedia.debug.redbug.REDLogLevels;
```

One of the first things to do is to initialize RED | bug's connection with your application. You can do this using the initialize method of the REDbug class.

The method takes three parameters: the ID for the application, the type of application it is, and whether you want the debug to be active. The application ID is an arbitrary string that will be used to identify the application in RED|bug. The application type is represented by a constant on the REDAppTypes class. It can be TYPE_AIR, TYPE_FLASH, or TYPE_FLEX. The third parameter is a boolean value that specifies whether you want debugging to be enabled. The code should go in the init method for the object you're debugging, generally the event handler for the creationComplete event:

```
private function init():void{
    REDbug.initialize("myApplication",REDAppTypes.TYPE_FLEX,true);
}
```

Now it is time to start thinking about which modules you want to initialize.

To use a module, instantiate it and store it. The modules take different parameters in their constructors, such as a debug message to display, but none of them is required. So, let's instantiate your logger, capabilities, and memory modules. The instantiation should go in the init method for the object you're debugging after the REDbug.initialize() call:

```
private var transferObj:RED_Logger;
private var transferMemStats:RED_MemUtil;
private var transferCapabilities:RED_Capabilities;

private function init():void{
    REDbug.initialize("myApplication",REDAppTypes.TYPE_FLEX,true);

    transferObj = new RED_Logger();
    transferMemStats = new RED_MemUtil();
    transferCapabilities = new RED_Capabilities();
}
```

To start the logging of memory usage in the application, you need to start the timer for the memory usage graph. This is done with the static startTimer method of the RED_MemUtilTimer class. You pass it the number of milliseconds since the application has begun running, or you can just start it at 1 to start the graph. Place this code after the instantiation of the RED_Capabilities object:

```
RED_MemUtilTimer.startTimer(1);
```

When you want to send a message to the RED|bug console, you have two different options. One is the send method, and the other is to create dynamic logging functions. Let's tackle the send method first. That method takes a transfer object as a parameter. In this case, that just means an instance of the RED_Logger, which you happen to have stored as transferObj.

You can set the log level, data object, and message in the transfer object and then send it. The log level is set in the level property of the object and is best set using constants from the REDLogLevels class. The levels still correspond to the standard Logging API levels, but you can set your own custom levels if you so desire. The message is set in the msg property, and the data object you want to inspect is set in the debugObj property. We'll use some dummy data here, but in real life, you'd probably be doing this in response to an event and outputting data from it. However, for the exercise here, just put this after the startTimer function call:

```
transferObj.level = REDLogLevels.LEVEL_DEBUG;
transferObj.msg = "Testing Logger";
transferObj.debugObj = {a:"123",b:"456",c:["one","two","three"]};

REDbug.send(transferObj);
```

The other means of sending data is a bit more complex in the setup but easier to use in the long run. RED | bug also allows you to set up custom function names to send data through.

The first step of the process is to call the addTransferManager method of the REDbug class to tell RED | bug the name of the function and the logger object that will handle it. This is very cool, because you can give it your preferred name, but it does have the drawback that it won't show up in code hinting. You can assign different functions to work with different loggers, but for this case, we'll again use your existing transferObj logger and add this line next:

```
REDbug.addTransferManager("myLog",transferObj);
```

Now you have a method on the REDbug object. Because this isn't a static method, you need to get an instance of the REDbug object on which to call the method. To get an instance, use the static gi method of the REDbug class. It returns an instance of the REDbug class.

From that instance, you can now call your function to output information to the console. The parameters it takes are the log level, the debug object, the message to display, whether to send the message to the trace panel, whether to send the message to the Firebug debugging browser plug-in, and whether the data should be hidden from RED | bug.

The last three parameters are Booleans and default to false. In the logger module of RED | bug, you can expand the debug objects you send and view their properties and their properties' properties.

```
REDbug.gi().myLog("My Custom Level",{fType:"banana",color:"green"},
                  "Testing Logger with a Piece of Fruit");
```

The finished code for this example should look like this:

```
import com.realeyesmedia.debug.redbug.REDAppTypes;
import com.realeyesmedia.debug.redbug.REDbug;
import com.realeyesmedia.debug.redbug.modules.RED_Capabilities;
import com.realeyesmedia.debug.redbug.modules.RED_Logger;
import com.realeyesmedia.debug.redbug.modules.RED_MemUtil;
import com.realeyesmedia.debug.redbug.modules.RED_MemUtilTimer;
import com.realeyesmedia.debug.redbug.REDLogLevels;

private var transferObj:RED_Logger;
private var transferMemStats:RED_MemUtil;
private var transferCapabilities:RED_Capabilities;

private function init():void{
    REDbug.initialize("myApplication",REDAppTypes.TYPE_FLEX,true);

    transferObj = new RED_Logger();
    transferMemStats = new RED_MemUtil();
    transferCapabilities = new RED_Capabilities();
```

```
        RED_MemUtilTimer.startTimer(1);

        transferObj.level = REDLogLevels.LEVEL_DEBUG;
        transferObj.msg = "Testing Logger";
        transferObj.debugObj = {a:"123",b:"456",c:["one","two","three"]};

        REDbug.send(transferObj);

        REDbug.addTransferManager("myLog",transferObj);
        REDbug.gi().myLog("My Custom Level",{fType:"banana",color:"green"},
                          "Testing Logger with a Piece of Fruit");
    }
```

This should be it for the code you need. Keep in mind that this is a full-featured usage of RED|bug. You can leave out the modules you don't need, and if you use the dynamically defined functions, there will be fewer lines of code. Start the RED|bug console, and if all is well with the world, when you debug your application, you will receive output in RED|bug.

LuminicBox FlashInspector

Another third-party resource for debugging your application is LuminicBox FlashInspector (http://www.luminicbox.com/blog/default.aspx?page=post&id=2), which is similar to the logger module of RED|bug. It simply traces output from your application, and like the logger console of RED|bug, it allows you to expand complex objects to view their properties, including subobjects that can in turn be inspected.

FireBug

FireBug (http://www.getfirebug.com/) is a browser plug-in for Firefox that allows you to see the network calls made by Flash. It also allows you to see messages output by Flash movies that are sent to it. The fact that it works while you're debugging your application in a browser is one reason why RED|bug provides a way for you to also send messages to FireBug.

Summary

In this chapter, we went over how you can optimize the way your application performs and utilizes memory, looked at means of monitoring that performance and memory usage, covered debugging applications in Flex, explored the Logging API, covered how to create a custom logger, and explained how to use a third-party debugging console. Don't you feel smarter? Remember, making your application perform better and use less memory will make all users happier, but especially users with slower computers. Keep in mind that best coding practices are a great way to optimize your application without breaking a sweat, so it is totally worth it for the benefits you will reap. Also, make sure you hunt for and eradicate bugs in your applications using the bevy of tools available for that purpose. Users will be even happier if your sleek application has no bugs.

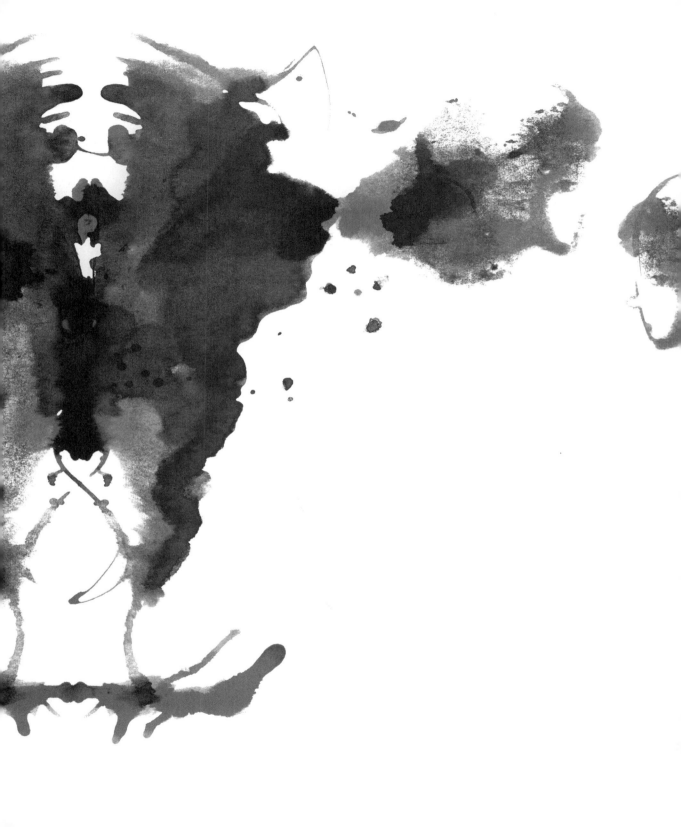

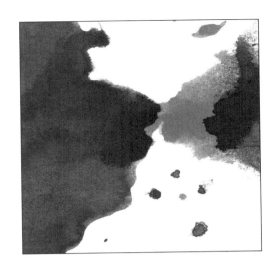

Chapter 8

GETTING THE MOST OUT OF APIS

In this chapter, we'll look at opportunities for finding interesting uses for the data exposed by different mashups, as well as discuss the best ways to access a particular API using ActionScript 3.0.

Finding inspiration

In his book *Analog In, Digital Out*, interaction designer Brendan Dawes talks about one of the new challenges facing the music industry. With the increased popularity of pay-per-song digital music stores such as iTunes, consumers are no longer buying whole albums but are instead choosing to purchase individual tracks. As a result, the concept of album artwork is becoming less relevant to the user, because it may not aid recognition of a particular song. Hence, this exposes the need for unique artwork per song.

However, is it economically viable for record labels to commission a unique piece of artwork for each song on an album? In an industry that is seeing increasingly smaller profit margins per album as it moves into the digital arena, it is certainly not a suggestion that would go over too well!

Dawes suggests a solution to this: using mathematics to generate a set of swirls, colors, and ink blots that are unique to the frequency peaks and waveform signatures of a piece of music. Although this is an innovative solution, we can't help but wonder whether an algorithmically generated image could ever capture the same raw emotion of a piece of artwork produced by an artist.

Mashups might provide a solution to the problem, because web applications such as Flickr and YouTube contain vast amounts of user-generated, visual content. Although this content is often lacking a professional touch, it can certainly capture emotions.

With this in mind, this chapter will explore ways to provide passive visualizations of data using these web services. These can be something to add some visual shine to an application or (as you'll see when we cover how to develop these applications for the desktop) something that can run in the background as a widget providing passive content and entertainment.

Abstracting data services

The services we'll use for this example are LastFM and Flickr. LastFM is a social music website that provides custom radio streams and gathers statistics about its users' listening habits, which allows the service to offer personalized recommendations and match-making services. Flickr, as you probably know, is a photo-sharing site.

For this application, LastFM will be the primary data source, providing information relating to a user's favorite songs and artists. The application will then use this information to retrieve relevant images from Flickr and display them, creating a visual experience unique to a particular user.

LastFM's back-end is a database called Audioscrobbler, which tracks users' listening habits. Data is fed into this system by plug-ins available for popular media players, such as WinAmp or iTunes. This data is then analyzed, processed, and added to a user profile *before* being exposed using web services.

In many ways, LastFM's web services are a data gold mine. LastFM offers access to data specific to users, artists, songs, albums, tags, and groups, including everything from obtaining a user's profile to providing numerically ranked friend/music/group recommendations based on the data contained within Audioscrobbler.

Different types of data are available in different forms, be it plain text, XML, XSPF, iCal, or RSS.

> *XSPF stands for XML Sharable Playlist Format, a format specifically designed for sharing track, artist, and album information. It was proposed by the Xiph.org Foundation, but it is not currently recognized by any other standards body.*

We'll primarily use the plain XML feeds because of the ease and efficiency of parsing XML data using the ActionScript 3.0 APIs. In most cases when it comes to mashups, XML is preferable for data exchange. For these reasons, it rarely makes sense to write a custom parser for a particular data type unless it is your only option.

A quick Google search for *LastFM ActionScript libraries* yields none for accessing its web services, at least none that are at all similar to the ones we'll be using later in this book to interface with other services. Although connecting to these web services and XML feeds directly is not a problem, any code written would need to be specific to our application, which limits its reusability in other projects. This is why it is often good practice to first create your own interface.

The interface in this chapter will serve two purposes:

- It will manage and choreograph any network communications with the remote services, including handling any authentication that may be required and error conditions such as receiving malformed data responses.

- It will abstract the data contained within the service responses, parsing the XML responses into specific data objects and allowing easy access to this data within the application.

For readers familiar with software design patterns, this approach is reminiscent of the Facade pattern, because the interface will provide a simplified way of working with the services offered by LastFM from within Flash- or Flex-based applications.

This interface is intended to be reusable across different applications, so we'll show how to give it its own package structure so that it can be easily imported. All the LastFM web services will be accessible through methods within the LastFM class, with data being returned using the data objects contained in the lastfm.data package—each data object corresponds to a type of data that will be returned, such as Users, Friends, Songs, Artists, and Albums.

The following is the LastFM user profile XML feed:

```
<?xml version="1.0" encoding="UTF-8"?>
<profile id="3409793" cluster="2" username="ckorhonen">
    <url>http://www.last.fm/user/ckorhonen/</url>
    <realname>Chris Korhonen</realname>
    <mbox_sha1sum>
            1cba39b8761c045b4cdc4b120cabc500f9613461
    </mbox_sha1sum>
    <registered unixtime="1141600970">Mar 5, 2006</registered>
    <age>24</age>
    <gender>m</gender>
    <country>United Kingdom</country>
    <playcount>1010</playcount>
    <avatar>
            http://panther1.last.fm/avatar/724c4aebd5c6a8099716526.jpg
    </avatar>
    <icon>http://panther1.last.fm/depth/global/icon_user.gif</icon>
</profile>
```

If you look at the construction of the data objects, you will see that each data object maps to the content of a particular XML feed, created as an ActionScript class. In the previous code, you have a typical response from the user profile XML feed. This contains all the available information specific to a given user. You can view this and many more XML feeds at www.audioscrobbler.net/data/webservices/.

Within this data object, you would encapsulate all the XML data that you are interested in and want to expose to your application. It's reasonable to expose everything available in order to future-proof your interface. In most cases, you won't incur any performance penalties for this, unless you are working with a web service or XML document that contains *considerably* more data. Usually, in that instance, you would notice a delay in XML parsing and a jump in client-side CPU usage, in which case you might want to consider the XML parsing overhead and look to other methods of integration.

The LastUser class, listed next, shows that you are storing all the data returned from the XML feed. The code also includes a class constructor method, which allows for instantiation and data population.

```
package sourcebottle.lastfm.data
{
    public class LastUser
    {
        public var id:Number;
        public var username:String;
        public var realname:String;
        public var url:String;

        public var gender:String;
        public var age:Number;
        public var country:String;

        public var playCount:Number;
        public var registered:String;

        public var avatarURL:String;
        public var iconURL:String;

        function LastUser(user:Object){
            id          = user.id;
            username    = user.username;
            realname    = user.realname;
            url         = user.url;
            gender      = user.gender;
            age         = user.age;
            country     = user.country;
            playCount   = user.playCount;
            registered  = user.registered;
            avatarURL   = user.avatarURL;
            iconURL     = user.iconURL;
        }
    }
}
```

(We show the full source code for the LastFM interface, including the full set of data objects, later in this chapter.)

With the data objects defined, you can now build the logic associated with calling the web services—the LastFM class. This class extends the ActionScript 3.0 EventDispatcher class that allows you to dispatch your own events. This is important because you will be using this class to make calls to various remote services, which occur asynchronously with program execution. By leveraging the event model that exists within Flash, this provides you with a mechanism to return data to your application once these calls have received a response.

If you examine Listing 8-2, you have a version of your LastFM class that contains the functionality to load a user's profile. Each call to a data service is handled by an instance of a URLLoader, which is instantiated in the class constructor:

```
private var _userLoader:URLLoader;
```

This is the standard method used with ActionScript 3.0 to load data from a remote location. If you were developing an ActionScript 2.0 version of this interface, then you would instead use either an XML or LoadVars object to load your data.

> *If you experience issues loading external data with the* URLLoader *class, then the usual suspect is often the Flash Player's cross-domain security model. Ensure that the service you are trying to access has an appropriate* crossdomain.xml *file setup.*

Within the constructor, you are attaching several event listeners to the URLLoader. When a given URL is loaded successfully, a COMPLETE event is broadcast. You are listening for this and executing the userHandler function in this instance. In addition, you are also listening for error events and triggering the errorHandler in this event.

```
_userLoader.addEventListener(Event.COMPLETE,userHandler);
_userLoader.addEventListener(IOErrorEvent.IO_ERROR,errorHandler);
_userLoader.addEventListener(SecurityErrorEvent.SECURITY_ERROR,
                                             errorHandler);
```

> *In terms of error handling, you are simply printing the error text to the console, which will provide useful information for debugging. However, this does not give any immediate feedback to an application using this class, which is patiently waiting for a data response.*
>
> *If such feedback were necessary, then there are a couple of options:*
>
> - *Broadcast a general Error event back to the expectant application. In this case, the application would need to include the logic to realize the response indicates there is an error so that it can deal with it accordingly.*
> - *Implement a timeout within the application. So after a period of waiting, the assumption is made that an error has occurred, and this is handled accordingly.*
>
> *Once tested, any errors are likely to be the result of (or lack of) network connectivity. So, often a timeout is the best option.*
>
> *In upcoming chapters, you will be taking a closer look at debugging your Flex applications and also at integration with popular browser plug-ins, such as Firebug, in order to perform live debugging.*

The userHandler function is triggered once you have successfully loaded some data. Because this is in XML format, you can simply instantiate it as an XML object and take advantage of the E4X XML parser that is present in ActionScript 3.0:

```
var xml:XML = new XML(_userLoader.data);
```

E4X makes it simple to work with XML data within ActionScript, allowing you to extract data using the dot (.) and attribute (@) identifiers. For example, in the sample profile XML document, once instantiated, you can access the username attribute using xml.@username. Similarly, you can access node content using simple dot notation, so it's xml.realname.

> Unfortunately, E4X is not available in ActionScript 2.0 applications, leaving you with several options. Either use the built-in XML functionality and parse the DOM tree "the old fashioned way" by traversing element nodes and their children, extracting data as you go, or you can use a third-party XML parsing library, such as ForX (http://www.orionsyndrome.com/), which is an E4X-like XML manipulator class.

From the XML data, you can extract the data you are interested in, and in this case you use it to create a new instance of the LastUser data object:

```
var user:LastUser = new LastUser({ realname:xml.realname,
                                    username:xml.@username,
                                    age:xml.age,
                                    url:xml.url,
                                    country:xml.country,
                                    playCount:xml.playcount,
                                    registered:xml.registered,
                                    gender:xml.gender,
                                    iconURL:xml.icon,
                                    avatarURL:xml.avatar});
```

You then take this newly created LastUser and add it to an array (in case you want to return multiple data objects). This array becomes the data object contained within a LastEvent class and is dispatched:

```
package sourcebottle.lastfm.events{
    import flash.events.Event;

    public class LastEvent extends Event{
        public static const ON_USER_PROFILE_RESULT
                        = "onUserProfileResult";

        private var _data:Object = new Object();
```

```
        public function LastEvent(type:String,
                            bubbles:Boolean = false,
                            cancelable:Boolean = false){
              super(type,bubbles,cancelable);
        }

        public function get data():Object{
              return _data;
        }

      public function set data(d:Object):void{
            _data = d;
      }

    }
  }
```

The LastEvent class is simply an extension of the standard ActionScript event, with relevant getter/setter methods, which allow it to return a data object:

```
package sourcebottle.lastfm{
      import flash.net.*;
      import flash.xml.*;
      import flash.events.*;
      import sourcebottle.lastfm.data.*;
      import sourcebottle.lastfm.events.LastEvent;

      [Event(name="onUserProfileResult",
                  type="sourcebottle.lastfm.events.LastEvent")]

      public class LastFM extends EventDispatcher{
            private var _userLoader:URLLoader;


            function LastFM(){
                  _userLoader = new URLLoader();

                  _userLoader.addEventListener(Event.COMPLETE,userHandler);
                  _userLoader.addEventListener(IOErrorEvent.IO_ERROR,
                                          errorHandler);
                  _userLoader.addEventListener(SecurityErrorEvent.
                                          SECURITY_ERROR,errorHandler);


            }
```

```
private function scrobblerRequest(url:String):URLRequest{
    var req:URLRequest = new URLRequest(url);
    return req;
}

public function loadUserProfile(s:String):void{
    _userLoader.load(scrobblerRequest(
            "http://ws.audioscrobbler.com/1.0/
                user/" + s + "/profile.xml"));
}


private function userHandler(e:Event):void{
    var xml:XML = new XML(_userLoader.data);
    var userArray:Array = new Array();

    var user:LastUser = new LastUser({realname:xml.realname,
                                      username:xml.@username,
                                      age:xml.age,
                                      url:xml.url,
                                      country:xml.country,
                                      playCount:xml.playcount,
                                      registered:xml.registered,
                                      gender:xml.gender,
                                      iconURL:xml.icon,
                                      avatarURL:xml.avatar});
    userArray.push(user);

     var response:LastEvent =
         new LastEvent(LastEvent.ON_USER_PROFILE_RESULT);
    response.data = userArray;
    dispatchEvent(response);
}


private function errorHandler(error:IOErrorEvent):void{
    trace(error.text);
}
        }
    }
```

Using the interface

Now that you have created the LastFM library encapsulating your data and service requests by using events to broadcast data back to the calling application, we'll show you how to use the functionality you have just created within a typical ActionScript application.

Within this application, you first want to import the classes that you will be utilizing:

```
import sourcebottle.lastfm.LastFM;
import sourcebottle.lastFM.events.*;
import sourcebottle.lastFM.data.*;
```

> If you develop an ActionScript library and want to distribute it without revealing the source code, then there is always the option to make it available as a compiled SWC file. This allows developers to harness functionality by simply importing it into their project.

With your classes now accessible from within your application, you need to instantiate the library:

```
var lastfm:LastFM = new LastFM();
```

and call the relevant method:

```
lastfm.getUserProfile('ckorhonen');
```

while listening for the response:

```
lastfm.addEventListener(LastEvent.ON_USER_PROFILE_RESULT,displayUser);
```

That's it!

The displayUser function is triggered when you get a response and should contain all the logic to do something with the data you have just received:

```
var user:LastUser = e.data[0];
```

The data objects now give you easy access to all the data contained within, which can be used to populate the user interface or to drive other functionality within the application.

Now that you have developed a straightforward and standardized method of extracting data from LastFM's APIs, you can begin thinking about how you intend to utilize it in conjunction with the data available from Flickr's API.

As you are attempting to create a passive visualization, you need to decide what data you are going to base this upon. For now, let's assume you want to present a visual slide show of imagery associated with a user's top-ten favorite artists.

Using the LastFM interface, you first need to retrieve the list of top artists:

```
lastfm.getTopArtists('ckorhonen');
```

and then do something with the result:

```
lastfm.addEventListener(LastEvent.ON_TOP_ARTISTS_RESULT,
                        processArtists);
```

Once you have the data within your application, you need to do some further data extraction before you can begin retrieving data from Flickr. If you examine the output from the LastFM web service, you'll see that it returns up to 50 results ranked in order of preference; in addition, several artists may share the same ranking if they are tied for position:

```
<artist>
    <name>Baskervilles</name>
    <mbid>041907cf-881a-42e1-83ac-0cb10e43ad2e</mbid>
    <playcount>39</playcount>
    <rank>4</rank>
    <url>http://www.last.fm/music/Baskervilles</url>
     <thumbnail>
          http://static3.last.fm/storable/image/54014/small.jpg
     </thumbnail>
    <image>
          http://cdn.last.fm/proposedimages/sidebar/6/1260910/82879.jpg
    </image>
</artist>
```

In the interface, you take this information and group it into its own data object, called LastArtist:

```
package sourcebottle.lastfm.data
{
    public class LastArtist
    {
        public var name:String;
        public var url:String;

        public var playCount:Number;
        public var rank:Number;

        public var thumbURL:String;
        public var imageURL:String;

        function LastArtist(artist:Object){
            name       = artist.name;
            url        = artist.url;
            playCount  = artist.playCount;
            rank       = artist.rank;
            thumbURL   = artist.avatarURL;
            imageURL   = artist.iconURL;
        }
    }
}
```

Within the LastFM class, you have written a handler for responses from the top artists web service. This examines the response and creates a LastArtist instance for each artist and returns these as an array through the TOP_ARTISTS_RESULTS event:

```
private function topArtistsHandler(e:Event):void{
    var xml:XML = new XML(_topArtistLoader.data);
    var artistArray:Array = new Array();

    for each(var tempXML:XML in xml.children()){
        var artist:LastArtist =
            new LastArtist({name:tempXML.name,url:tempXML.url,
                playCount:tempXML.playcount,rank:tempXML.rank,
          thumbURL:tempXML.thumbnail,
          imageURL:tempXML.image});
        artistArray.push(artist);
    }

     var response:LastEvent = new LastEvent(
        LastEvent.ON_TOP_ARTISTS_RESULT);
    response.data = artistArray;
    dispatchEvent(response);
}
```

Within the application, you are listening for this ON_TOP_ARTISTS_RESULT event, and you then process the array of artists that is returned:

```
lastfm.getTopArtists('ckorhonen');
lastfm.addEventListener(LastEvent.ON_TOP_ARTISTS_RESULT,
                        processArtists);
```

> You may ask, why are we bothering to go to Flickr to retrieve imagery when there is a selection of album artwork accessible through the LastFM APIs? There are two reasons for this. First, the imagery available from LastFM is often low resolution, which limits what you can do with it. Second, you are trying to create a more abstract visualization experience, and you simply require a larger set of imagery than what is available from a single data source.

Because you are interested in only the top-ten artists for a particular user, you need to take the data returned and pull out what you need:

```
var top10:Array = new Array:

...

private function processArtists(e:LastEvent):void{
    for(var i =0;i<10;i++){
        if(e.data[i]){
            var artist:LastArtist = e.data[i];
            top10.push(artist);
        }
    }
}
```

171

Thankfully, the results from LastFM are sorted in order of preference, which saves you from having to do any additional processing here. However, if the results were out of order or you wanted to retrieve a different range of data, then you could access the ranking by using the rank attribute of a LastArtist object.

Now you have the data that you require to begin extracting data from the Flickr APIs. Like you did for the LastFM web services in Chapter 4, you have abstracted the Flickr APIs in order to make it straightforward to retrieve data from those APIs.

Before using these APIs, you first need to set your API key, which grants you permission to access data:

```
FlickrService._apiKey = apiKey;
FlickrService._secret = secret;
```

Now you need to obtain a singleton instance of the interface, which means that throughout execution only a single instance of the Flickr service will exist:

```
flickr = FlickrService.getInstance();
```

And now you are ready to begin retrieving data.

Considering performance

With any web application, performance should be a consideration when you work with data exchanges. Modern programming languages and compilers are often sufficiently advanced that many programming inefficiencies and bottlenecks are removed in the compilation process. What this means for client-side web applications is that data requests can often be the number-one performance bottleneck impacting performance and, by extension, degrading the user experience of your application.

For smaller applications and widgets, especially small components of larger pages, responsiveness is important. If you are waiting for data to be returned, then you cannot offer much for the user to interact with. So, you risk being ignored.

In larger applications, you can usually get away with a loading delay because it often is within the realm of the user's expectations. However, you can usually either offer portions of the interface, which the user can interact with sans data, or present portions with loading indicators that help give a facade of responsiveness. The challenge here is to make your application feel as responsive as a desktop application, because whether you like it or not, this is what it will be compared against in the eyes of the end user.

To optimize the performance of your applications, you have several possible avenues of optimization that can lead to significant gains.

Optimizing asset loading

Optimizing asset loading is perhaps the simplest area of performance optimization and often results in the discovery of lots of low-hanging fruit for harvest. Simply put, how many HTTP requests is your application making? How many assets are loaded over the lifetime of your application? By *assets*, we are talking about any external file dependency, be it an image, XML file, or something completely different.

Once you have a picture of what is being loaded, it is often worth breaking the list down further. Which items are required before the application can be considered fully rendered and interactive, and which are loaded as the user interacts with the application? Often, the largest bottlenecks are caused by the former.

There are often cases where it is a requirement to load external files. For example, you may want to keep the SWF's background image in an external JPG file so that it can be changed in the future without having to recompile. Similarly, you could be using data files in order to pass configuration information into your application, as well as be using an external CSS file to control text styling.

Dynamically driven applications have the advantage of allowing applications to be maintained with simple content updates that can be performed by non-Flash developers. It saves having to recompile the application with each update, which in turn reduces the risk of errors being introduced. For instance, perhaps the person responsible for the compile didn't have the same version of the fonts used on their workstation, ever so slightly changing how they appear.

It is often useful to take a step back and consider where particular assets may be better stored, internally within a SWF or externally. If you list each one, along with the frequency of expected updates, this can yield many opportunities to reduce either the number of external assets loaded or the file size of these assets.

Granted, much of this optimization is at the cost of the SWF file size. However, this occupies only a single HTTP request and, with inclusion of preloader screens and animation, need not compromise the user experience.

Caching

In this example, you are not interested in continually refreshing data. Rather, you want to obtain all the data that you need up front before you begin rendering anything to the user.

In many mashups, this is the approach adopted, simply because of the core dependency of application functionality upon its constituent data sources. Without data, many applications are simply an empty shell because there is no content to render. With web applications, this usually is not a problem, but the idea of occasionally connected (offline) clients comes into play when you consider offline web applications and, eventually, desktop applications.

One consideration here is the "freshness" of data. For example, a user's musical tastes are unlikely to change overnight. An avid Beethoven fan is unlikely to convert suddenly and begin holding Rammstein in high regard. On the other hand, thousands of new photos and images are uploaded to Flickr every day. It is a constantly changing data source.

In this case, you are already making a call to LastFM when your application initializes. From here, you will be making multiple calls to Flickr, followed by calls to download actual images. If LastFM is down, or performing slowly, then the entire application will suffer. So, let's look at ways you can optimize this.

First you can begin looking at your calls and seeing whether there are opportunities to cache responses. LastFM is an obvious contender, because data is unlikely to change significantly with any regularity. Refreshing cached data once per week should be sufficient. Unfortunately, Flickr presents you with fewer opportunities for data caching if you want to keep your content current and interesting. A typical search response would have a lifetime of a day at best.

Without any web-based database, the best solution in this instance is to store a representation of this data within a *shared object*. A shared object is to Flash developers what a cookie is to web developers; in other words, it gives you the ability to store data that persists on the user's machine and that is available on subsequent visits.

For security reasons, a shared object can be read by only those Flash applications that reside on the same domain as the Flash application that initially created the shared object. However, developers should be aware that shared objects are stored on a user's filesystem in an unencrypted state, making them impractical for storing private data unless it is in some way encrypted.

By default, the size limit on a shared object is 100KB. If a shared object exceeds this size, then the user will be prompted to either accept it or reject it.

Within ActionScript 3.0, the process of setting a shared object is relatively straightforward:

```
import flash.net.SharedObject;

...

var so:SharedObject = SharedObject.getLocal("example");
so.data.setProperty("myMessage" ,"Hello World!");
so.flush();
```

This creates a shared object of the name example. To write a shared object to disk, you use the flush() method. This is also called automatically when an application is closed.

The contents of a shared object can be simply extracted:

```
so.data.myMessage
```

> *Shared objects are also used within Flash applications as a means of sharing data in real time between a remote server and potentially other users who are also connected to that server. In this case, one would connect to a remote shared object stored on a web server, which can be shared between multiple clients. As properties within the shared object are updated, the server is notified of the change, and it is synchronized between connected clients.*

In any web application where there is a dependency on data upon initialization, caching can result in a major performance gain, with the application hitting the ground running with regard to data.

This is particularly important when you consider user experience, where the user does not want to wait for a page to load but instead wants to begin interacting as soon as possible. Having the data available from a previous session can make a huge difference in the usability of your application.

The tricky part comes when you are defining rules for refreshing the data. As with the shared object example, date stamping is a solution that can work well in certain circumstances, when you have seldom-modified data. However, when a data source is more dynamic, then this can prove less effective because data is more likely to be noticeably out of date.

A solution to this could involve some smoke and mirrors, whereby you choose to cache every piece of data utilized by a web application so that when a user returns, load/initialization time is reduced. Once the application is initialized, then you can begin making HTTP requests and service calls in order to refresh this data.

The only challenge here is managing how these post-load data updates are handled without disrupting the user, who probably would be a bit confused if the data they were interacting with suddenly flickered out of existence only to be replaced by a fresher version. The traditional web metaphor, and user expectation, is to expect content to be refreshed as part of the initial load of a page, rather than following the load and initialization of an application. This is important to remember when considering updating an application's user interface with fresh data.

Consolidating

With caching taken care of, you have another opportunity for performance gains, and this is by consolidating HTTP calls. You want to retrieve images and then consolidate them into a visualization. So in this case, you might as well bundle your calls to the Flickr API. Rather than making a call per artist, you can include all artists within your search parameters and have the query return results that match any single artist.

This approach is likely to have a major impact on reducing the actual initialization time of an application, especially when you consider how the Flash Player interacts with the network through the web browser. Out of the box, most web browsers are limited to four concurrent HTTP requests spread across two different domains. So, the last thing you want is to have critical HTTP requests queued up while something else is downloaded.

Web application developers have been aware of this for a while, and many techniques are available to reduce the number of HTTP requests upon the load of a particular page. Consolidating CSS and JavaScript files and using CSS sprites are examples of ways to optimize the number of HTTP requests. If your application is making multiple data calls, which are adversely impacting performance, then consolidation may be the way forward.

A good technique is to call many different web services from your own web server, consolidating the responses from each into a single response that a web application can consume. Another advantage of this approach, beyond reducing HTTP requests, is to leverage the processing power of the web server to reformat/restructure data into a more consumable data format. This is especially useful when working with large quantities of XML-based data, whose parsing takes its toll on the client.

From a data owner's perspective, consolidation is also preferred, because it reduces the load on a particular web service (along with CPU/bandwidth costs). In fact, many service providers take additional steps to prevent application developers from overusing a service and often imposing restrictions on how often, or how many times a day, a particular application can request data.

Summary

In this chapter, we covered the key considerations when working with different APIs and web services in order to create your mashups. These considerations include ways you can optimize your developer workflow and share code between applications by abstracting an API into a reusable library and ways you can optimize the performance of an application.

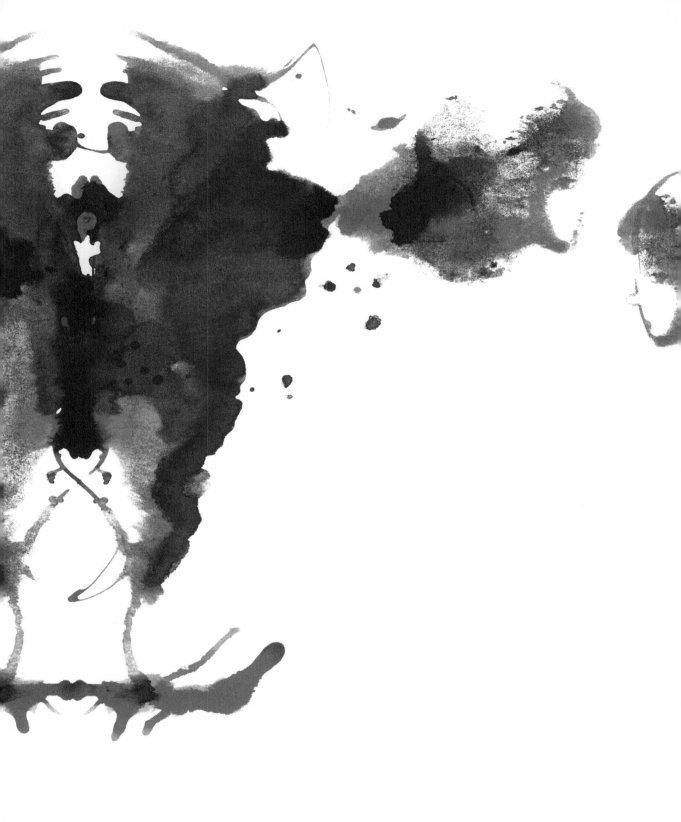

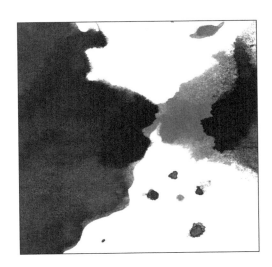

Chapter 9

MASHING UP FUNCTIONALITY

In this chapter, we'll cover mashups that concentrate on application functionality, rather than data source–centric mashups. You can use these mashups to provide the infrastructure that supports your applications.

In previous chapters, we discussed the Flash Platform as used to develop mashups that gather information from multiple data sources. For example, you can quickly build applications that display images from a web service, allow two-way interaction with various social networks, and do other straightforward tasks. However, as mashups become more complex, they put greater demands on the infrastructure required to support them.

So far, the mashups in this book have been client-side applications that execute within Flash Player. We have not shown how to use any server-side technologies to process or manage data, but as applications grow, this becomes more desirable. For instance, to allow a user to select a photo from Flickr, edit it within a Flex-based image processor, and then store it somewhere, it is often desirable to use the server both to store data and to orchestrate the flow between different web services. Similarly, if you are developing a mashup intended for use by a specific group of people, perhaps within a company, then you may want to securely authenticate users to limit access to authorized users only.

In this chapter, you'll examine external services such as Amazon S3, Amazon Simple DB, and OpenID to leverage the functionality they provide as part of your mashup.

This distributed approach can have many benefits. For starters, you don't need to concern yourself with developing the inner workings of these functional elements. All you need to know is how to use them—what goes in and what comes out. This will give your application greater flexibility and scalability, because the application infrastructure is being provided and maintained by a third party with much vaster resources than you probably have and that is accountable to a large number of customers.

Of course, you'll need network connectivity if you develop around such a distributed architecture. This is usually not a problem, since we are talking about building mashups after all; however, it may not be suitable for intranet applications. And, although many of these services offer security and encryption, they may also not be the ideal approach if you are dealing with sensitive personal information.

Using Amazon S3 as a data store

When building any kind of web application, you need somewhere to host your files, whether they are simple HTML, SWF, and image files that make up your application or whether they consist of content that is consumed by your application. With most web hosting packages, you are given a limited amount of disk space per month and a bandwidth allowance to account for the traffic generated by people visiting your site and downloading content. It is perfectly feasible for you to host your own files, but you will often be limited in several ways:

- **Storage capacity**: Your storage capacity will be limited depending on the specifics of your hosting plan. Although you can increase the capacity, additional storage is usually sold in set increments, rather than by actual usage. When dealing with user-generated content, especially multimedia content, the storage requirements to support an application can increase rapidly.

- **Bandwidth limitations**: Exceeding this limit often results in either penalty charges or the website being shut down for a period, depending on your agreement with your hosting provider. It obviously is no good if your new mashup is promoted on several websites, attracting many new users, and then unceremoniously pulled because you are exceeding your bandwidth limit.

- **Network factors**: Web content is usually hosted in a single location that corresponds to the physical location of the web server. The network location and connection speed of this server will have a huge bearing on the performance of your website because it dictates the number of "steps" between a user and your content, as well as the limiting speed at which content can be downloaded.

For example, content hosted on a server in Phoenix, Arizona, is likely to offer reasonable response times for users in San Francisco and on the West Coast; however, for a user in Australia, response times may be significantly less. Companies such as Akamai offer content acceleration solutions that work by hosting copies of web content on servers locally, around the world. However, these services are often financially prohibitive for the lone developer.

Amazon S3 avoids all these common limitations. It leverages the infrastructure of Amazon.com to provide vast storage capabilities accessible through a set of APIs.

> You can find more information on the Amazon S3 APIs at http://aws.amazon.com/s3.

Amazon runs a network of global websites, and S3 is part of this infrastructure, delivering the benefits of service reliability, architecture, and response times. Amazon is so confident in its solution that the company offers a service-level agreement of 99.9 percent monthly uptime.

With the S3 APIs, you can read and write as many items of data as required, with each data item having a maximum file size of 5GB. Data is stored in *buckets*, the S3 equivalent of folders, which you can use to categorize and organize content. In addition, you can enforce specific access rights in order to protect stored data.

All of this comes under a totally different pricing structure than standard web hosting offers. Rather than paying a flat monthly fee, you pay for what you use each month, which at the time of this writing is $0.15 per 1GB of storage and $0.18 per 1GB of bandwidth usage. This pricing model means that the upkeep cost of a web application using S3 is comparable to the costs of a standard hosting package, with the additional peace of mind that you don't need to worry about the actual implementation or maintenance of the system.

Within your applications, you can utilize S3 in two primary ways, either by using it simply to host static files that you then consume or by using it interactively from within your application to access and store data. Let's take a closer look.

Getting started with S3

Before you can begin looking at the S3 APIs, you need to first register for the service. You can do this by visiting http://aws.amazon.com/s3 and signing up for the service. Your S3 account is associated with your Amazon username and password, so if you already use Amazon for shopping, then the sign-up process is quite straightforward, with your registered credit card used for monthly billing.

To find your access key ID and secret access key, visit your Amazon Web Services account page. You'll use these keys to securely access the S3 service, and you will be using them in your applications.

It is important to remember that the secret access key is exactly that, a secret. As such, it should not be shared; otherwise, third parties will be able to access your account.

Hosting content with S3

Storing assets is quite straightforward. Many tools allow you to upload and manage files on S3, but for this example, we'll stick with the S3 Firefox Organizer plug-in (Figure 9-1). It's available at `https://addons.mozilla.org/en-US/firefox/addon/3247`.

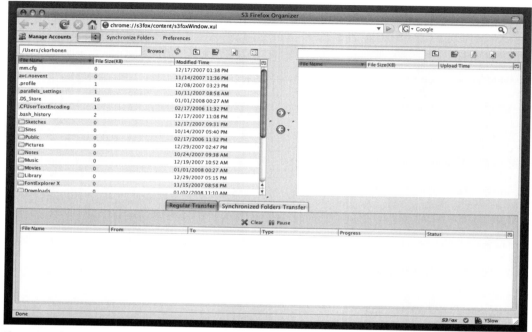

Figure 9-1. The S3 Firefox Organizer plug-in

If you want to host a file within S3, follow these steps:

1. In the plug-in, click Manage Accounts, and enter your access key. Once you have installed the plug-in, you need to enter your access keys, which you can do by clicking Manage Accounts in the top left of the user interface. Then you can connect to S3.

2. Once connected, create a new bucket where you will store your content. In this case, create a bucket named `mysite.files`.

3. You can now double-click the newly created bucket `mysite.files` icon and begin uploading files in the same manner you would use with an FTP client.

4. Right-click the file, and select Edit ACL. A list of permissions should appear (Figure 9-2). Choose Everyone, and click the Read check box so that the file can be viewed by anyone using your application.

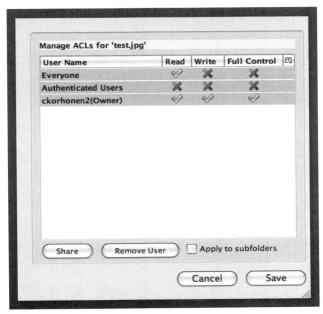

Figure 9-2. File permissions on an uploaded file, set to allow full read access

5. Now you should be able to access your file over HTTP. URLs of files stored on S3 are constructed in the following format:

`http://<bucket name>.s3.amazonaws.com/<item name>`

So, a file named `test.jpg` would be accessible at the following URL:

`http://mysite.files.s3.amazonaws.com/test.jpg`

You have now successfully set up an S3 bucket that you can use for file hosting.

To make it appear as if files are hosted on your domain name, `files.mysite.com`, set up a CNAME record for the subdomain "files" on `mysite.com` that points to your S3 host name. This functionality is usually located within your domain name control panel.

Accessing hosted files from Flash applications

To access these files from a SWF file hosted on another domain, you need to set up a crossdomain.xml file within your bucket:

```
<?xml version="1.0"?>
<cross-domain-policy>
    <allow-access-from domain="*" />
</cross-domain-policy>
```

To prevent access from certain domains, you can restrict your list of allowed domains as necessary from within the crossdomain.xml file:

```
<?xml version="1.0"?>
<cross-domain-policy>
    <allow-access-from domain="*.mydomain.com" />
</cross-domain-policy>
```

Reading and writing data

In addition to hosting files, you can create your own S3 client, allowing you to read and write files from within your applications. To store data files, configuration information, or user-generated content, you can simply upload this into an S3 bucket and access it later.

Next, we'll show how to develop a simple example to access S3, shown in Figure 9-3. First, download Christian Cantrell's ActionScript 3.0 library for interacting with Amazon S3 (http://code.google.com/p/as3awss3lib/), which requires that you also download AS3 Crypyo (http://crypto.hurlant.com/) and AS3 Core (http://code.google.com/p/as3corelib/).

> The downloadable SWC version of AS3CoreLib does not include the class com.adobe.net.MimeTypeMap. *If you experience problems, then download the precompiled version from Google Code page for the S3 Library.*

We'll show how to create a simple file browser for S3, allowing users to view the contents of buckets, create new buckets, and manage files.

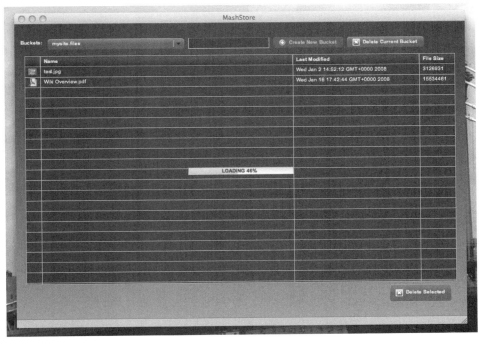

Figure 9-3. The interface of the S3 example application, showing the contents of the bucket uploaded during the web hosting example

The user interface

You can begin by creating the MXML file that will define the application interface.

In this example, you are creating two distinct application states to define the user interface in two different modes of operation. There is one state for browsing your S3 buckets and manipulating the files within and another state for the user to enter the S3 API keys, which are needed before you can view any files. An additional state displays a loading indicator, which will appear when you are waiting for an operation to complete.

```
<?xml version="1.0" encoding="utf-8"?>
<mx:WindowedApplication
    xmlns:view="com.realeyes.mashstore.view.*"
    xmlns:mx="http://www.adobe.com/2006/mxml"
    layout="absolute"
    minWidth="800" minHeight="600"
    creationComplete="_onCreationComplete();"
    currentState="{model.currentState}">
```

```
<mx:Style source="styles/mashStore.css" />
<mx:Script source="_includes/_MashStore.as" />

<mx:states>
  <mx:State name="welcome">
          <mx:AddChild position="lastChild">
          <view:Welcome id="welcome_view" horizontalCenter="0"
                          verticalCenter="0"/>
      </mx:AddChild>
  </mx:State>

  <mx:State name="default">
    <mx:AddChild position="lastChild">
          <mx:HBox id="buckets_hb" top="30" left="10">
              <mx:Label id="bucket_lbl"  text="Buckets:"
                          fontWeight="bold" />
              <mx:ComboBox id="buckets_cb" left="84"
                          top="25"
                          dataProvider="{ model.buckets }"
                          labelField="name"
                          change="model.currentBucket =
    Bucket(ComboBox(event.target).selectedItem).name"/>
              <mx:TextInput id="createBucket_ti" />
              <mx:Button id="createBucket_btn"
                      label="Create New Bucket"
                      enabled="{Boolean( createBucket_ti.text.length )}"
                      click="_onCreateBucket( event )"
                      icon="@Embed(source='icons/add.png')"/>
              <mx:Button id="deleteBucket_btn" label="Delete Current Bucket"
                      icon="@Embed(source='icons/delete.png')"
                      click="_onDeleteBucket( event );"/>
          </mx:HBox>
      </mx:AddChild>
      <mx:AddChild position="lastChild">
          <view:FileManager id="addFiles_view" top="55" right="10"
                          left="10" bottom="10"/>
      </mx:AddChild>
  </mx:State>

  <mx:State name="loading" basedOn="default">
    <mx:AddChild position="lastChild">
          <mx:ProgressBar id="loading_prg" horizontalCenter="0"
                          verticalCenter="0"
                          labelPlacement="center"
                          mode="polled"
                          source="{service}"/>
```

```
        </mx:AddChild>
            <mx:SetProperty target="{loading_prg}" name="source"
                            value="{service}" />
        </mx:State>
    </mx:states>

</mx:WindowedApplication>
```

When you return to your main application MXML file, you are referencing the external file _MashStore.as, which contains ActionScript code relating to your user interface:

```
import com.adobe.webapis.awss3.AWSS3Event;
import com.adobe.webapis.awss3.Bucket;
import com.realeyes.mashstore.business.MashStoreService;
import com.realeyes.mashstore.events.InitializeServiceEvent;
import com.realeyes.mashstore.model.MashStoreModel;

import flash.events.Event;
import flash.events.MouseEvent;

import mx.controls.Alert;
import mx.events.CloseEvent;

private var _defaultBucket:String = "jccrosby";

[Bindable]public var model:MashStoreModel;
[Bindable]public var service:MashStoreService;
```

With your user interface initialized, you get an instance of your application's model (we are using the Model View Controller architecture here) and add application event listeners, like so:

```
private function _onCreationComplete():void{
    model = MashStoreModel.getInstance();
    welcome_view.addEventListener(
            InitializeServiceEvent.INITIALIZE_SERVICE,
            _initService );
    model.addEventListener( MashStoreModel.CHANGE_CURRENT_BUCKET,
                            _onChangeCurrentBucket );
}
```

The listener initializes the S3 service and initially retrieves a list of available buckets. This is fired once the user has provided their API keys:

```
private function _initService( p_event:InitializeServiceEvent ):void{
    service = MashStoreService.getInstance();
    service.listBuckets(); // get the initial data
}
```

185

The other event listeners relate to your user interfaces, responding to events as the user interacts with the UI controls:

```
private function _onChangeCurrentBucket( p_event:Event ):void{
    // Now that we have a new bucket, list the objects in that bucket
    service.listObjects( model.currentBucket );
}

private function _onDeleteBucket( p_event:MouseEvent ):void{
    Alert.show( "Are you sure you want to delete the " +
                     model.currentBucket + " bucket?",
                     "Delete Bucket!", Alert.YES|Alert.NO,
                     this, _onConfirmDeleteBucket );
}

private function _onConfirmDeleteBucket( p_event:CloseEvent ):void{
    if( p_event.detail == Alert.YES ){
        service.deleteBucket( model.currentBucket );
    }
}

private function _onCreateBucket( p_event:MouseEvent ):void{
    if( createBucket_ti.text == "" ){
        Alert.show( "You must enter a name for the new bucket!",
                     "Bucket Name Error!" );
    } else {
        service.createBucket( createBucket_ti.text );

        var newBucket:Bucket = new Bucket();
        newBucket.name =  createBucket_ti.text;
        newBucket.creationDate =  new Date();

        model.buckets.addItem( newBucket );

        createBucket_ti.text = "";
    }
}
```

As the user interacts with your application, the user interface will move between the various states. Explicitly specifying these states here allows you to easily reconfigure your user interface at runtime.

For the welcome and default state, you are referencing separate MXML components that provide portions of the user interface for these states (Figure 9-4).

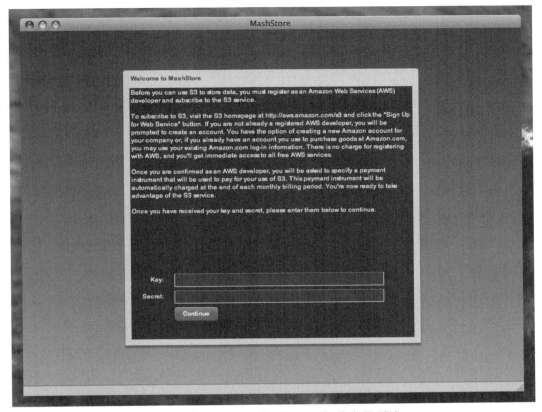

Figure 9-4. The initial state of your application, prompting the user for their S3 API keys

The welcome screen

Within Welcome.mxml, you define the look and feel of the prompt that is used to ask the user for their API key (Figure 9-5):

```
<?xml version="1.0" encoding="utf-8"?>
<mx:Panel xmlns:mx="http://www.adobe.com/2006/mxml"
    layout="absolute"
    width="472" height="454"
    title="Welcome to MashStore"
    creationComplete="_onCreationComplete();">
```

187

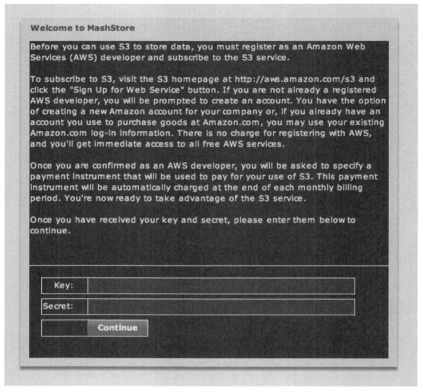

Figure 9-5. The interface element defined in `Welcome.mxml`

Metadata is used in order to define events that are dispatched from this view. This allows the Flex IDE to offer code hinting and autocompletion for this component.

```
<mx:Metadata>
    [Event(name="initializeService",
        type="com.realeyes.mashstore.events.InitializeServiceEvent")]
</mx:Metadata>

<mx:Script>
    <![CDATA[
        import com.realeyes.mashstore.events.➥
                 InitializeServiceEvent;
        import mx.controls.Alert;
        import com.realeyes.mashstore.model.MashStoreModel;
        import com.realeyes.mashstore.business.MashStoreService;
```

To avoid the user entering their API keys each time they load the application, in this example you are storing the API keys in a shared object so the user doesn't need to enter them each time. If they already exist, then you change the application state to `default` and initialize the application.

```
private var _so:SharedObject;

private function _onCreationComplete():void{
    _so = SharedObject.getLocal( "mashstore" );

    // If we've entered our data already
    if( _so.data.key && _so.data.secret ){
        // Set the key and secret
        MashStoreService.KEY = _so.data.key;
        MashStoreService.SECRET = _so.data.secret;

        // Change to the default State
        MashStoreModel.getInstance().currentState =
            ViewStates.DEFAULT;
        _initApp();
    }
}

private function _onContinue( p_event:MouseEvent ):void{
    key_valid.validate();
    secret_valid.validate();

    // Set the key and secret
    MashStoreService.KEY = key_ti.text;
    MashStoreService.SECRET = secret_ti.text;

    _so.data.key = MashStoreService.KEY;
    _so.data.secret = MashStoreService.SECRET;

    // Kick-start the app
    _initApp();
}

private function _initApp():void{
    // Broadcast an event saying we're ready to
    // initialize the application
    dispatchEvent( new InitializeServiceEvent(
        InitializeServiceEvent.INITIALIZE_SERVICE));

    // Change to the default View State
    MashStoreModel.getInstance().currentState =
            ViewStates.DEFAULT;
}
    ]]>
</mx:Script>
```

In this code, you are using the built-in Flex validators to authenticate the user's input, ensuring that they have entered a value for the API key before allowing them to proceed.

This is just the beginning when it comes to the Flex validators. In more complex form-based applications, you can perform much more advanced data validation, including validation by minimum and maximum values and by regular expression.

```
<mx:Validator id="key_valid"
              required="true"
              requiredFieldError="You must specify a Amazon S3 Key!"
                  source="{key_ti}"
                  property="text" />
<mx:Validator id="secret_valid"
              required="true"
              requiredFieldError="You must specify a Amazon S3 Secret!"
              source="{secret_ti}"
              property="text" />

<mx:VBox x="0" y="0" width="100%" height="100%">
    <mx:Text width="100%" height="285">
        <mx:htmlText><![CDATA[<p>Before you can use S3 to
            store data, you must register as an Amazon Web
            Services (AWS) developer and subscribe to the S3
            service.</p>
            <p>To subscribe to S3, visit the S3 homepage at
            http://aws.amazon.com/s3 and click the "Sign Up
            for Web Service" button. If you are not already a
            registered AWS developer, you will be prompted to
            create an account. You have the option of creating a
            new Amazon account for your company or, if you
            already have an account you use to purchase goods
            at Amazon.com, you may use your existing
            Amazon.com log-in information. There is no charge
            for registering with AWS, and you'll get immediate
            access to all free AWS services.</p>
            <p>Once you are confirmed as an AWS developer,
            you will be asked to specify a payment instrument
            that will be used to pay for your use of S3. This
            payment instrument will be automatically charged at
            the end of each monthly billing period. You're now
            ready to take advantage of the S3 service.</p>
            <p>Once you have received your key and secret,
            please enter them below to continue.</p>]]>
        </mx:htmlText>
    </mx:Text>
    <mx:VBox width="100%" height="100%">
        <mx:Form width="100%" height="100%">
            <mx:FormItem label="Key:">
                <mx:TextInput id="key_ti" width="335" />
            </mx:FormItem>
```

```
            <mx:FormItem label="Secret:">
                    <mx:TextInput id="secret_ti" width="335" />
            </mx:FormItem>
        <mx:FormItem>
                <mx:Button id="continue_btn" label="Continue"
                        click="_onContinue( event );"/>
            </mx:FormItem>
        </mx:Form>
    </mx:VBox>
  </mx:VBox>
</mx:Panel>
```

The File Manager

The other MXML component you are using in your state is for your File Manager. This component uses a DataGrid in order to display files (Figure 9-6).

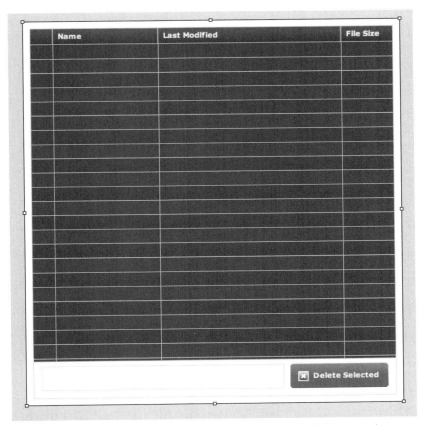

Figure 9-6. The File Manager state, with a DataGrid for displaying file listings and controls to perform various operations

```
<?xml version="1.0" encoding="utf-8"?>
<mx:Canvas
    xmlns:mx="http://www.adobe.com/2006/mxml"
    width="100%" height="100%"
    creationComplete="_onCreationComplete();">

    <mx:Metadata>
        [Event(name='uploadFiles', type=
                    'com.realeyes.mashstore.events.UploadFilesEvent')]
    </mx:Metadata>

    <mx:Script>
        <![CDATA[
            import mx.events.CloseEvent;
            import mx.controls.Alert;
            import com.adobe.webapis.awss3.S3Object;
            import com.realeyes.mashstore.business.MashStoreService;
            import com.realeyes.mashstore.events.UploadFilesEvent;
            import com.realeyes.mashstore.model.MashStoreModel;
            import mx.events.DragEvent;
            import mx.utils.ObjectUtil;
            import mx.collections.ArrayCollection;

            private var _service:MashStoreService;

            [Bindable]public var model:MashStoreModel;
```

Next, you initialize the user interface and register its events. As a user adds or removes files from this view, the following code will trigger your S3 service to upload or remove files:

```
            private function _onCreationComplete():void{
                model = MashStoreModel.getInstance();
                _service = MashStoreService.getInstance();

                addEventListener( NativeDragEvent.NATIVE_DRAG_ENTER,
                                    _onDragEnter );
                addEventListener( NativeDragEvent.NATIVE_DRAG_DROP,
                                    _onDragDrop );
            }

            private function _onRemove( p_event:MouseEvent ):void{
                var fileString:String = "";

                Alert.show( "Are you sure you want to delete the
                                selected files?", "Delete Confirmation",
                                Alert.YES|Alert.CANCEL, this,
                                _onConfirmDelete, null, Alert.YES );
            }
```

```
private function _onConfirmDelete(
            p_event:CloseEvent):void{
    if( p_event.detail == Alert.YES ){
        var objects:Array = files_dg.selectedItems;
        for each( var object:S3Object in objects ){
            // Remove the selected items from S3
            _service.deleteObject(model.currentBucket,
                                    object.key );

            // Remove selected items from the model
            var itemIndex:int =
                model.objects.getItemIndex(
                        files_dg.selectedItem);
                model.objects.removeItemAt( itemIndex );
        }
    }
}
```

For your application to respond to drag-and-drop events, you must create the appropriate methods that indicate that the component should accept files dropped onto it:

Once a file is dropped, it will be uploaded to S3.

```
private function _onDragEnter(
            event:NativeDragEvent ):void {
    NativeDragManager.acceptDragDrop( this );
}

private function _onDragDrop(
            event:NativeDragEvent ):void {
    NativeDragManager.dropAction =
            NativeDragActions.COPY;

    var newFiles:Array = event.clipboard.getData(
            ClipboardFormats.FILE_LIST_FORMAT )
                    as Array;

    for each( var file:File in newFiles ) {
        _addDroppedFile( file.nativePath, file.name );
    }
}

private function _addDroppedFile( nativePath:String,
            fileName:String ):void {
    var droppedFile:File =
        File.userDirectory.resolvePath( nativePath );
    var newObject:S3Object = new S3Object();
```

```
                                // Create a new object locally
                                newObject.key = droppedFile.name;
                                newObject.bucket = model.currentBucket;
                                newObject.lastModified =
                                    droppedFile.modificationDate;
                                newObject.size = droppedFile.size;

                                // Add to the objects model
                                model.objects.addItem( newObject );

                                // Push to S3
                                MashStoreService.getInstance().saveObject(
                                    model.currentBucket,
                                    droppedFile.name, droppedFile );
                        }
                ]]>
            </mx:Script>
```

The DataGrid contains columns indicating the name, size, and last-modified date for each file. In addition, you use a custom item renderer for each file.

```
            <mx:DataGrid id="files_dg"
                        dataProvider="{model.objects}"
                        allowMultipleSelection="true"
                        left="10" top="10" bottom="62" right="10"
                        change="model.currentObject =
                        S3Object( DataGrid( event.target ).selectedItem )">
                <mx:columns>
                    <mx:DataGridColumn width="30" headerText=""
                            itemRenderer="com.realeyes.mashstore.
                                    itemrenderer.FileTypeRenderer" />
                    <mx:DataGridColumn headerText="Name" dataField="key"/>
                    <mx:DataGridColumn width="250" headerText="Last Modified"
                                    dataField="lastModified"/>
                    <mx:DataGridColumn width="70"  headerText="File Size"
                                    dataField="size"/>
                </mx:columns>
            </mx:DataGrid>

            <mx:ControlBar left="10" right="10" bottom="10">
                <mx:Spacer width="100%" height="100%"/>
                <mx:Button id="removeFiles_btn" click="_onRemove( event );"
                        label="Delete Selected"
                        con="@Embed(source='../../../../icons/delete.png')"
                        height="35"/>
            </mx:ControlBar>
        </mx:Canvas>
```

Rendering file icons

To render distinct icons for each file, based on its file type, you use a custom item renderer.

The item renderer consists of an Image component and a snippet of ActionScript.

To determine the file extension of the file, you access the S3 Object, which represents the file to access the filename.

We assume that the filename is of the format [filename].[extension], so you split the string and return the extension.

```xml
<?xml version="1.0" encoding="utf-8"?>
<mx:Image
    xmlns:mx="http://www.adobe.com/2006/mxml"
    horizontalAlign="center" verticalAlign="middle">

    <mx:Script>
        <![CDATA[
            import com.realeyes.net.FileIconMap;
            import com.adobe.webapis.awss3.S3Object;

            private var _data:Object;
            private var _object:S3Object;


            override public function get data():Object{
                return _data;
            }
            override public function set data(p_value:Object):void{
                _data = p_value;
                _object = S3Object( _data );

                // Get the file extension from the key
                var ext:String = _object.key.split( "." )[ 1 ];
                // Look up the image Class in FileIcon dictionary
                var icon:Class =
                    FileIconMap.getInstance().getIcon( ext );

                // Set the image source
                this.source = icon;
            }
        ]]>
    </mx:Script>
</mx:Image>
```

To find an icon for the extension, you need to look it up in your FileIconMap class. This provides a mapping between the file extension and the icon reference.

195

Each icon is a PNG file that you load into your application. If an icon does not exist for a specific file type, then a default icon is returned.

```
package com.realeyes.net{
    import flash.utils.Dictionary;

    public class FileIconMap{
        static private var _instance:FileIconMap;

        [Embed(source="../../../icons/text.png")]
        private var  textDoc:Class;

        [Embed(source="../../../icons/flash.png")]
        private var  flash:Class;

        [Embed(source="../../../icons/html.png")]
        private var  html:Class;

        [Embed(source="../../../icons/icons.png")]
        private var  ico:Class;

        [Embed(source="../../../icons/image.png")]
        private var  image:Class;

        [Embed(source="../../../icons/msg.png")]
        private var  msg:Class;

        [Embed(source="../../../icons/coldfusion.png")]
        private var  coldfusion:Class;

        [Embed(source="../../../icons/zip.png")]
        private var  zip:Class;

        [Embed(source="../../../icons/word.png")]
        private var  word:Class;

        [Embed(source="../../../icons/pdf.png")]
        private var  pdf:Class;

        [Embed(source="../../../icons/rss.png")]
        private var  rss:Class;

        [Embed(source="../../../icons/code.png")]
        private var  code:Class;

        [Embed(source="../../../icons/video.png")]
        private var  video:Class;
```

```
[Embed(source="../../../icons/unknown.png")]
private var  defaultIcon:Class;

private var icons:Dictionary;

public function FileIconMap( ){
    _init();
}

private function _init():void{
    icons = new Dictionary();

    icons["txt"] = textDoc;
    icons["xml"] = textDoc;
    icons["fla"] = flash;
    icons["html"] = html;
    icons["htm"] = html;
    icons["ico"] = ico;
    icons["png"] = image;
    icons["jpg"] = image;
    icons["gif"] = image;
    icons["bmp"] = image;
    icons["tiff"] = image;
    icons["tiff"] = image;
    icons["msg"] = msg;
    icons["cf"] = coldfusion;
    icons["zip"] = zip;
    icons["7z"] = zip;
    icons["rar"] = zip;
    icons["doc"] = word;
    icons["docx"] = word;
    icons["pdf"] = pdf;
    icons["rss"] = rss;
    icons["js"] = code;
    icons["php"] = code;
    icons["mxml"] = code;
    icons["rb"] = code;
    icons["flv"] = video;
    icons["mpg"] = video;
    icons["mov"] = video;
    icons["avi"] = video;
}

static public function getInstance():FileIconMap{
    if( !_instance ){
        _instance = new FileIconMap( );
    }
    return _instance;
}
```

```
                    public function getIcon( p_extension:String ):Class{
                        var icon:Class;

                        if( icons[ p_extension ] == null ){
                            icon = defaultIcon;
                        } else {
                            icon = icons[ p_extension ];
                        }

                        return icon;
                    }
                }
            }
```

Modeling S3 data

We'll use the application's model to keep track of the current state, including which S3 bucket is currently selected and whether the application is currently loading any data:

```
        package com.realeyes.mashstore.model{

            import com.adobe.webapis.awss3.S3Object;
            import com.realeyes.mashstore.view.ViewStates;

            import flash.events.Event;
            import flash.events.EventDispatcher;

            import mx.collections.ArrayCollection;

            [Event(name='changeCurrentBucket',
                        type='com.realeyes.mashstore.model.MashStoreModel')]

            [Bindable]
            public class MashStoreModel extends EventDispatcher{
                static private var _instance:MashStoreModel;

                static public const CHANGE_CURRENT_BUCKET:String =
                            "changeCurrentBucket";

                // Tracks the currently selected bucket to DL from
                private var _currentBucket:String;

                // Controls the loading state
                private var _isLoading:Boolean;

                public var currentObject:S3Object;
                public var currentState:String = ViewStates.WELCOME;

                // Tracks all the buckets for an S3 account
                public var buckets:ArrayCollection;
```

```
// Tracks all the objects for a bucket
public var objects:ArrayCollection;

public function MashStoreModel( ){
    _init();
}

static public function getInstance():MashStoreModel{
    if( !_instance ){
        _instance = new MashStoreModel(   );
    }
    return _instance;
}

private function _init():void{
    objects = new ArrayCollection();
}

[Bindable(event="changeCurrentBucket")]
public function get currentBucket():String{
    return _currentBucket;
}
```

When the bucket is changed, you dispatch an event to indicate this, which triggers the S3 service to download the listing for the contents of the newly selected bucket:

```
public function set currentBucket(p_value:String):void{
    _currentBucket = p_value;
    dispatchEvent( new Event( CHANGE_CURRENT_BUCKET ) );
}
```

If you begin a large operation with the S3 URLs, you will set the _isLoading indicator. Because you have defined a custom getter/setter for this variable, you can ensure that the appropriate state is set.

```
public function get isLoading():Boolean{
    return _isLoading;
}

public function set isLoading(p_value:Boolean):void{
    _isLoading = p_value;
    if( isLoading ){
        currentState = ViewStates.LOADING;
    } else {
        currentState = ViewStates.DEFAULT;
    }
}
    }
}
```

Controlling your S3 service

The S3 service contains all the business logic to manage the interaction between the application and the S3 web services. It uses the S3 libraries in order to work with files and buckets, dispatching events upon the completion of operations so that the main application can respond.

```
package com.realeyes.mashstore.business{

    import com.adobe.net.MimeTypeMap;
    import com.adobe.webapis.awss3.AWSS3;
    import com.adobe.webapis.awss3.AWSS3Event;
    import com.adobe.webapis.awss3.Bucket;
    import com.realeyes.mashstore.model.MashStoreModel;
    import com.realeyes.mashstore.view.ViewStates;

    import flash.events.EventDispatcher;
    import flash.events.ProgressEvent;
    import flash.filesystem.File;

    import mx.collections.ArrayCollection;
    import mx.controls.Alert;
    import mx.utils.ObjectUtil;

    public class MashStoreService extends EventDispatcher{
        static private var _instance:MashStoreService;

        static public var KEY:String;
        static public var SECRET:String;

        private var _aws:AWSS3;
        private var _model:MashStoreModel;
        private var _mimeMap:MimeTypeMap;

        private var _bytesLoaded:Number;
        private var _bytesTotal:Number;
        private var _bucketToDelete:Bucket;

        public function MashStoreService( ){
            _init();
        }

        static public function getInstance():MashStoreService{
            if( !_instance ){
                _instance = new MashStoreService(  );
            }
            return _instance;
        }
```

On initialization, you create an instance of your AWSS3 library, using the user's API and secret keys.

In addition, you register events for each of the file transfer operations to which you will respond:

```
private function _init():void{
    _aws = new AWSS3( KEY, SECRET );

    _model = MashStoreModel.getInstance();

    _mimeMap = new MimeTypeMap()

    _aws.addEventListener( AWSS3Event.BUCKET_CREATED,
                                        _onCreateBucket );
    _aws.addEventListener( AWSS3Event.LIST_BUCKETS,
                                        _onListBuckets );
    _aws.addEventListener( AWSS3Event.BUCKET_DELETED,
                                        _onDeleteBucket );
    _aws.addEventListener( AWSS3Event.LIST_OBJECTS,
                                        _onListObjects );
    _aws.addEventListener( AWSS3Event.OBJECT_RETRIEVED,
                                        _onObjectRetrieved );
    _aws.addEventListener( AWSS3Event.OBJECT_SAVED,
                                        _onObjectSaved );
    _aws.addEventListener( AWSS3Event.OBJECT_DELETED,
                                        _onObjectDeleted );
    _aws.addEventListener( ProgressEvent.PROGRESS,
                                        _onProgress );
    _aws.addEventListener( AWSS3Event.REQUEST_FORBIDDEN,
                                        _onRequestForbidden );
    _aws.addEventListener( AWSS3Event.ERROR, _onError );
}
```

The following are methods for each of the operations you can perform with the S3 APIs, wrapping the functionality for interacting with buckets:

```
public function deleteBucket( p_name:String ):void{
    _aws.deleteBucket( p_name );

    for each( var bucket:Bucket in _model.buckets ){
        if( bucket.name == p_name ){
            _bucketToDelete = bucket;
        }
    }
}

public function createBucket( p_name:String ):void{
    _aws.createNewBucket( p_name );
}

public function listBuckets():void{
    _aws.listBuckets();
}
```

And here's the code for individual objects within the buckets:

```
public function saveObject(p_bucketName:String,p_name:String,
                          p_objectFile:File):void{
    // Get the MIME-Type or use default because S3
    // requires a content type
    var mimeType:String = _mimeMap.getMimeType(
            p_objectFile.extension );
    mimeType = mimeType != null ?
            mimeType : "application/octet-stream";

    _model.currentState = ViewStates.LOADING;

    _aws.saveObject( p_bucketName, p_name, mimeType,
                          p_objectFile );
}

public function listObjects( p_bucketName:String,
                             p_prefix:String=null,
                             p_marker:String=null,
                             p_maxKeys:int=-1 ):void{
    _aws.listObjects( p_bucketName, p_prefix, p_marker,
                          p_maxKeys );
}

public function deleteObject( p_bucketName:String,
                              p_objectName:String
    ):void{
    _aws.deleteObject( p_bucketName, p_objectName );
}
```

You can also have your event handlers that are triggered once an operation has completed.

For example, once you have created a new bucket, you will want to call the S3 APIs and retrieve a list of all the buckets, of which your newly created one should be a part:

```
private function _onCreateBucket( p_event:AWSS3Event ):void{
    listBuckets();
}

private function _onListBuckets( p_event:AWSS3Event ):void{
    _model.buckets = new ArrayCollection( p_event.data );
    if( _model.buckets.length){
        _model.currentBucket = Bucket(
                _model.buckets[ 0 ] ).name;
    }
}
```

```
private function _onDeleteBucket( p_event:AWSS3Event ):void{
    trace( ObjectUtil.toString( p_event ) );
    _model.buckets.removeItemAt(
            model.buckets.getItemIndex( _bucketToDelete ) );
}

private function _onListObjects( p_event:AWSS3Event ):void{
    _model.objects = new ArrayCollection(
        p_event.data as Array );
}

private function _onObjectSaved( p_event:AWSS3Event ):void{
    // Reset bytes loaded/total values for the progress bar
    bytesLoaded = 0;
    bytesTotal = 0;

    _model.currentState = ViewStates.DEFAULT;
}

private function _onObjectRetrieved(p_event:AWSS3Event):void{
    trace( "Object Retrieved: " +
            ObjectUtil.toString( p_event ) );
}

private function _onObjectDeleted( p_event:AWSS3Event ):void{
    trace( "Object Deleted: " +
            ObjectUtil.toString( p_event ) );
}

private function _onProgress( p_event:ProgressEvent ):void{
    trace( "Loaded: %" +
            (p_event.bytesLoaded / p_event.bytesTotal ) * 100 );
    bytesLoaded = p_event.bytesLoaded;
    bytesTotal = p_event.bytesTotal;
}

private function _onRequestForbidden(p_error:AWSS3Event):void{
    Alert.show( "Details:\n\n " + p_error.data,
                    "Request Forbidden!" );
}

private function _onError( p_error:AWSS3Event ):void{
    Alert.show( "Details:\n\n" + p_error.data, "Error" );
}
```

```
            public function get bytesLoaded():Number{
                return _bytesLoaded;
            }

            public function set bytesLoaded(p_value:Number):void{
                _bytesLoaded = p_value;
            }

            public function get bytesTotal():Number{
                return _bytesTotal;
            }

            public function set bytesTotal(p_value:Number):void{
                _bytesTotal = p_value;
            }
        }
    }
```

Other services

We have focused on Amazon S3 in this chapter simply because of the ease with which Flash and Flex applications can access it. But several other online services can provide functionality for applications and mashups.

Amazon Simple DB for data storage

Amazon Simple DB is a step up from S3. Rather than storing files, Simple DB provides an infrastructure for creating a database and running queries. This is especially useful when you are working with large sets of data, such as thousands of user profiles or data items. It also frees up the developer from having to worry about the operational maintenance of the database or from investing in hardware.

Like with S3, you can use a simple web services interface to access a Simple DB instance, and it is available on a pay-as-you-go basis.

> *At the time of this writing, users of SimpleDB are charged $0.14 per machine hour of processing used for database queries, $0.10 per gigabyte of data added, and $0.18 per gigabyte of data retrieved.*

Because this is still a relatively new service, there are not yet any ActionScript APIs for interacting with this service; however, this will likely change as the service develops and developers begin leveraging its power in their Flash and Flex applications.

You can find out more about Amazon Simple DB at http://aws.amazon.com/sdb.

OpenID for user identity

Many web applications require registration before permitting access to any functionality. Since new web applications spring up every day, the process of registering the same information numerous times quickly becomes tedious. However dull it is for users, pity the poor developers who have to create a secure authentication scheme and user database when they could be spending their time on more creative tasks.

Enter OpenID, a system that provides an open and decentralized solution for online identity that can be used across disparate sites.

The idea is simple. A user chooses a trusted OpenID provider that meets their needs. This ID is completely free and can be moved around between providers. With a single registration, the OpenID can be used as a means to logging into every web application with OpenID support.

When you enter your OpenID—for example, `http://chris.provider.com/`—the web application redirects the login to `provider.com`, which would challenge the user to authenticate themselves. Upon successful completion of this process, you're returned to the original site with a token that allows you to log in.

With both Yahoo and AOL signed up as OpenID providers, the OpenID movement certainly has some weight behind it. In addition, its support in popular PHP, Python, and Ruby on Rails plug-ins makes it relatively straightforward to implement if you are looking for a way to secure your web applications and mashups.

> For more information on OpenID, you can visit `http://openid.net`. In addition, if you are looking for information on implementing OpenID in various web application frameworks, then you can find more information at `http://wiki.openid.net/Libraries`.

Summary

Mashups are not just about the flow of data, but they can also encompass functionality. As you have seen, solutions such as S3 help developers set up the foundations for a new web application, offering solutions to common problems that are often time-consuming or costly to implement.

As you explore the Web, you can find many such services that are often worth a look if they meet the needs for a particular project.

In addition, it often makes sense to look at the standards that are emerging on the Web. Initiatives such as OpenID have community backing and look to make things easier for developers and users alike.

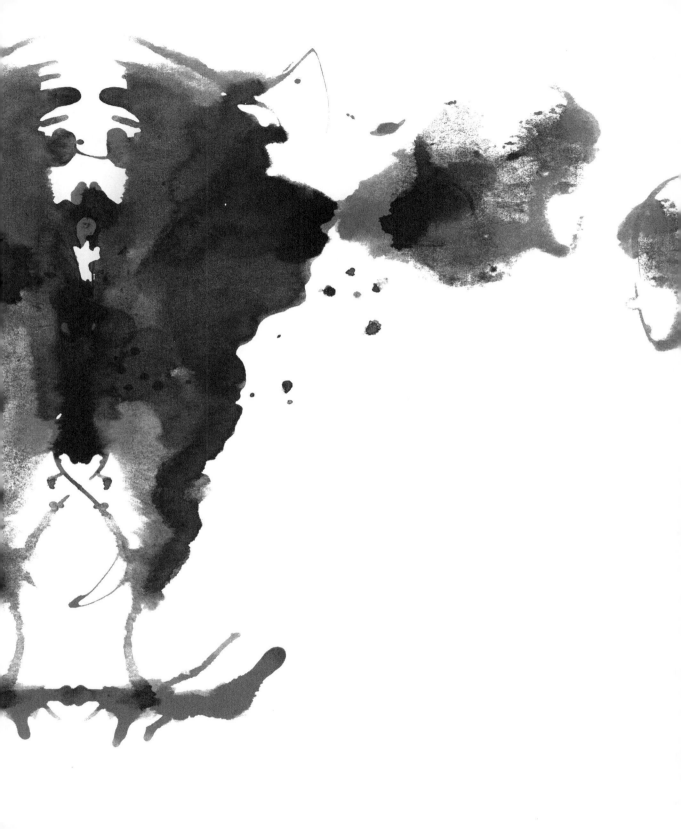

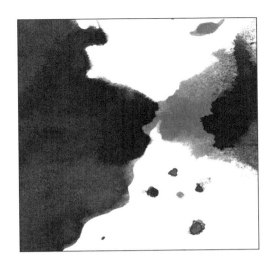

Chapter 10

SWX: A NATIVE FLASH DATA FORMAT

Having covered data exchange using popular formats such as XML, we'll now shift our focus to something completely different, a new technology called SWX, which is a perfect tool with which to build mashups.

Introducing SWX

SWX is a fairly new kid on the block, with its first implementation released in March 2007. Developed by Flash guru Aral Balkan, SWX represents a new way of working with data within Flash applications. It offers support for both Flash applications and applications built using Flash Lite, making it an excellent choice for developing mashups for mobile devices such as phones, personal digital assistants (PDAs), and Chumbys.

The philosophy behind SWX is that of simplicity. It is intended to make it easy for developers to get started with the development of mashups and other data-driven applications. Like other technologies, such as Ruby on Rails, much of the hard and repetitive work is already taken care of, leaving the door open for developers to craft compelling user experiences and even have fun doing it!

Unlike traditional data formats such as XML, SWX is the only native Flash data format. Based upon Flash's SWF file format, a SWX SWF file is dedicated to storing data.

You can think of it as a serialized data object that can be loaded into a Flash application just like any MovieClip.

Since SWX is a native format, you do not incur any of the processing overhead you'd expect when processing XML data. Data is instantaneously available and usable by the application without the need for parsing. This is another reason why SWX is an excellent choice for developing mobile or embedded applications, where processing power is often limited.

SWX also includes its own RPC protocol, which is used to define a method of calling server-side functions, with the results returned as a SWX object. At the time of this writing, the only implementation of SWF RPC is PHP-based. However, you should expect more implementations to become available, supporting popular server-side technologies such as J2EE, Ruby on Rails, and .NET.

In addition, a set of SWX tools are available to aid the developer. The tools were developed using Flex and reflect the underlying simplicity of the technology.

The SWX Service Explorer works with SWX RPC implementations to provide a simple interface for exploring server-side services (Figure 10-1). This is an excellent tool for testing and debugging server-side functionality, providing a comprehensive interface for viewing the data exchange, and getting statistics on the performance and response times of the data services. In the event of an error on the server side, the Service Explorer captures a debugging trace output and gives you all the information you need to track down the most elusive bug.

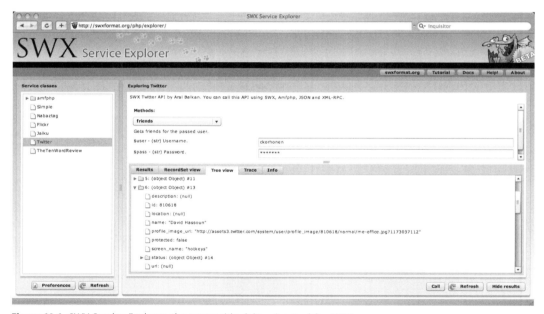

Figure 10-1. SWX Service Explorer, the server-side debugging tool for SWX

SWX Data Analyzer lets you probe the data going back and forth between server and application (see Figure 10-2). This is useful for those times when perhaps something isn't appearing as expected within your application and you need to take a closer look at the input data.

In addition to being available in your web browser, the SWX Data Analyzer is also available as a cross-platform desktop application, built with AIR. SWX applications are also fully compatible with AIR, meaning that they can be converted into cross-platform desktop applications.

To debug something like this, you would usually insert trace statements into your code or use a debugging application such as X-Ray, LumnicBox, or RedBug. In the case of SWX, all that is necessary is to set the debug property of the SWX instance to true, and debugging output will automatically be captured in the Data Analyzer.

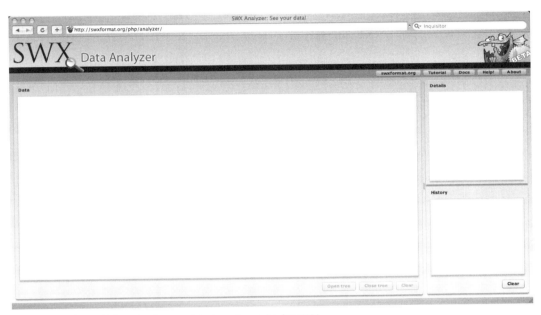

Figure 10-2. The SWX Data Analyzer, a data transfer probe for SWX

Getting started

To demonstrate the simplicity of working with SWX, we will show the steps required to build a simple mashup that pulls data from the Twitter API. Then we'll follow up by covering some of the more advanced concepts.

Twitter (www.twitter.com) is fast becoming the "Hello World" application of the Web 2.0 age, with hundreds of implementations based upon its simple API. It is a social utility that allows you to maintain a list of friends and post updates about yourself. Updates are "automagically" sent to all your friends, and the updates appear on your profile page. In many ways, it is a cross between a lifestream and an instant messaging application, allowing you to keep track of people who are in some way relevant to you.

In this case, we'll show how to retrieve the public timeline from the Twitter API and also provide an interface where users can post new updates.

The first step is to create a new Flash file. On the stage, open the Actions panel, and create a new MovieClip:

```
var loader_mc:MovieClip =
this.createEmptyMovieClip("loader_mc",this.getNextHighestDepth());
```

With this MovieClip, you can add several parameters before making the call to the SWX gateway. In this case, we are using the SWX public gateway, available on www.swxformat.org. This provides services that access several common APIs.

```
loader_mc.serviceClass = "Twitter";
loader_mc.method = "publicTimeline";
loader_mc.debug = true;

loader_mc.loadMovie("http://www.swxformat.org/php/swx.php","GET");
```

The serviceClass parameter is the PHP class being called on the server side, and it is used to specify the method that you are calling. You can find method signatures and listings of any required input parameters using the SWX Service Explorer.

You are also setting the debug parameter to true so you can capture data using the SWX Data Analyzer and check to make sure everything is working. When you compile your movie and switch to the Data Analyzer, you should be able to see data flowing from the server, as illustrated in Figure 10-3.

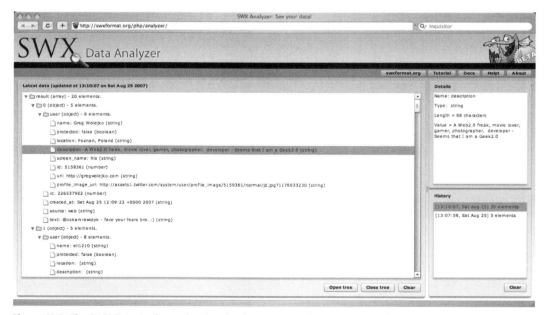

Figure 10-3. The SWX Data Analyzer, showing the data response from a service call

You should now be successfully loading data into your application. At this stage, you can manipulate and utilize it however you want within the context of your application.

> When testing your application within the Flash IDE, you will see a "Security Sandbox Violation" message printed in the console when you run your application. This is simply a result of running your SWF locally using the `file://` protocol as opposed to from a website, downloaded using the `http://` protocol. The different protocols reside within different security sandboxes, which is why you get the warning message. Once you deploy your application on a website, it will function as expected, and you can ignore this warning.

Obviously, you can't even begin to do anything with your data until you know that it has been downloaded. Data returned from a SWX call is stored within the `result` attribute of the loader instance as an array of objects. So, for example, you would be able to access the text of a Twitter update using the following syntax:

```
loader_mc.result[0].user.description
```

> The basis for SWX data is the JSON format, which is becoming one of the dominant formats for data interchange within web applications. It is used both for data received and for data parameters submitted when calling SWX RPC services.

It's necessary to keep an eye on the `result` attribute so that you know when your request has been completed and it has been populated with the data from your SWX service response. A straightforward way to do this is to use the `onEnterFrame` function. This is executed during each frame of the movie, so it provides a good mechanism for polling your loader to see whether a result has been returned.

If a result has been returned, then you can execute a function that will do something with the data. In this case, you will begin rendering the UI. Otherwise, you will continue polling until you receive a response.

```
function onEnterFrame(){
    if(loader_mc.result){
        renderInterface();
        this.onEnterFrame = null;
    }
}
```

It's important to note that once a result has been received, you are removing the `onEnterFrame` function. Otherwise, it would be executed again and again, potentially causing performance issues down the line.

It may be desirable to set a timeout on this service call, with either a fallback to default content or a notification informing the user that the service is being unresponsive. This is certainly an essential consideration when it comes to delivering the best user experience, and we will be covering this in greater depth later.

Once you know that your data has been downloaded, you can begin rendering the user interface.

The result attribute should now contain an array of user objects, which contain the information you want to display. In the `renderInterface` method, you can place these into a logical component, such as a DataGrid.

In this example, we have placed a data grid component onto the stage and given it the instance name `results_grid`. Now you can populate it with data from the SWX service call.

```
function renderInterface():Void{
    for(var i:Number = 0;i<loader_mc.result.length;i++){
        var twitterUpdate:Object = new Object();
        twitterUpdate.update = loader_mc.result[i].text;
        twitterUpdate.name = loader_mc.result[i].user.name;

        results_grid.addItem(twitterUpdate);
    }
}
```

In this case, you are simply taking the response from the service, creating an object, and adding it to your DataGrid (see Figure 10-4).

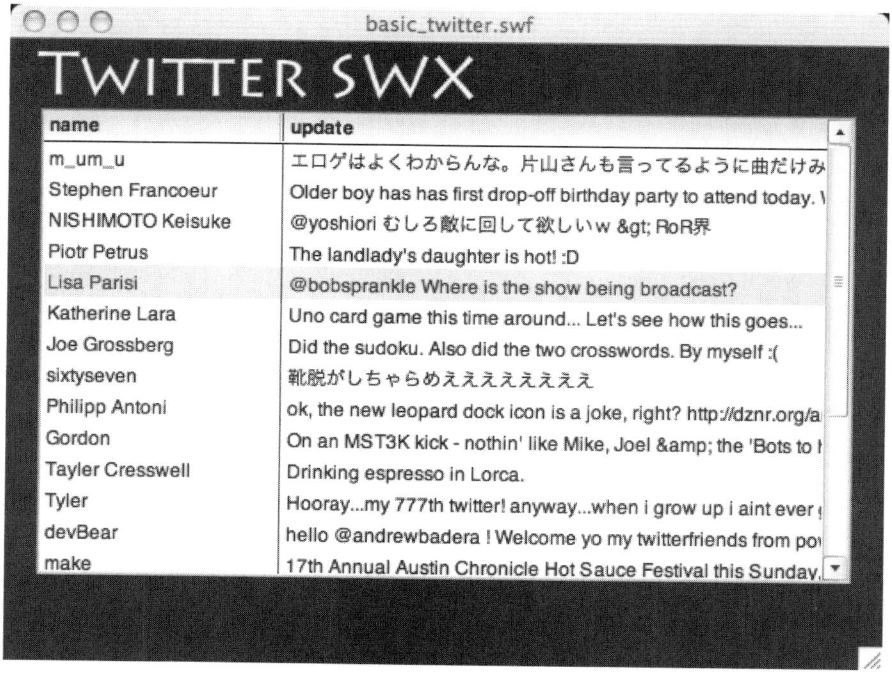

Figure 10-4. The SWX application, displaying live data from Twitter!

You could spend more time making the interface look pretty, experimenting with item renderers, and setting up the response object as a data provider for the grid component, but for the purposes of this example, we have shown how simple it can be to work with data APIs using SWX. Before we move on to some more advanced features, we'll demonstrate the process of data submission.

As mentioned, Twitter allows you to update your status for all to see, so let's do it!

First you need to modify the interface of your application slightly by adding a standard text input user interface component and a button. You will be giving the text input box the instance name status_txt and the button the instance name submit_btn. Figure 10-5 shows the updated UI.

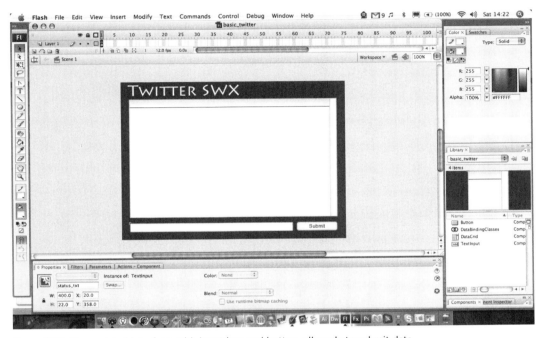

Figure 10-5. The updated interface, with input box and button, all ready to submit data

Within the ActionScript, you now need to define an onRelease function for the button, which will trigger data submission. So, create a new MovieClip on the stage in the same manner that you used initially to retrieve data from the service. The difference in this case is that you need to use a different method name, which you can find using the Service Explorer.

```
var submitter_mc:MovieClip = this.createEmptyMovieClip("submitter_mc",
    this.getNextHighestDepth());
submitter_mc.serviceClass = "Twitter";
submitter_mc.method = "update";
```

213

If you examine the method description in the Service Explorer, you can see that it takes three or four input parameters. These are listed in Table 10-1.

In the case of optional parameters, it's worth noting that if these are to be left to their default values, then they should not be passed at all. In the current version of SWF, passing in a null or empty string gives the parameter this value, rather than any default that is specified.

Table 10-1. API Listing for the Twitter Update Method

Parameter Name	Data Type	Description
$update	String	The text of your Twitter update
$user	String	Your Twitter username
$pass	String	Your Twitter password
$source	String	Optional; your Twitter source string (this denotes where you are making the update from)

These parameters need to be set within a JSON string, bound to the args property of the MovieClip:

```
submitter_mc.args = "['" + status_txt.text + "','yourusername',
                                    'yourpassword','']";
```

Now, if you call the SWF service, the update should be posted:

```
submit_btn.onRelease = function(){
    var submitter_mc:MovieClip = this.createEmptyMovieClip("submitter_mc",
        this.getNextHighestDepth());

    submitter_mc.serviceClass = "Twitter";
    submitter_mc.method = "update";

    submitter_mc.args = "['" + status_txt.text + "','yourusername',
        'yourpassword','']";
    submitter_mc.debug = true;
    submitter_mc.loadMovie("http://www.swxformat.org/php/swx.php","GET");
}
```

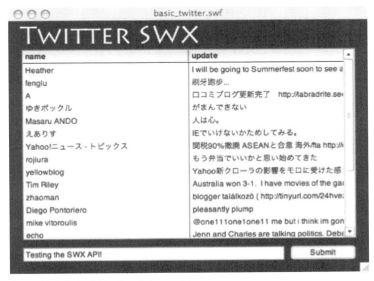

Figure 10-6. Submitting the status update.

Now let's check the website to see whether it has been posted; see Figure 10-7.

Figure 10-7. The data has been posted!

Since the status message is encoded as a JSON string, you should ensure that special characters contained within the string do not cause problems. To be on the safe side, it is a good idea to escape all strings being used as method arguments.

You can escape a string using the escape(string) command, which will convert all spaces and special characters to their equivalent character codes. So, for example, Hello World becomes Hello%20World.

In general, this is good practice when working with strings regardless of the data format being used. It helps prevent unexpected application behavior and can also guard against SQL injection or other means of code injection, thus protecting the integrity and security of data.

Next steps

We have spent some time demonstrating the simplicity of SWX, as proven by the ease of working with an API such as that provided for Twitter. The next steps in SWX development involve moving away from reliance on the SWX public gateway and setting up your own SWX gateway. This will allow you to develop your own server-side classes, which can interact with other APIs and web services in order to deliver data in your application. We will also be covering how the SWX ActionScript libraries can make application development even easier.

From the SWX website, you can download the server-side component either as a stand-alone package, which should be placed within the web root of your web server, or as a MAMP installation composed of MySQL, Apache, PHP, and several other components required to get started. Before we cover any server-side development, we'll talk about the SWX ActionScript libraries, which are also part of this distribution.

SWX library

Using the SWX ActionScript Library, you can rewrite the earlier Twitter example to use this library quite simply. To begin with, you need to add it to your project's class path so that the Flash compiler knows where to find it when you build your application.

You can do this in two ways. You can copy the library's directory structure within the same directory as the FLA file, or if you prefer to keep external libraries separate from the source code of an individual project, you can tell the Flash IDE to specifically search a directory for external classes and libraries from within the Preferences panel. If you open ActionScript preferences, then you can specify specific locations under the ActionScript 2.0 Settings and ActionScript 3.0 Settings options.

```
import org.swxformat.*;

var swx:SWX = new SWX();
swx.gateway = "http://www.swxformat.org/php/swx.php";
swx.encoding = "POST";
swx.debug = true;
```

```
var callParameters:Object =
    {
        serviceClass: "Twitter",
        method: "publicTimeline",
        args: [],
        result: [this, renderInterface],
        timeout: [this, timeoutHandler]
    }

swx.call(callParameters);
```

You also need to slightly rewrite the renderInterface method in order to work with the new results object:

```
function renderInterface(event:Object):Void{
    for(var i:Number = 0;i<event.result.length;i++){
        var twitterUpdate:Object = new Object();
        twitterUpdate.update = event.result[i].text;
        twitterUpdate.name = event.result[i].user.name;

        results_grid.addItem(twitterUpdate);
    }
}
```

The status update could also be rewritten simply by specifying a different callParameters object:

```
submit_btn.onRelease = function(){
    var callParameters:Object =
        {
            serviceClass: "Twitter",
            method: "update",
            args: [ status_txt.text, username, password],
            result: [this, resultHandler],
            timeout: [this, timeoutHandler]
        }

    swx.call(callParameters);
}

function timeoutHandler(event:Object){
    trace("Call timed out!");
}
```

Using the SWX Library has a clear benefit that it produces much cleaner code without much of the plumbing usually required, such as creating empty MovieClips or polling the loader object to check whether a response has been returned. All of this functionality is taken care of internally by the library itself.

In addition, the library provides many other powerful features such as the following:

- Triggering a function callback once a response has been received.
- Handling service timeouts (using either a default or user specified value) and performing a callback to the appropriate handler method.
- Monitoring load progress when interacting with data-heavy services. This can be used to trigger callbacks as desired.
- Support for loading external assets specified in data responses, such as images.
- Call queuing and management.
- Utility functions used to safely convert arrays, strings, or objects into the correct JSON notation.

For lightweight applications and widgets, the bulk of this functionality may be redundant. But once we move on to developing more complex applications, which may feature many different data calls, then functionality such as queuing multiple service calls and event callbacks become essential.

Application development with SWX PHP

We'll now cover SWX PHP and show how you can build a SWX-based application that incorporates a server-side component in order to provide you with an end-to-end understanding of SWX.

Specifically, we'll show how to build a simple application that displays the weather at a user-specified location. The client-side application will make a request to the web server using SWX, which will in turn make a request to the Weather.com web services, which will return the current weather.

Assuming you have already installed the SWX distribution onto a compatible web server, the first step is to create a new PHP SWX service class named Weather.php, which is to be located in the php/services folder.

The class itself is fairly simple comprising a single method called getWeather, which takes a location code as an input parameter. You are constructing the URL of the Weather.com service using the API key (free upon registration at Weather.com) and location code. From there, you parse the XML response and return the value of the current temperature. For simplicity, you are using the PHP SimpleXML extension in order to quickly and easily parse the response.

```php
<?php
class Weather{
    function getWeather($locationCode){
        $partnerId  = [Insert Partner ID Here];
        $licenseKey = [Insert Key Here ];
         $serviceUrl = "http://xoap.weather.com/weather/local/" .
            $locationCode . "?cc=*&dayf=2&prod=xoap&par=" .
            $partnerId  . "&key=" . $licenseKey
        $response = fopen($serviceUrl,"r");
```

```
        while(!feof($response))
            $xml .= fgets($response,4096);
        fclose($response);
        $xml = new SimpleXmlElement($xml);
        $temperature = $xml->cc->tmp;
        return $temperature;
    }
}
?>
```

You can begin testing this class before you even get started on your client-side code using the SWX Service Explorer, as shown in Figure 10-8.

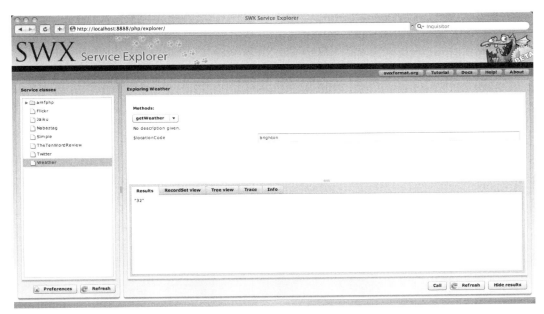

Figure 10-8. The getWeather service as viewed in the Service Explorer

If you open Flash CS3 and create a new file, you can begin to create the client. You'll use the SWX ActionScript library in order to simplify the creation and management of the service calls:

```
import org.swxformat.*;

var swx:SWX = new SWX();

function init():Void{

    swx.gateway = "http://localhost:8888/php/swx.php";
    swx.encoding = "POST";
    swx.debug = true;
```

```
        var callParameters:Object =
            {
                serviceClass: "Weather",
                method: "getWeather",
                args: ['UKXX0215'],
                result: [this, resultHandler],
                timeout: [this, timeoutHandler]
            }

    // location code for Brighton, UK = UKXX0215

    swx.call(callParameters);

}

function resultHandler(event:Object):Void{
    temp_txt.text = event.result +"°C";
}

function timeoutHander(event:Object):Void{
    temp_txt.text = "n/a";
}

init();
```

In this example, you are simply retrieving the temperature data for Brighton, United Kingdom, from the PHP service and using this to populate temp_txt, a dynamic text field within the application.

You should now have a working PHP service class, which is returning data that is loaded into the Flash application using SWX, similar to the rather simplistic example you have in Figure 10-9.

When connecting to other data sources using SWX, you will follow the same approach for working with your data: either using the supplied SWX ActionScript library or using your own code to specify a method belonging to a class on a SWX gateway server you want to call. Parameters can be passed as an array of arguments or potentially as a JSON object if you are dealing with complex data structures.

Figure 10-9. The PHP service is working and returning data to the application.

Any response is returned in the result object without any additional parsing requirements. What you do with the result largely depends on the individual application, but getting at the raw data is as simple as iterating through arrays and interrogating objects.

Why choose SWX?

As you have seen, SWX is just one of many communication mechanisms that can be used to work with data from within Flash applications. In any mashup, the choice of data format is one that is going to be made early on in a project. In many cases, it will be driven by what data sources you are looking to consume and interact with.

Earlier we mentioned that SWX's method of providing serialized data can offer significant performance gains over XML-based data. Though it may be difficult to perceive the performance impact for a given mashup, once you begin to exchange large quantities of data, the XML parsing overhead becomes greater and the potential for bottlenecks increases dramatically.

This is especially important when you consider ActionScript 2.0 development, where applications are not privy to the significant performance improvements offered by ActionScript 3.0 and Flash Player 9 when it comes to CPU-intensive operations such as XML parsing. And it becomes even more important when you look beyond the desktop realm and toward other devices with limited CPU resources. (This may or may not be limited to Flash Lite.)

SWX offers a solution where all of the heavy lifting of data is taken care of on the server side, which takes the load off the processing power of the client and creates a more consistent experience for all users. In addition, it is perhaps currently the best solution for mobile devices.

> As an example of what the performance benefits of SWX could mean to the end user, let's look at an application written in Flash 7/ActionScript 2.0. It dynamically generates a page layout consisting of various text, image, and UI components based upon an XML feed pulled from the server. So far, so good.
>
> In many circumstances, XML-driven layouts work effectively, creating a metalanguage in which an application can be described. In this case, we had two XML inputs, the application layout descriptor and a lookup table, weighing in at nearly 200KB between them.
>
> The page would load, HTTP requests were being observed in the background, and the user was left staring at the loading icon for a good three to six seconds after the data had been downloaded. Behind the scenes, CPU usage would shoot up to 100 percent while the XML was being parsed and merged into something that the application could then render; it was not a nice user experience at all and one that contributed to a high user abandonment of the web page.
>
> What had worked effectively on a small scale, with simple/well-defined inputs, was then used for a much larger task, and guess what? It didn't scale!
>
> In contrast, a reengineered version of the application, not using SWX but having the majority of the data required to render serialized within the SWF file, was much more responsive and without the huge loading bottleneck.

As we have also observed, SWX lends itself well to rapid development of data-driven applications. It has an excellent set of tools that further simplifies the already straightforward process of connecting to remote data sources. It helps insulate the developer from a lot of the technical complexity and gotchas, making it worthy of consideration if you are new to Flash development or prefer to spend time focusing on the design and user experience side of things.

One point that we haven't yet touched on is how SWX makes it extremely simple to manage cross-domain data access to your SWX gateway. By default, access is restricted to allow only those SWF files resident on the same domain as the gateway. However, access can be granted to all SWF files hosted on external domains or selectively to a list of domains from which SWF files can access SWX data stored in the SWX PHP configuration file (swx_config.php):

```
$allowedDomains = array('http://www.domain1.com',
                        'http://www.domain2.com');
```

Of course, SWX may not be the ideal choice for everyone. Currently, there is no official support for ActionScript 3. However, when we consider ActionScript 3, it is important to realize that not only is XML parsing performance significantly enhanced but also the E4X parser makes accessing data properties almost as simple as SWX.

> *Technically, you can access SWX SWF files in ActionScript 3. Provided that the SWX debug parameter is set, the SWF can be loaded and the* LocalConnection *object can be used in order to extract data. This is the same method used by the SWX Data Analyzer tool, and although it is inventive, it is not optimal and results in impaired performance.*

SWX may also not be the ideal solution for high-traffic websites. Because it is a fairly new technology and still under active development, it is built without many of the optimizations that one might expect. This could lead to scalability challenges and performance degradation when under heavy load; however, in such a high-load environment, it is probably worth considering using Flash Remoting, LiveCycle Data Services, or an open source alternative such as Red5.

Summary

In this chapter, we showed you a different way to work with data within your Flash applications. SWX is unique in being a native data format; it eliminates overheads caused by parsing and also offers a free open source solution that makes it suitable for smaller widgets and content aimed at mobile and embedded versions of the Flash Player.

Although it is not suitable for everyone, it does greatly simplify working with data, leaving you as the developer free to explore your creativity and develop new and creative uses for the data that is available for consumption.

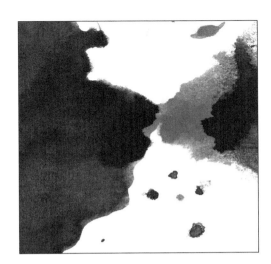

Chapter 11

TAKING IT TO THE DESKTOP

In this chapter, you will take the next step on your journey by looking at options available to developers who want to make their applications available offline on users' desktops.

In previous chapters, you looked at the steps involved in developing Flash- and Flex-based applications that consume feeds and services. You can use these technologies to make web applications that offer the user a great deal of functionality within a compelling user experience. But, you are missing one piece of the puzzle and placing one requirement upon the user—you are limiting them to accessing your applications only from within a web browser.

Typically web applications have two common constraints:

- A web application requires the user to be connected to the Internet in order to access and utilize data and functionality.

- It is difficult to offer integration with desktop applications in a reliable and consistent manner across different web browsers and platforms. Traditionally, it was accepted that you could not access offline data while you were not connected to the Internet. Today, however, this attitude is changing—users are placing a heavier reliance on online applications storing their data.

For example, a user might use Google Mail for their e-mails, Flickr for photo storage, and a calendar application such as 30 Boxes in order to stay organized. In addition, they might store contacts in Google Mail alongside transcripts of instant-messaging conversations. Without connectivity, the user will have *no access* to any of this functionality or their data. For some, this might not be of large concern, but for others it could be a major disadvantage.

Table 11-1 lists the common web-based alternatives for web applications.

Table 11-1. Common Computing Tasks and Their Desktop and Web Clients

Task	Desktop Application	Web-Based Alternative
E-mail	Outlook, Mac Mail, Thunderbird	Google Mail, Yahoo Mail
Calendar	Outlook, iCal, Lotus Notes	Google Calendar, 30 Boxes
Word processing	Microsoft Office, Open Office	Google Documents
Spreadsheets	Microsoft Office, Open Office	Google Spreadsheets
Photos	iPhoto, Picasa	Flickr
Project management/ organization	OmniProject, Microsoft Project	Basecamp

Of course, tools do exist that can be used to access some of this data offline. For example, Google Mail offers POP access so that users can download their e-mail messages to a desktop client. Software also exists to synchronize Google Calendar with most common desktop calendars.

The disadvantage of these is that you are forcing the user to maintain their data through multiple software interfaces that are different. So, a user can still access their data offline but can't access any of the functionality of a given web application. Google Mail is a good example of this—when you download your e-mails using POP, you lose all of the labeling and filtering functionality that is offered by the web application, and you also no longer have access to your address book or the all-important search functionality.

The only solution for creating a uniform user experience, whether online or offline, is to create a desktop application that serves as a companion application for a given web application, offering access to functionality whether the user is online or offline.

A desktop application can also offer many integration opportunities. For example, imagine you wanted to offer a user an opportunity to import some data from your web application into their address book (Figure 11-1). There is no reliable and predictable method for you to do this—the best method is to make the data available as a vCard, a standard format for address book entries. Beyond this, it all becomes a big question mark.

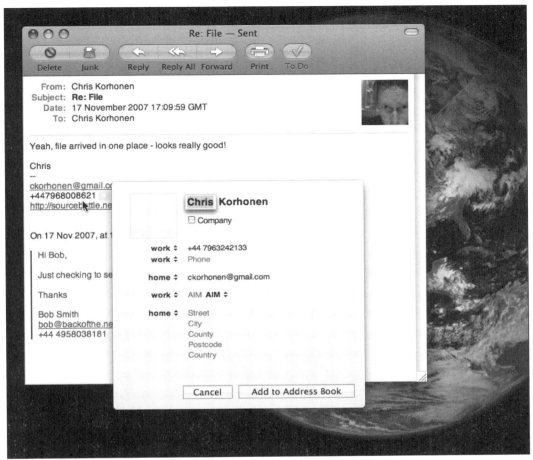

Figure 11-1. An example of data in Mac OS's e-mail client being detected and seamlessly imported into the system's address book

How will the user's browser handle a vCard? Will it attempt to render it as user-unfriendly gibberish? Will it attempt to pass it to an external application?

How will the user's operating system handle the vCard? Does the user have the appropriate file associations set up to handle the vCard? Does the user even have a compatible application installed? See Figure 11-2.

With all of these potential points of failure, it may just be easier to ask the user to copy and paste the data into their address book manually—although this might be a bad experience, it might also be more likely to work!

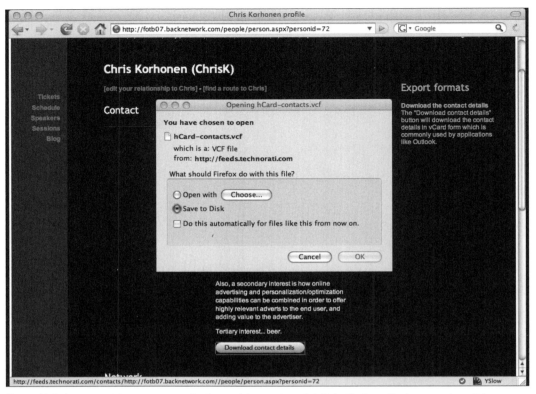

Figure 11-2. An attempt to consume a vCard containing contact details in Firefox—the browser doesn't know what to do with it!

Aside from exchanging data between applications, a web application cannot hope to offer much integration with the local file system or the operating system. To achieve this, you need a desktop application.

Microformats could potentially be one solution to this problem. They are small tidbits of HTML used to describe the semantic meaning of data contained within a document. They are commonly used to describe people in the form of an hCard, a derivative of the vCard format. Microformats can also be used to describe more complex items such as events, résumés, geographical coordinates, and so on. For more information, you can visit microformats.org *or* whymicroformats.com. *Currently, microformats are supported through browser plug-ins, such as Operator, WebCards, and Tails, which are all available as extensions for Firefox. Native microformat support is planned for Firefox 3.0, and this capability is also planned for several other browsers including Internet Explorer.*

By having this capability built into the browser, or as a plug-in, you can significantly reduce the points of failure when attempting to integrate with desktop applications, because the system integration will be handled for you through the browser, configured centrally by the user where necessary.

Why develop for the desktop?

From a technical perspective, desktop can offer solutions to the problems of integrating with other applications and with the user's operating system. A desktop application can also offer opportunities to provide seamless offline access to functionality and data offered by a web application. But why should you do a development U-turn, shifting your focus from developing web applications and moving it toward the desktop?

The simple answer is that there are many things you can offer on the desktop—things that either cannot be implemented in a web application or things that can be implemented within a web application only in a suboptimal manner, in terms of either technology or user experience.

For example, take a look at DropSend (www.dropsend.com), a web application that enables users to upload large files and send them via e-mail. The e-mail recipient will receive a link where they can download the file.

One of the main tasks of the application is to allow users to upload files, a function that is traditionally done very badly within web applications. Because of the limited function of the web browser, a user must select each file individually in order to upload it. When sending large numbers of files, this tends to be a pain. Hence, the creators of DropSend decided to create a desktop application.

This desktop version of DropSend allows the user to simply drag and drop files onto the application that will be uploaded to the web application, ready to send (see Figure 11-3). It offers simplicity and convenience, following a user interface metaphor that the user will already be familiar with.

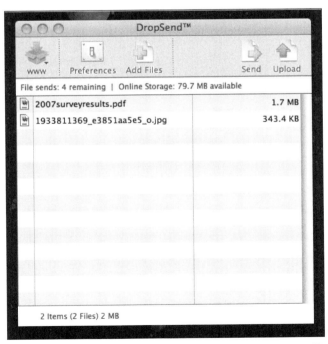

Figure 11-3. The DropSend desktop client. A user can simply drop files onto the window and upload them to online storage.

LastFM (`www.last.fm`) uses a desktop application to similar effect. The web application works by keeping track of what users listen to and cataloging the popular songs. It would obviously be too much to ask the user to manually add information about every song they listen to, each time they listen to it. In order for LastFM to be a success, the developers saw the need to automate this data collection.

And so a desktop application was born that automates the process of integrating with the user's music player and submitting that data to the web application (see Figure 11-4).

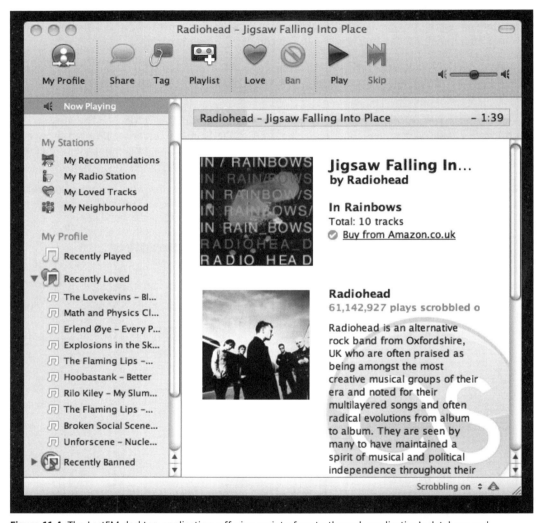

Figure 11-4. The LastFM desktop application, offering an interface to the web application's database and streaming media files while also tracking the music the user listens to in other clients such as iTunes

Desktop applications can help complement your web application by making a user's data portable and always available. They can also encourage participation, as in the case of LastFM, by taking something very time-consuming for the user and making that functionality available in a more accessible and convenient form.

Development options

You have several options when it comes to building a desktop application—you can look toward native applications where you want to offer complex functionality and interaction or toward widget platforms for smaller amounts of functionality and less complex applications. Or, you can look to see whether there are any opportunities to leverage your skills of building web applications in order to develop on the desktop.

Native applications

The obvious solution when developing a desktop application is to write it as a system native application, built around the frameworks and functionality offered by the host operating system. This gives the application developer full access to the system, including its hardware—something that is not always possible with other development techniques.

Most desktop programming environments, whether they be C++, C#, Java, or something completely different, provide a huge set of features including all that you need in order to construct fully feature-rich user interfaces and, if you so desire, a common API for working with elements such as 2D and 3D graphics, connected peripherals, and other capabilities provided by the operating system.

This approach does, however, require the developer to use a totally different set of skills compared to web development. There is often the increased complexity of memory management, user interface toolkits, device management, and so on, to worry about. The technical learning curve means that as a web developer you would probably want to avoid thinking about building a native desktop application unless the following is true:

- You want to outsource the development of your desktop application to another developer who has experience in this area.
- You have no other choice. For example, if you need access to specific hardware connected to a computer, such as a Bluetooth connection or a printer.

Also, do not underestimate the complexity of this approach—developing a polished desktop application is usually not quick and easy, especially when compared to developing a website. See Figure 11-5.

Figure 11-5. iTunes, an integrated music and video player application, offering deep filesystem integration when managing files and also rich data-driven visualizations. In this instance, albums are seen represented as 3D objects.

Widget platforms

Over the past few years, widgets have gained popularity as a means of making small amounts of functionality or information available on users' desktops. They are generally interactive, with a small footprint, and optimized to perform a single task. Examples of desktop widgets include the following (see Figure 11-6):

- A world clock widget that shows multiple time zones
- A conversion widget that allows the user to convert between specific units.
- Weather widgets that connect to an online service and display the current weather for a specific country or region

Widgets can be stand-alone applications, compiled as system native executables, or they can run within a widget engine—a software runtime environment in which a widget will execute. The widget engine provides all the necessary functions required by the widget in order to integrate with the operating system and to send and retrieve data across the network. Widgets are often defined using XML and/or a scripting language such as JavaScript.

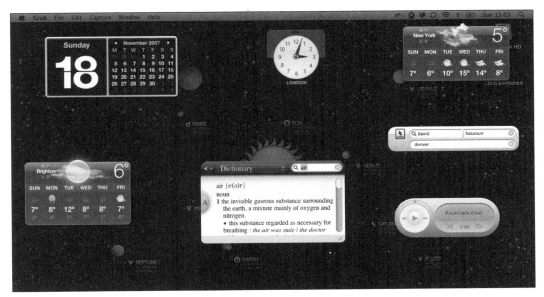

Figure 11-6. An example of a set of OS X dashboard widgets

Because the widget engine often removes most of the complexity associated with developing a desktop application, a widget platform can be an attractive choice for developers, who can develop small applications quickly and easily. In many cases, the platform will also provide the developer with a means of running their widget on multiple platforms.

The challenge for developers is often choosing which widget engine to build their application around. There are several major platforms, each with their own advantages and disadvantages.

Windows Vista supports its own form of widgets, called *gadgets*. These offer extensive capabilities for integrating with other applications and the Windows operating system, and developers can quickly build simple applications using a combination of HTML and VBScript, a scripting language based on Visual Basic. Gadgets have one major advantage to users—the runtime is part of the Windows operating system, meaning that users do not have to download any additional components in order to use gadgets. The downside, of course, is that developers are limited to running gadgets on Windows machines.

Mac OS X has had support for its own dashboard widgets since version 10.4. These function in a similar way to Microsoft's gadgets; however, they are built using standard CSS, HTML, and JavaScript. Again, this is integrated into the operating system, so the user does not need to download any additional software, but this time a Mac is required!

For developers seeking to build cross-platform widgets, both Google and Yahoo offer cross-platform widget engines. These allow quick, easy widget development using HTML and JavaScript. However, they do require the end user to have either Google Desktop or the Yahoo! Widget Engine installed—which could restrict the use of a particular widget and also make them unsuitable for deployment in corporate environments where steps are taken to prevent the user from installing any software. Table 11-2 compares the major widget platforms.

Table 11-2. Comparison of Major Widget Platforms

Platform	Operating Systems	Development Language
Microsoft Gadgets	Windows Vista	HTML/VBScript
Mac OS Dashboard	Mac OS 10.4+	HTML/CSS/JavaScript
Google Gadgets	Mac/Windows	HTML/JavaScript
Opera Widgets	Mac/Windows/Linux	HTML/CSS/JavaScript
Klipfolio	Windows	Proprietary
Yahoo! Widget Engine	Mac/Windows	HTML/JavaScript

So, although many of these solutions for developing widgets provide developers with a quick and easy means of developing simple applications, they do have a limited reach—you have to pick a single platform and concentrate on educating your users on what they need to do to install your widget. Or you could take the scattergun approach and develop several widgets for a selection of the major platforms.

The advantage of the scattergun approach is that most code should be easily portable, because most of the major platforms use similar technologies for their widgets. The disadvantage is that there is the potential for this approach to become a software maintenance nightmare, with multiple widget versions to maintain, each with their own platform-specific quirks and eccentricities.

In addition, although widgets are often suited for delivering small amounts of complex functionality and data, as a developer you are often limited to a simple scripting-based programming environment. This makes it very difficult, if not impossible, to develop larger and more complex applications—in this case, a widget platform is probably not an ideal choice.

Web technologies

In this chapter, you've seen both native applications and some of the popular widget platforms; however, neither of these really provides web developers with an optimal solution. If you want to build native applications, then you need to learn an entirely new skill set, and if you decide to build widgets, then you are limited in both application complexity and coverage of the user base.

What you really need is a way you can use your existing web development skills in order to develop complex and integrated desktop applications. Here you have three options, covered in the following sections.

Zinc

Zinc is a long-standing solution that allows Flash applications to be converted to native Windows or Mac OS X applications. It works by taking a SWF file and combining it seamlessly with a stand-alone Flash Player application, similar to the Flash Projector. In addition, it offers additional functionality such as the following:

- DLL linking, allowing Flash to interface with external libraries written in native code that can trigger external applications and commands

- A windowing API that offers skinning and application transparency

- Access to the local file system

- The ability to create custom installers for applications and trial versions

All this functionally comes with the advantage that no additional files are required to run a Zinc application—they can be distributed as standard executables. However, although it is possible to package applications as native Windows or OS X applications, cross-platform differences need to be accounted for in the application code itself, which creates more work for the developer.

You can find more information about Zinc at `www.multidmedia.com`.

Adobe Integrated Runtime

Previously known under the code name Apollo, Adobe Integrated Runtime (AIR) is Adobe's answer to the challenge of creating cross-platform desktop applications using the tools and skills familiar to a web developer (see Figure 11-7).

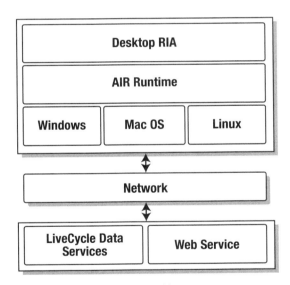

Figure 11-7. AIR application architecture

AIR allows web developers to build desktop applications using their favorite technology, be that Flash, Flex, HTML, or JavaScript/Ajax. The application can then be packaged as a platform-independent `.air` file and distributed.

Users can then download the application and install it in much the same way they would install a native application, the only requirement being that they have the AIR runtime installed, which is available on Windows and Mac OS X, with a Linux version in the works. Adobe also has plans for the provision of the AIR runtime on mobile devices such as PDAs and smart phones.

AIR also puts additional features at the developer's fingertips, which are suited to developing a desktop application. These include the following:

- A file I/O API for accessing items on the local file system
- SQLite database that can be used for local data storage
- A windowing API
- Clipboard support
- Drag-and-drop support
- PDF support
- Enhanced HTML support

Of particular note is the enhanced support for HTML content—something that has been lacking in Flash for many years. AIR introduces an HTMLControl component, which can be used to render HTML, CSS, and JavaScript. This is pretty much a mini–web browser, based on the standards-compliant WebKit page-rendering engine, which is used in Safari on Mac OS X. This is used to render all HTML content within an AIR application.

The key value of AIR to developers is the ability to take their existing web development skill set and utilize it to build cross-platform desktop applications quickly and easily. As you will explore in the next chapter, the process of converting a web application to an AIR application is smooth and straightforward, often with only minimal changes required. From there, the developer has a solid foundation upon which to begin crafting user experiences that leverage the unique capabilities of AIR in order to enhance their application.

AIR offers a more feature-rich runtime compared to the widget platforms examined earlier in the chapter; it also allows developers to use familiar web technologies and facilitates cross-platform development, with a single code base regardless of platform, unlike other similar technologies such as Zinc.

Google Gears

Google Gears is a browser extension that is designed to add support for offline functionality, which can be leveraged by web application developers.

The philosophy behind Google Gears is to address the main limitation of the web browser so that developers can craft a better user experience. Although Google Gears is currently a separate extension, the long-term plan is to submit it to the W3C, the web standards body, in the hopes that the application will one day be built into standards-compliant web browsers. In the interim, Google is working closely with the Mozilla Foundation and Adobe to integrate this technology with the Firefox browser and the Adobe Integrated Runtime.

Although it remains to be seen whether Google Gears can be decoupled from its specific browser dependencies, the collaboration with Adobe makes it worth considering if you are developing HTML-based AIR applications.

> *At the time of this writing, this technology is currently in beta and supports Internet Explorer 6 on Windows and Firefox 1.5+ on Windows, Mac OS, and Linux. A version of the extension with support for Safari is currently in development.*

As part of the extension, three core components are installed:

- **The local server**: This is essentially a local web server that allows key application components such as HTML, CSS, JavaScript, and images to be cached offline so that they are always accessible.
- **The database**: This is a local database, built around the SQLite database engine, that can be used to store web application data. This also incorporates some of the Google Search "magic," enabling fast text searching within the database.
- **The WorkerPool**: This is a mechanism that allows potentially processor-intensive data-processing tasks to be run in the background so that the responsiveness of the web application is not compromised.

All of these components are accessed through a JavaScript API; this means you can use Google Gears to add offline support to both HTML/JavaScript and Flash/Flex-based applications. In the case of a Flash application, a developer would make JavaScript calls using the ExternalInterface class in order to interact with Google Gears.

Let's take a look at how to use Google Gears, from both HTML and Flash.

The simplest use of Google Gears is to store an item in the local database, allowing it to be accessed when the page is viewed offline.

Before you can access the functionality of Google Gears, you need to include the gears_init.js file on your web page. This is provided by Google and creates the factory through which you can access the full functionality of Google Gears. If the user does not have Google Gears installed, then you can also specify conditional logic to direct them to the download page or provide an alternate experience.

The first step is to create an HTML page that will form the example application (see Figure 11-8):

```
<!DOCTYPE html PUBLIC "-//W3C//DTD XHTML 1.0 Strict//EN"
    "http://www.w3.org/TR/xhtml1/DTD/xhtml1-strict.dtd">
<html xmlns="http://www.w3.org/1999/xhtml">
    <head>
        <meta http-equiv="Content-Type"
            content="text/html; charset=utf-8" />

        <title>Google Gears Example</title>

        <script type="text/javascript" src="gears_init.js"
            charset="utf-8">
        </script>

        <script type="text/javascript" src="example1.js"
            charset="utf-8">
        </script>
    </head>
    <body>
        <h1>Database Example</h1>
```

```
<form onsubmit="storeData();return false">
    <label for="data">Enter some data:</label>
    <input type="text" id="data" />
    <input type="submit" />
</form>

<hr/>

<div style="border:1px dashed #ccc;width:70%;
    background-color:#eee;padding:5px;">
    Stored Value:<br />
    <span id="stored"></span>
</div>
    </body>
</html>
```

Once you have the simple HTML page built, you can begin interacting with Google Gears using JavaScript.

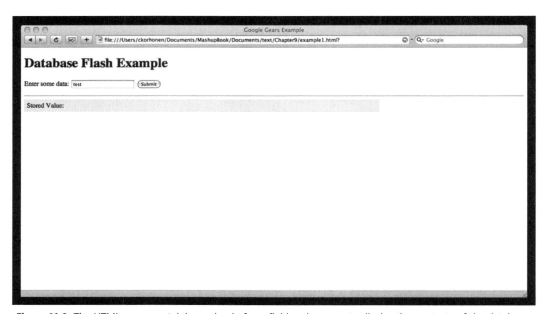

Figure 11-8. The HTML page, containing a simple form field and an area to display the contents of the database

In the example1.js file, referenced in the HTML page, the first thing you need to do is create your database if it does not already exist:

```
var db;
initDb();

function initDb(){➥
' (Phrase VARCHAR(255), Timestamp INT)');
}
```

In this code, you access the Gears factory and create a new database instance. Once you have a database, you can open and manipulate it using familiar SQL statements. Here you create a simple table called EXAMPLE, with two columns—one for the text string and one for an integer timestamp.

Once the database is created, you are also calling the displayData() function, which will update the HTML page with a listing of all the items stored:

```
function displayData(){
}
```

Data is returned in a record set containing multiple rows. As you can see, you are able to iterate through this data structure and extract values from specific columns.

With the database created and set up, you can use it to store data:

```
function storeData(){
    if(!window.google || !google.gears){
        //Gears is not installed
        return;
    }

    //Let's create our database
    try{
        db = google.gears.factory.create('beta.database','1.0');
    } catch(e){
        alert("Could not create database: " + e.message);
    }

    //Create the data table
    if(db){
        db.open('database-demo');
        db.execute('CREATE TABLE IF NOT EXISTS EXAMPLE' +


        displayData();
    }
    var output = "";
    try{
        var resultset =
        db.execute('SELECT * FROM EXAMPLE ORDER BY Timestamp DESC');

        //Iterate through resultset
        while(resultset.isValidRow()){
            output += resultset.field(0) + "<br />";
            resultset.next();
        }
        resultset.close();
    } catch(e){
        alert("Error " + e.message);
    }
```

```
        //Dump results into a div
        document.getElementById('stored').innerHTML = output;
        if(!google.gears.factory || !db){
            //Gears is not installed, or we don't have a database
            return;
        }

        //Get the value and create a timestamp
        var value = document.getElementById('data').value;
        var timestamp = new Date().getTime();

        //Insert the value into our database
        db.execute('INSERT INTO EXAMPLE VALUES (?,?)

        //Update the page
        displayData();
    ', [value, timestamp]);
    }
```

This function is executed when the user clicks the form's Submit button, and the function again uses a SQL statement in order to update the database.

If you open your HTML page, notice that Google Gears asks for the user's permission before any of its functionality becomes available. If you allow access, you should be able to see Google Gears in action, storing values entered in the text field. Switching your browser to offline mode should confirm that this data is available offline.

As it stands, in order to use these examples, you need to have loaded the pages from your web server before you actually go offline. If you wanted to take this further, you could use the local server functionality in order to actually store actual HTML files, CSS files, JavaScript files, SWF files, and images offline so that they are always accessible.

To do this, you would create a manifest file—a list of files that are to be mirrored locally:

```
{
  "betaManifestVersion": 1,
  "version": "version_string",
  "entries": [
      { "url": "application.html"},
      { "url": "application.js"},
      { "url": "gears_init.js"}
    ]
}
```

This file should be named manifest.json and placed in the root directory of your web application.

The manifest file is specified as JSON, and alongside the list of filenames is a version string—changing this as files are updated indicates updates and triggers Google Gears to refresh the local versions.

> JSON is shorthand for JavaScript Object Notation, essentially a JavaScript data structure that can be easily written and parsed.

Within your JavaScript code, you would need to initialize the local server and create a data store on page load:

```
if (!window.google || !google.gears) {

} else {
    var localServer = google.gears.factory.create("beta.localserver",
                                                   "1.0");
    var store = localServer.createManagedStore("my_store_name");
}
```

By passing a relative or absolute URL to a manifest file and checking for an update, a local mirror of the specified files will be created:

```
store.manifestUrl = "http://mydomain.com/manifest.json";
store.checkForUpdate();
```

When working offline, you can access stored files as usual, without a need for the user to enter a different URL.

Flash integration

As mentioned earlier, nothing is preventing a Flash or Flex application from utilizing Google Gears in order to store data. Let's take a look at how you would adapt the previous database example to work with a Flash front-end.

Although this example was developed using Flash CS3, nothing would step you from adapting this technique for Flex and/or ActionScript 2.0 applications.

Within the Flash application, you need to identify the instances where you want to exchange data with Google Gears. Once you have those instances identified, you can create functions within your JavaScript that will handle the passing of data:

```
function storeData(e:MouseEvent):void{
    var dataValue:String = text_mc.text;

    if(dataValue){
        ExternalInterface.call("storeData",dataValue);
    } else{
        // Do Nothing
    }
}
```

241

Notice how you are using ExternalInterface to call the JavaScript function called storeData:

```
function storeData(s){
    if(!google.gears.factory || !db){
        //Gears is not installed, or we don't have a database
        return;
    }

    var timestamp = new Date().getTime();

    //Insert the value into our database
    db.execute('INSERT INTO EXAMPLE VALUES (?,?)', [s, timestamp]);

    flashObject.storeSuccess();

}
```

You are also attempting to call a function within your Flash application, in this case signaling that the data has been stored successfully.

Within the Flash application you are registering the callback and assigning it to a function named success:

```
ExternalInterface.addCallback("storeSuccess",success);

function success():void{
    //Code to execute upon success
}
```

> For more intensive integration of Flash applications with Google Gears, developers are advised to take a look at the Flash-Gears Bridge, created by Scott Hyndman, at www.scotthyndman.ca.

You can follow a similar method when you want to retrieve data that is stored within the Google Gears database—you make an ExternalInterface call to the JavaScript function retrieveData, and the data is passed as an array.

The only disadvantage of integrating with Google Gears in this way is the potential performance hit that comes with using ExternalInterface. For the occasional call, this isn't usually something a developer should worry about, but if you get into a situation where multiple simultaneous calls are being made or large amounts of data are being transferred back and forth, then it may be worth reconsidering the approach.

In the case of a Flash/Flex application, then using shared objects (Flash cookies) may be sufficient for small amounts of data that need to be stored offline, such as configuration settings. Once you start developing AIR applications, you also have the SQLite database and the local file system at your disposal if you need to store more substantial amounts of offline data.

Comparison of desktop development approaches

Table 11-3 offers a comparison of development approaches offered by the various desktop technologies covered in this chapter.

Table 11-3. A Comparison of Development Approaches for AIR, Zinc, Widgets, and Native Applications

Feature	AIR Application	Zinc	Widget Platform	Native Application
Cost	Free SDK download, plus various free or commercial IDE options	Various pricing options for Zinc (depending on whether you want to develop for Mac and/or PC); IDE is also required for Flash applications	Usually free SDK provided	Depends on languages used, usually many different free/paid SDKs available for common desktop programming applications
Technologies	Flash, Flex, HTML/JavaScript	Flash/Flex	HTML/CSS/JavaScript	Usually a language such as C++, Java or C#
Platforms	Windows/Mac	Windows/Mac	Dependent on widget platform	
Runtime required?	Yes	No	Yes	No
Application installation required?	Yes	No	Yes	No
Filesystem access	Yes	Yes	No	Yes
Clipboard access	Yes	Yes	No	Yes
Out-of-the-box access to local hardware/peripherals	Web cam/microphone	Web phone/microphone	No	Yes
Access to external libraries and DLLs	No	Yes	No	Yes
Support for audio/video playback	Yes	Yes	No	Yes
Suitable for stand-alone kiosks?	No	Yes	No	Yes

Summary

In this chapter, you examined many of the common options for developing desktop applications and looked their advantages and disadvantages. As you move forward, you will be taking a more in-depth look at AIR and exploring the features and opportunities that it offers to developers.

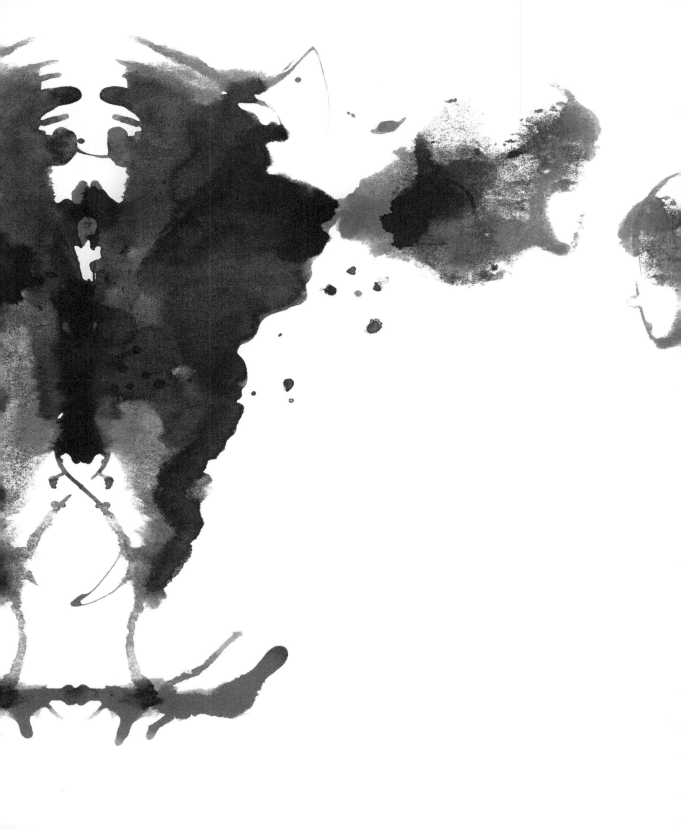

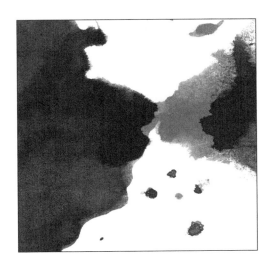

Chapter 12

DEVELOPING FOR THE DESKTOP WITH AIR

Now that you have explored the ins and outs of building Flash- and Flex-based mashups on the Web, in this chapter you'll take a closer look at AIR and see how you can use it to bring the skills you have learned to the desktop.

As we touched upon in the previous chapter, Adobe Integrated Runtime (AIR) is a model for deploying Flash-, Flex-, and HTML-based content onto a user's desktop, whether that be a PC or a Mac.

AIR takes care of all the cross-platform operating system integration, leaving the developer free to think about the look, feel, and functionality of their application without worrying about how to read a file from a Mac OS filesystem or how to display a Windows Vista system notification. For web developers, a good analogy is being able to develop a complex CSS page layout without having to worry about how it will render in different web browsers!

In addition to implementing a consistent cross-platform runtime environment, AIR also offers functionality that developers can leverage in their Flex or HTML/JavaScript applications, which is often desirable when you consider the context within which users often interact with desktop applications. This includes local filesystem access and storage, the ability to respond to drag-and-drop interactions, and the integration with the user's Dock or system tray, all of which you will explore as go on in this book.

Before exploring many of the advanced features, we'll cover how you can create AIR applications and also how you can take your preexisting Flex applications and get them running on the desktop.

Creating an AIR application

To build a Flex-based AIR application, you need a copy of Flex Builder 3, or you can use the free AIR SDK (www.adobe.com/go/getairsdk), which is provided by Adobe and can be used in conjunction with any IDE in order to compile and debug your AIR application.

You also need a copy of AIR installed when developing an AIR application.

Starting a new project

Within Flex Builder, you follow a similar process used to create a new Flex application. First select File ➤ Flex Project, and then select Desktop Application as the application type in the wizard that appears (see Figure 12-1).

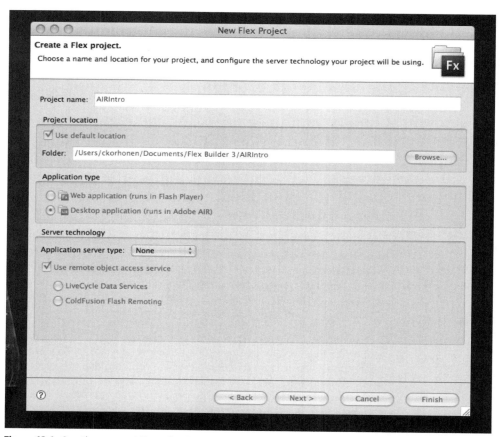

Figure 12-1. Creating a new AIR application

As before, you can leave the other options in the wizard alone unless you want to change file locations, import external libraries, or integrate your application directly with an application server.

When you click Finish, Flex Builder will generate the application structure. The folder structure generated for your AIR application is nearly identical to what you would get if you were building a Flex application. You have your src directory where your source code resides, your libs directory for any external libraries you may want to use, and your bin directory where your application will be generated.

You may notice that you no longer have an html-template directory, where the files used as a base for your HTML page would normally reside. The reason for this is quite simple: you are no longer integrating your application on a web page. Instead, it will be running natively on the user's desktop—no HTML template required.

If you take a look within your src directory, you will see you have two files, your familiar MXML file and a new file ending in -app.xml, which is the AIR application descriptor that contains specific parameters used when installing and running applications. You will be looking at this in more detail later, but first, let's open the MXML file:

```
<?xml version="1.0" encoding="utf-8"?>
<mx:WindowedApplication xmlns:mx="http://www.adobe.com/2006/mxml"
                        layout="absolute">

</mx:WindowedApplication>
```

This should look similar to your Flex application, with the only difference being the primary tag name. In Flex, this would be <mx:Application>. With AIR, it's <mx:WindowedApplication>. The difference is that WindowedApplication inherits additional functionality that applies specifically to desktop applications.

Because there are no fundamental differences between Flex applications built for the Web and those built for the desktop, porting existing applications is a relatively painless process. If you refer to the Twitter application you developed in Chapter 3 and copy the files to your new Flex project, you can quickly and simply port it to AIR.

If you open the MXML file for your Flex application, you'll see the following:

```
<?xml version="1.0" encoding="utf-8"?>
 <mx:Application xmlns:mx="http://www.adobe.com/2006/mxml"
                 layout="absolute"
                 creationComplete="twitterFeed.send()">
    <mx:HTTPService id="twitterFeed"
         url="http://www.twitter.com/statuses/friends_timeline/25883.rss" />

    <mx:List left="10" right="10" top="41" bottom="62" id="tweets"
         dataProvider="{twitterFeed.lastResult.rss.channel.item}"
         itemRenderer="Tweet">
     </mx:List>

    <mx:Label x="10" y="10" text="My Super Twitter Application!"
              fontFamily="Arial" fontWeight="bold"
              fontSize="15"/>
```

```
<mx:TextArea bottom="10" left="10" right="112" id="tweet_txt"
             maxChars="160"/>
<mx:Button label="Post" bottom="10" right="10" height="44"
           width="94"
           id="submit_btn" click="postData()"/>

<mx:Script>
    <![CDATA[
        import mx.rpc.events.ResultEvent;
        import com.dynamicflash.util.Base64;

        public function postData():void{
            var request:HTTPService = new HTTPService();
            request.url = "http://twitter.com/statuses/
                                      update.xml";
            request.method = "POST";
            request.addEventListener(ResultEvent.RESULT,
                                      handleComplete);

            var username:String = "username";
            var password:String = "password";
            var encodedCredentials:String = Base64.encode(
                             username + ":" + password);

            var headerArray =
                    new Array(
                    new URLRequestHeader("Authentication",
                             "Basic " + encodedCredentials));

            request.headers = headerArray;
            request.request = { status: tweet_txt.text };
            request.send();
        }

        public function handleComplete(e:Event):void{
            tweet_txt.text = "";
            twitterFeed.send();
        }]]>
    </mx:Script>
</mx:Application>
```

Paste this code into the MXML file for your AIR application, changing <mx:Application> to
<mx:WindowedApplication>:

```
<?xml version="1.0" encoding="utf-8"?>
<mx:WindowedApplication xmlns:mx="http://www.adobe.com/2006/mxml"
                        layout="absolute"
                        creationComplete="twitterFeed.send()">
    <mx:HTTPService id="twitterFeed"
            url="http://www.twitter.com/statuses/friends_timeline/25883.rss" />
```

```
<mx:List left="10" right="10" top="41" bottom="62" id="tweets"
        dataProvider="{twitterFeed.lastResult.rss.channel.item}"
        itemRenderer="Tweet">
</mx:List>

<mx:Label x="10" y="10" text="My Super Twitter Application!"
        fontFamily="Arial" fontWeight="bold"
        fontSize="15"/>

<mx:TextArea bottom="10" left="10" right="112" id="tweet_txt"
        maxChars="160"/>
<mx:Button label="Post" bottom="10" right="10" height="44"
        width="94"
        id="submit_btn" click="postData()"/>

<mx:Script>
    <![CDATA[
        import mx.rpc.events.ResultEvent;
        import com.dynamicflash.util.Base64;

        public function postData():void{
            var request:HTTPService = new HTTPService();
            request.url = "http://twitter.com/statuses/
                                update.xml";
            request.method = "POST";
            request.addEventListener(ResultEvent.RESULT,
                                handleComplete);

            var username:String = "username";
            var password:String = "password";
            var encodedCredentials:String =
                    Base64.encode(username + ":" + password);

            var headerArray =
              new Array(new URLRequestHeader("Authentication",
                            "Basic " + encodedCredentials));

            request.headers = headerArray;
            request.request = { status: tweet_txt.text };
            request.send();
        }

        public function handleComplete(e:Event):void{
            tweet_txt.text = "";
            twitterFeed.send();
        }]]>
    </mx:Script>
</mx:WindowedApplication>
```

Now you can compile and run the application, and you should see it running in all its desktop glory. Compare the web version (see Figure 12-2) to the desktop version (see Figure 12-3).

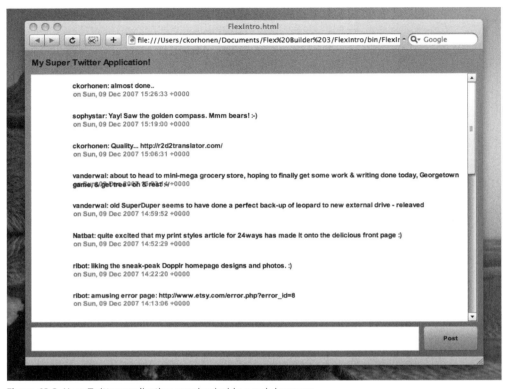

Figure 12-2. Your Twitter application running inside a web browser

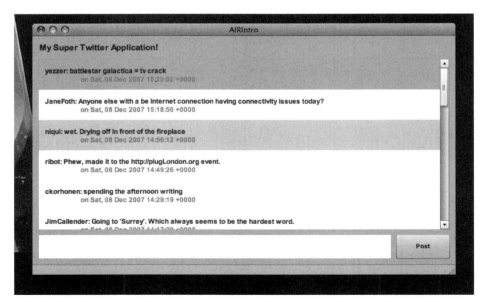

Figure 12-3. Your Twitter application running on the desktop

It really is this simple to repurpose existing applications for the desktop, and this was one of the key priorities of Adobe when designing and building AIR—it needs to be something that web developers can jump right into and leverage their existing skillsets, without requiring any mass rewrite of code. Although it may be prudent to spend more time tailoring applications for the desktop, there is certainly nothing stopping developers from quickly porting web content.

Now that you have a working desktop application, let's take a look at your -app.xml file to see how you can begin to customize your application.

Defining and customizing your application

Now that you are developing for the desktop, you have an extra degree of control that you can exert upon your application. This includes the specific elements displayed to the user; the size, position, and appearance of the application window; and even how the application integrates with the local filesystem with regard to handling different file types.

All of these elements are defined in your -app.xml file.

If you look the file that was generated with your Twitter application, you can see that it is vary sparse:

```xml
<?xml version="1.0" encoding="UTF-8"?>
<application xmlns="http://ns.adobe.com/air/application/1.0.M6">
    <id>AIRIntro</id>
    <filename>AIRIntro</filename>
    <version>v1</version>

    <initialWindow>
        <content>
            [This value will be overwritten by Flex Builder in
            the output app.xml]
        </content>
    </initialWindow>
</application>
```

If you step through the XML document, the first thing of note is the XML namespace attribute (xmlns), which is used to denote the specific version of AIR that is required in order to run the application. In this case, your application requires AIR 1.0 Milestone 6 or greater to be installed, because this is the version of the AIR SDK that we are using here.

> When a user installs AIR, they install a specific version of the runtime. Because it is upgraded, rather than overwritten, each specific version remains available for applications to use. This means backward compatibility should in most cases not be a worry for developers. An application targeting a specific version will continue to behave as expected, even if the user upgrades to a newer version of the runtime.
>
> If a user attempts to install an AIR application but does not have the required version of the runtime installed, there are strategies for dealing with this, including leveraging the ExpressInstall functionality within Flash Player. We'll cover this in more detail when we talk about distributing your AIR application later in this chapter.

Within your <application> node, you have additional nodes that describe different properties of the application:

- The <id> node is used to uniquely identify your application to AIR; it should usually be the name of your application.

- The filename of the resulting AIR application is defined by the <filename> node; this can be anything you want provided it does not contain special characters that the host operating system may not allow to be used in filenames. The filename also acts as the default window title for your application if none is provided elsewhere.

- The <version> node denotes the version of your application; it can take whatever format is desired.

- Finally, you come to the <initialWindow> node, which describes the initial window that will be viewable when the application is launched. In this case, the content for this window is automatically inserted by Flex Builder during the compilation process; however, this can be replaced by a SWF or HTML file reference if desired.

Modifying the application window

When you consider the initial window, you may decide you want to modify how this window appears and behaves. Fortunately, there are many optional parameters you can use to do this.

The first thing you can do is to change the window title of your application; in this case, use My Twitter Application:

```
<title>My Twitter Application</title>
```

AIR application windows utilize the default look and feel (often referred to as *system chrome*) provided by the host operating system, so on Windows the Maximize/Minimize/Close buttons will be on the right, and on Mac OS X they will be on the left. By default the systemChrome property is set to standard:

```
<systemChrome>standard</systemChrome>
```

To customize an application's look and feel, such as removing the window title bar altogether or replacing it with a custom skin, you can set the value of the systemChrome property to none.

This is especially important if you are building widgets on top of the AIR platform that often seek to visually distinguish themselves from the operating system's look and feel. We will be covering how to achieve this later.

By setting the transparent property, you can control whether your application window can have transparent segments. Unfortunately, this is available only when you are not using the standard system chrome.

```
<transparent>false</transparent>
```

With this property enabled, you can control transparency by setting the alpha property of WindowedApplication.

If you want to adjust the transparency of only the components within the application, rather than the application window itself, then you do not need to set this property.

If you want to develop an application that perhaps performs a background task, or by default is minimized in the system tray, then you can use the `visible` property to define whether a window is displayed when an application is launched:

```
<visible>true</visible>
```

The functionality of a window can be controlled, giving the developer control over whether a user can minimize, maximize, or resize it. In addition, you can also choose to restrict the minimum and maximum sizes of an application in order to prevent the user interface layout from breaking down and becoming unusable in extreme circumstances. In the case of applications with a fixed layout, restricting the resizing of an application may also be desirable.

```
<minimizable>false</minimizable>
<maximizable>false</maximizable>
<resizable>true</resizable>
<minSize>100,100</minSize>
<maxSize>600,800</maxSize>
```

Finally, you can also control the initial properties of your window, so you can set it to appear at a certain position and at a certain size:

```
<width>400</width>
<height>500</height>
<x>20</x>
<y>20</y>
```

By default, application windows should appear centered on the screen, taking on the width and height of the Flex application within.

Working with different types of content

To create AIR applications, the developer is in no way restricted to using Flex. Existing Flash applications can be packaged as AIR applications.

To achieve this, simply change the <content> node within `initialWindow` to point to a local SWF file, like so:

```
<content>myswf.swf</content>
```

When you compile your application, it will take the SWF file as the content for the initial window.

The only restriction when repurposing Flash content as a desktop application is that if you have an ActionScript 2.0–based application, then you will not be able to access any of the AIR-specific APIs because they are implemented in ActionScript 3.0. This means that such applications will not be able to access the local filesystem, use drag-and-drop events, or use some of the more advanced features of ActionScript 3.0, such as accessing SQLite databases.

In some cases, this may be a crippling restriction, but if you are simply looking to port existing web applications or movies to desktop applications without any additional development work, then AIR should be more than suitable for most needs.

An option for ActionScript 2.0 developers who want to offer enhanced desktop integration without moving to ActionScript 3.0 is Zinc, which we briefly discussed in Chapter 10.

Although a lot of AIR development is focused on building ActionScript 3.0 applications, by using Flash or Flex it is also possible to build applications that are entirely based on HTML.

AIR fully supports HTML-based applications that utilize CSS layout and JavaScript functionality. In addition, you can also use third-party JavaScript frameworks such as Prototype, jQuery, or Mootools in order to build applications.

The process for building an application around HTML content is the same as if you were dealing with an existing SWF file.

Here, in the content property, you are simply specifying an HTML file that exists within the AIR application package:

```xml
<?xml version="1.0" encoding="UTF-8"?>
<application xmlns="http://ns.adobe.com/air/application/1.0.M6">
        <id>HTMLApp</id>
        <filename>HTMLApp</filename>
        <version>v1</version>
        <initialWindow>
             <content>app.html </content>
         </initialWindow>
</application>
```

Within a HTML-based application, a developer has full access to the AIR and ActionScript 3.0 APIs through the JavaScript window.runtime object. For example, if you wanted to access the URLMonitor class, you would do it in the same way as you would in ActionScript, except through the window.runtime object in the HTML DOM:

```
var request = new window.runtime.flash.net.URLRequest( "http://www.foo.com" );

monitor = new window.runtime.air.net.URLMonitor( request );
monitor.addEventListener( window.runtime.flash.events.StatusEvent.STATUS,
                            doStatus );
monitor.start();
```

Adobe has also released a useful set of JavaScript aliases that you can use to further simplify the syntax and make code more readable. The set is available for download from Adobe's Developer website; in addition, plug-ins for Dreamweaver CS3 are available that simplify the process of packaging and deploying AIR applications. For more information, visit http://labs.adobe.com/wiki/index.php.

With these JavaScript aliases, rather than typing the fully qualified class path, they can be accessed as methods on the air object within the pace DOM:

```
var request = new air.URLRequest( "http://www.foo.com" );

monitor = new window.runtime.air.net.URLMonitor( request );
monitor.addEventListener( air.StatusEvent.STATUS, doStatus );
monitor.start();
```

Adding icons and folders

In addition to customizing your application's windows, you also have control over other elements of its visual and nonvisual appearance.

To add a custom icon, you can use the following XML snippet, which you would add to the application descriptor XML file, within the `<application>` node:

```
<icon>
      <image16x16>assets/icon-16x16.png</image16x16>
      <image32x32>assets/icon-32x32.png</image32x32>
      <image48x48>assets/icon-48x48.png</image48x48>
      <image128x128>assets/icon-128x128.png</image128x128>
</icon>
```

Here, you pass references to PNG files that are contained within your application's AIR package. These can be created in Adobe Photoshop or another tool and should be sized accordingly—either 16×16, 32×32, 48×48, or 128×128. This provides different-sized icons that are used in different locations.

When building your application, in this case, you would create an assets directory within the src folder into which you would place your PNG images. During the process of compiling the application, these files would be packaged automatically.

You can also customize several items that are used when the application is being installed, such as the default installation folder and the folder into which the program shortcut is placed in the Windows Start menu:

```
<installFolder></installFolder>
<programMenuFolder>Twitter</programMenuFolder>
```

Distributing an AIR application

Now that you have successfully transformed your Twitter mashup into an AIR application, it's worth spending some time considering how to export a release version that you can begin sharing with the world.

Installing an AIR application: the user's view

When an AIR application is distributed, it is done so in the form of an `.air` file, which is based on the file format of a `.zip` archive. The complier packages up the contents of your application into a single file, simplifying distribution considerably. This file is platform independent, so the same AIR file can be used on a Mac or a PC. In addition, in order to prevent its contents from being tampered with, it can also be digitally signed by the creator.

> *Digitally signing an AIR application is a way that a user can validate the authenticity of the application, ensuring that it is coming from a trusted party and has not been modified or tampered with.*

The file extension .air is registered to AIR when AIR is initially installed, so assuming the user has a version of AIR installed on their machine, they can simply double-click an AIR file (see Figure 12-4) to begin the install process.

When you double-click the AIR file, you are greeted with a window similar to the one in Figure 12-5, showing clearly the application name and publisher, along with details about whether the application has been digitally signed and the level of system access that the application will have.

Figure 12-4. An AIR application that has been downloaded

This serves as a notification to users that they are in fact installing something onto their computer. Because AIR applications can have access to the local filesystem, they should be viewed in the same way that a native application would be viewed. Common sense educates users that untrusted applications may be harmful, and the same applies to AIR applications.

Within the -app.xml file you can define some of the information that will appear during the installation process, such as the application name and publisher details:

```xml
<?xml version="1.0" encoding="UTF-8"?>
<application xmlns="http://ns.adobe.com/air/application/1.0.M6">
    <id>SimpleTwitter</id>
    <filename>SimpleTwitter</filename>
    <name>My First Twitter Application</name>
    <version>2</version>
    <description>
            An application which that demonstrates the capabilities of Flex,
            reading a Twitter Feed.
    </description>
    <copyright>Chris Korhonen, 2008.</copyright>

    <initialWindow>
            <content>
                    [This value will be overwritten by Flex Builder in the
                    output app.xml]
            </content>
            <title>My Twitter Application</title>
    </initialWindow>
</application>
```

At this point, the user can choose to install or cancel the process.

If the user chooses to continue with the installation, they are invited to select an installation path. On Windows this defaults to the Program Files directory, and on Mac OS X it defaults to the Applications folder (see Figure 12-6). As a developer, this does not matter because the AIR APIs provide a means to access file locations regardless of the host operating system.

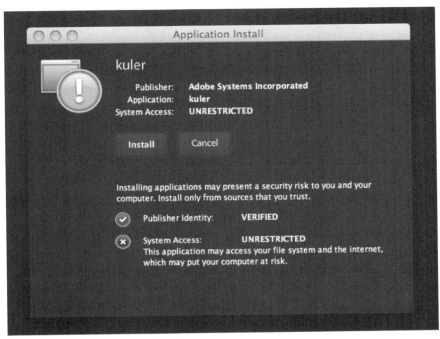

Figure 12-5. The AIR application installer

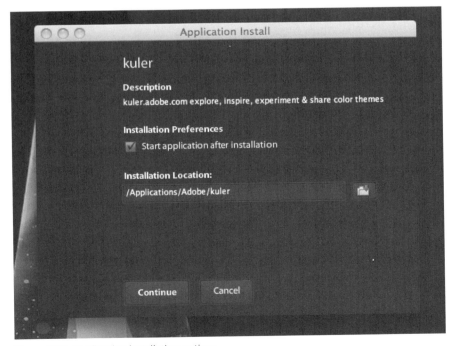

Figure 12-6. Configuring installation options

During the install process, AIR generates platform-specific code that allows the installed application to behave and execute in the same way as a native application. This is the only point in the process where platform-specific code is generated, and it is completely transparent to the developer.

Once installed, you can use the AIR APIs if you want to determine the host operating system or its specific capabilities with respect to operating system–specific features, which we will be covering later in this chapter.

Creating an AIR file

To create an AIR file for your application, open the Project menu, and select the option Export Release Build. This opens the export wizard (see Figure 12-7).

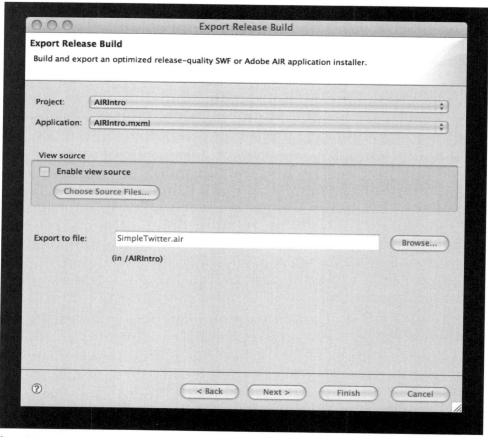

Figure 12-7. Exporting a release build

Here you can select the project and main MXML file that you want to export, as well as specify the path where your AIR file will be created.

In the next step, you will be asked whether you want to digitally sign your AIR file (see Figure 12-8). Generally this is recommended because it gives the application some level of legitimacy and because the presence of a certificate serves to reassure the end user during the install process.

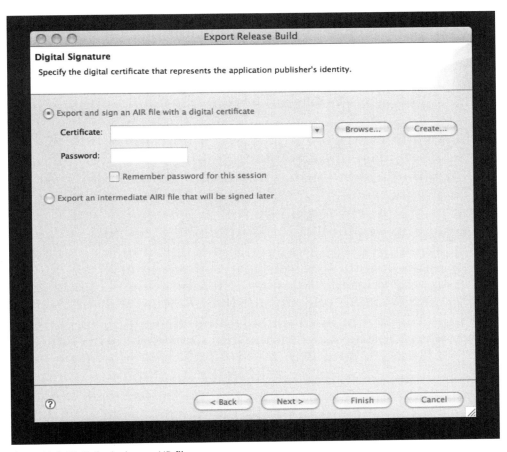

Figure 12-8. Digitally signing an AIR file

If you choose not to sign your AIR file, the installation experience for the user is similar to Figure 12-9. It isn't hard to imagine that the big red question mark and Xs could throw into doubt the legitimacy of the application and prompt the user to cancel the installation.

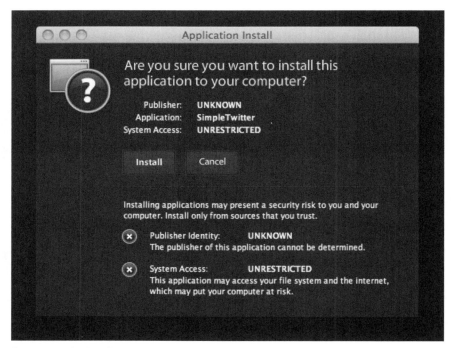

Figure 12-9. The installation process for an unsigned AIR file

Applications can be signed with a certificate such as those provided by secure certificate issuers like Thawte (www.thawte.com/) and VeriSign (www.verisign.com/); however, if you want to avoid that expense, you can generate your own certificate within Flex Builder.

To generate your own certificate, click the Create button. A window will open asking you to input the details you want to appear within your digital certificate (Figure 12-10). These may include your name, your organizational name, your department, and your geographical location.

You can also pick the type of certificate you want to generate; here it's safe to stick with the default 1024-RSA option.

You must also assign a password to the certificate that is required each time you sign an application.

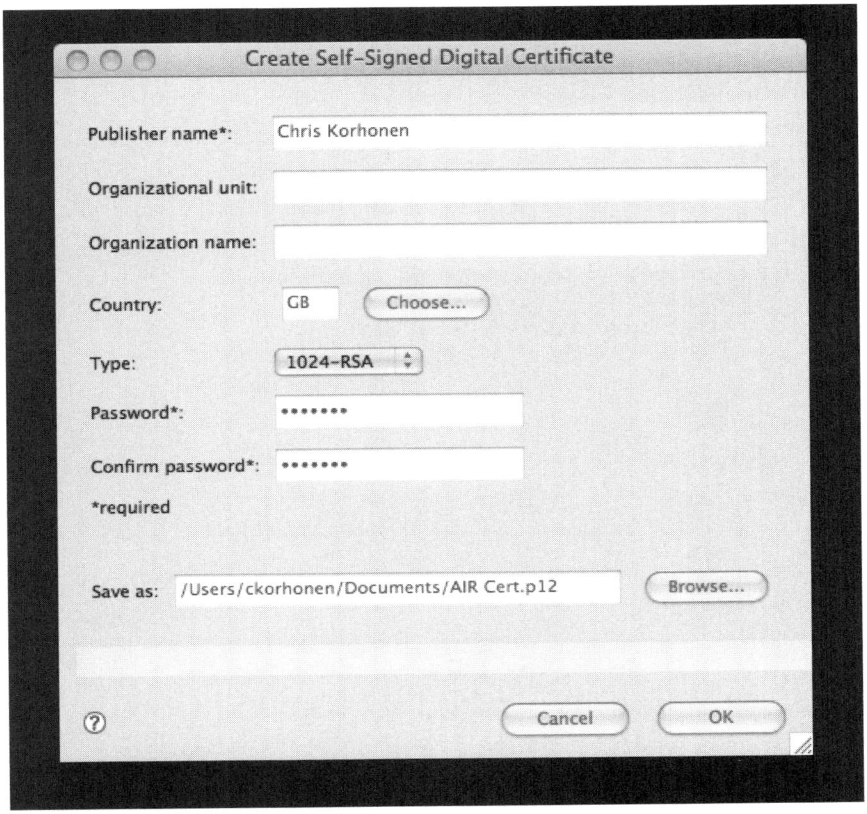

Figure 12-10. Generating a digital certificate

Once completed, click OK, and your certificate will be created. You will then be able to select it from the Certificate drop-down and use it to sign applications.

The final part in the export process (Figure 12-11) is to select the files that you want included in your AIR package. By default, the contents of the bin directory are included; however, for security and to keep the file size down, it makes sense to exclude any files that you know are not being used by the application.

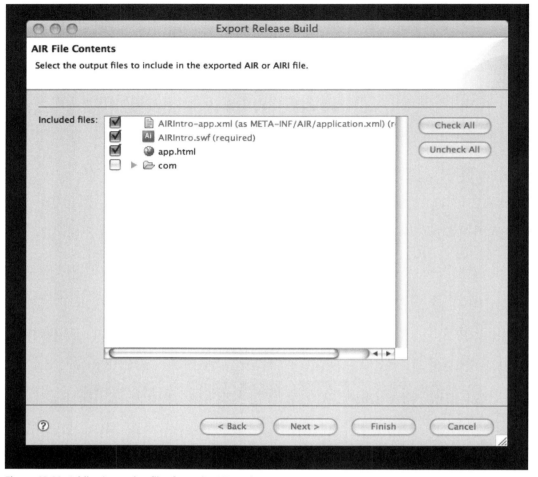

Figure 12-11. Adding/removing files from the AIR package

Now you should have an AIR file in the specified output location that will install your application.

Distributing AIR

One challenge, especially because AIR is such a new technology, is the penetration of AIR among users. It is highly likely that most users will not have it installed on their machines, and this is something that it is important to be cognizant of when deciding on the best way to distribute your application.

One strategy is to include a link to Adobe's website where the user can download the latest version of the runtime, similar to what is often done when Adobe PDF files are made available on a page.

This, however, is less than ideal and goes against what a user has come to expect when installing desktop applications. Most people are used to downloading a file, executing it, and having an application installed. By introducing extra steps and dependencies, the process becomes more complex, and a user is more likely to walk away—unless of course your download is something that they particularly want.

Thankfully, Adobe has considered this and has came up with a solution—the SWF-based "install badge" system, which can be used to install both AIR and an application together. This is leveraging the ubiquity of Flash Player and its ExpressInstall functionality, which until now has been used only for installing new versions of Flash Player.

An *install badge* (Figure 12-12) is essentially a SWF that can be embedded onto a website. When a user clicks it, Flash Player's ExpressInstall functionality is used to install both the application and AIR (if required).

You can find a sample install badge within the AIR SDK, and by customizing the FLA file provided, you can blend it seamlessly with the look and feel of your website.

This creates a simple, effective process where a user can install an application and potentially the runtime, without leaving the web page.

Figure 12-12. A sample install badge

A second solution is also in development, allowing the creation of a platform-specific executable bundle containing both the runtime and an application that can be distributed in much the same manner as a regular desktop application.

Also in the works for a future release are tools that allow AIR applications to be remotely deployed within a managed computing environment.

Summary

In this chapter, we introduced you to the key components that make up an AIR application and how you can turn existing Flex applications quickly and easily into desktop applications.

However, this is just the beginning of what is possible now that you have made the jump from the Web to the desktop. Over the next few chapters, you will be looking at some of the functionality that is now possible thanks to AIR.

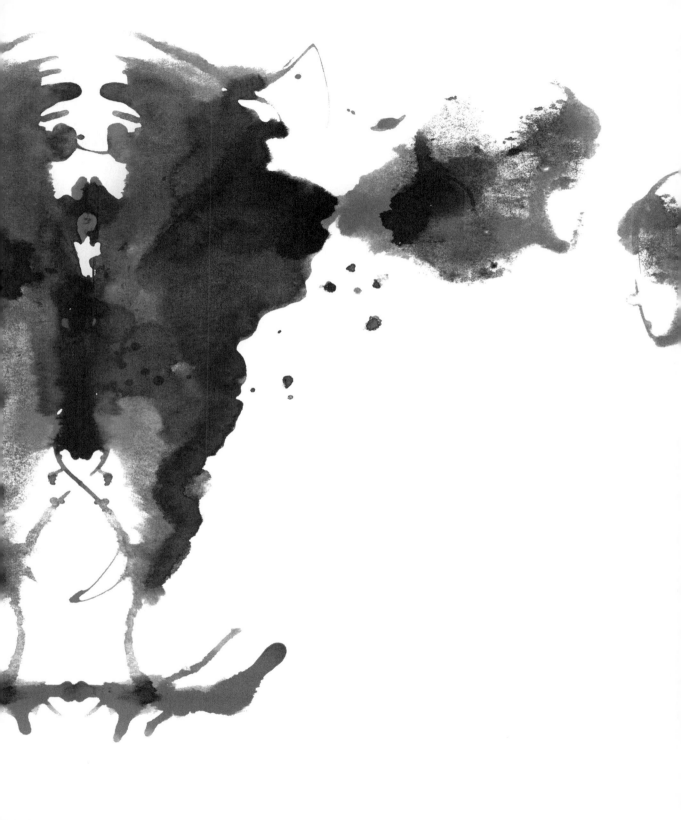

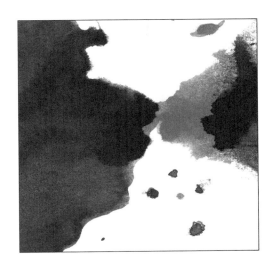

Chapter 13

ADDING MORE DESKTOP ELEMENTS TO THE WEB

In the previous chapter, you learned just how quickly and easily existing web-based content can be moved to the desktop; however, there is still much more of Adobe AIR to explore. In this chapter, you will learn how to incorporate some of the elements and functionality of the desktop user experience into your web applications.

You can work in two distinct development modes when using AIR. The first is where you transfer existing web functionality and you make it available on the desktop as an application or widget. This is an excellent approach when dealing with something fairly limited in functionality and complexity, such as a widget. This mode is also useful when you have constrained resources or are simply in a hurry and want to roll something out quickly as a trial or proof of concept.

The second development mode is where you set out specifically to exploit the added functionality available for an application running on a desktop as opposed to the Web. In this case, the application may contain more complex functionality, which lends itself to some of the features available within AIR, such as the embedded SQLite database. Or it may be that by delivering a piece of functionality in a manner similar to a desktop application, you actually have managed to solve a problem.

You can see good examples of web applications "going desktop" in many places. For instance, file uploads tend to be clumsily implemented in web applications. You can avoid the technical challenges and disconnects of browsing for files and uploading one at a time by creating a desktop application to take care of this kind of functionality.

Desktop tools such as the Flickr Uploadr, as shown in Figure 13-1, offer a solution by allowing users to select photo files and add metadata offline before uploading the files to the web application. The user is working with the local filesystem and a familiar operating system rather than a less-capable web-built interface. AIR makes this functionality available.

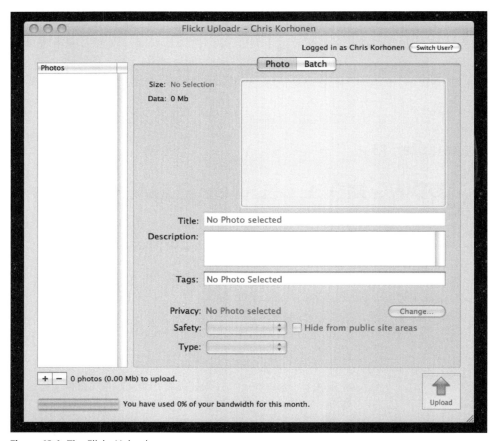

Figure 13-1. The Flickr Uploadr

Thanks to industry leaders Google, Yahoo!, Flickr, and Wikipedia, users have become used to web applications that are fast, usable, and feature rich. On the desktop, a user expects an application to function the same as any other application on their machine. This means supporting drag-and-drop inputs, using the clipboard, and adhering to familiar user interface conventions.

Just as experience can make or break a web application, the same is true on the desktop. The only difference is that what makes a good experience has subtly changed because our expectations as users are different on the Web than on the desktop.

One of the key distinguishers of a desktop application is the ability to access objects on the local filesystem through a variety of means. In this chapter, we'll cover each of these in detail and then show how they can be used in an example project.

Working with the filesystem

Through the File API provided in AIR, it is possible to perform numerous operations on the local filesystem including creating and deleting files and folders, reading and writing data, and managing files and folders.

Gaining local file access

You can find the classes for implementing these operations in the `flash.filesystem` package within the AIR APIs; they consist of the following:

- `File` represents a path to a file or folder and can be used as a pointer reference when interacting with the filesystem.
- `FileMode` defines string constants that determine which operations can be performed on a file once it has been opened. This includes whether the application has read/write access to the file and the various modes by which it can be updated.
- `FileStream` is used to open files for both reading and writing.

Synchronous or asynchronous file access

You can use the File API to manipulate files in two ways: synchronously or asynchronously.

If you choose to work in *synchronous* mode, this means that while you are reading from or writing to a file, no other code is executed in the background. This has the advantage that you do not need to set up any event listeners for the completion event. However, it also means that for the end user, the screen will freeze and will not be updated until the operation completes. You cannot provide any form of progress bar or visual feedback for the operation.

Asynchronous mode lets you read from or write to the file in the background while still executing code in the foreground. It is often the preferred option because the application is still interactive. However, this mode requires additional code in order to set up event listeners on the File and FileStream objects.

When working with the File API, rather than setting a flag that denotes synchronous or asynchronous, you have separate methods for the synchronous and asynchronous flavors of various operations.

Working with files and directories

Working with files means identifying file locations. The File API makes things easy by storing common system paths as static properties so they can be easily referenced. The following is a list of "special" file locations, common across operating systems, which are accessible through the File API:

- `File.appStorageDirectory` is the storage directory that is allocated to each AIR application when it is installed. This is the logical place to store any user preferences or cached data that is specific to a single instance of the application.
  - On Windows (usually): `C:\Documents and Settings\[username]\Application Data\[AIR Application ID]\Local Store`
  - On a Mac: `/Users/[username]/Library/Preferences/[AIR Application ID]/Local Store`

267

- `File.appResourceDirectory` is the directory where the files contained within AIR application are installed. This includes any files that were packaged inside the `.air` file during the build process.
  - On Windows: `C:\Documents and Settings\[username]\Local Settings\Application Data\ [AIR Application Name]`
  - On a Mac: `/users/[username]/Applications/[AIR Application Name]`

- `File.userDirectory` is the user's home directory.
  - On Windows: `C:\Documents and Settings\[username]`
  - On a Mac: `/users/[username]/`

- `File.desktopDirectory` is the user's desktop.
  - On Windows: `C:\Documents and Settings\[username]\Desktop`
  - On a Mac: `/users/[username]/Desktop/`

- `File.documentsDirectory` is the user's documents directory.
  - On Windows: `C:\Documents and Settings\[username]\My Documents`
  - On a Mac: `/users/[username]/Documents/`

- `File.currentDirectory` is the directory from which the AIR application was launched. Although this is often the same as the application resource directory, this may not always be the case because a user might choose to move an application following its installation.

As you leverage the File API and you begin to work with directories, you can now dig even deeper into the filesystem. For example, if you create an instance of the `File` object based on an existing directory, you can interrogate the filesystem for information related to the directory, like so:

```
var myFolder:File = File.documentsDirectory;

trace(myFolder.exists);
// true

trace(myFolder.isDirectory);
// true

trace(myFolder.nativePath);
// /users/ckorhonen/Documents/

trace(myFolder.url);
//  file:///users/ckorhonen/Documents

trace(myFolder.parent.url);
// file:///users/ckorhonen/
```

In this case, you're checking whether a specified directory exists and gathering information about its location and parent. A lot more information becomes available if you use the `File` object to point to a specific file rather than a directory, including file size, creation date, and last-modified date.

If you want it to point the `File` object to a specific file in a directory, you have several ways of doing this. To load an explicit file within documentsDirectory, you can resolve its path relative to that of documentsDirectory and assign it to the File object:

```
var myFile:File = File.documentsDirectory;
myFile = myFile.resolvePath("myFile.txt");
```

Alternatively, if you know either the URL or the native path to a specific file or directory, then you can use that in the class constructor or once you have instantiated the File object:

```
var myFile:File = new File();
myFile.url = "file:///Users/ckorhonen/Documents/myFile.txt";

var myFile:File = new File();
myFile.nativePath = "/Users/ckorhonen/Documents/myFile.txt";
```

> It is worth noting that file URLs are always URI encoded. This is often more noticeable under Windows where spaces in a directory path are replaced by %20.
>
> So, `C:\Documents and Settings\` becomes `C:\Documents%20and%20Settings\`.

To get a list of files within a directory, perhaps in order to populate a DataGrid or TreeView, the easiest option is to use one of the prebuilt Flex components available to you.

Within Flex 3 you have several components available to you (see Figure 13-2). The FileSystemDataGrid, FileSystemTree, and FileSystemList components all are pretty much self-descriptive and can be used to display filesystem data within a specific user interface control.

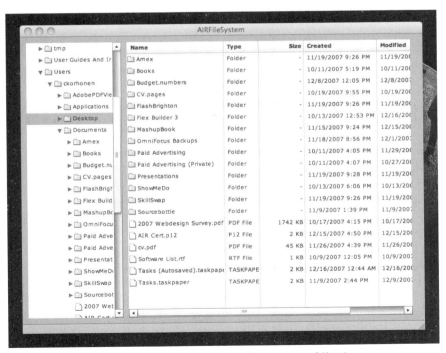

Figure 13-2. Some of the filesystem components available as part of Flex 3

These come complete with methods and events that allow users to select files and directories and have that data available to other components within an application.

You can also use the FileSystemComboBox and FileSystemHistoryButton components, which can be used with the tree or list components in order to navigate a filesystem, either upward through parent directories or backward and forward through their own navigation history.

Manipulating files

It is of little use to be able to view the local filesystem if you are unable to manipulate it, and this is where the FileMode and FileStream classes come in.

The FileMode class can determine how the application can interact with a given file, and this needs to be defined whenever you open a file for reading or writing. In many ways, this is useful because it reduces the chance of a developer accidentally writing a piece of code that has the unintended consequence of overwriting a file.

The file modes available are as follows:

- FileMode.READ is used when you want to open an existing file as read-only. If an application attempts to write to the file or the file does not exist, then an exception will be thrown.
- FileMode.WRITE is used to open a file with full read/write permissions, meaning that data can freely be read or written. If a file does not exist, then it will be created. *If the file already exists, then it will be overwritten.*
- FileMode.APPEND opens the file in full read/write mode. If the file does not exist, it will be created. Data is written at the end of the file, making this a useful file mode when dealing with application log files.
- FileMode.UPDATE opens the file in full read/write mode. If the file does not exist, it will be created. Data can be written to any position in the file, making this useful if you want to update a preference or application data file or similar.

The actual reading and writing of files is performed by the FileStream class, which contains numerous methods for reading and writing various data types, from text to binary data to serialized ActionScript objects.

To get an idea of how it works, let's take a look at some sample code for creating a new file containing the message "Hello World." First you need to create the File pointer:

```
var myFile:File = File.documentsDirectory.resolve("MyFile.txt");
```

Now that you have the File pointer, let's create a FileStream instance and set the FileMode:

```
var fileStream:FileStream = new FileStream();
fileStream.open(myFile, FileMode.WRITE);
```

As you can see, you are opening the file in full read/write mode, meaning that if it does not already exist, then it will be created for you.

Next you specify what you want to write to your file, so using the appropriate method, you write it to your file:

```
var message:String = "Hello World";
fileStream.writeUTFBytes(message);
```

Then, because you are now finished, you close the file:

```
fileStream.close();
```

Reading the data back from the file follows a similar process:

```
var myFile:File = File.documentsDirectory.resolve("MyFile.txt");
var fileStream:FileStream = new FileStream();
fileStream.open(myFile, FileMode.READ);

var message:String = fileStream.readUTFBytes();
fileStream.close();

trace(message);
// Hello World
```

In the previous example, you were using a synchronous method of creating and writing to your file. If you were to do it asynchronously, then you would still follow the same process of opening the file, reading data, and closing the file. The key differences are that you open the file in a different way and you use events as a means of monitoring progress.

```
var myFile:File = File.documentsDirectory.resolve("MyFile.txt");
var fileStream:FileStream = new FileStream();
fileStream.openAsync(myFile, FileMode.WRITE);

fileStream.addEventListener(Event.CLOSE, handleComplete);
fileStream.addEventListener(IOErrorEvent.IO_ERROR, handleError);
fileStream.addEventListener(OutputProgressEvent.OUTPUT_PROGRESS,
                                              handleProgress);

fileStream.writeUTFBytes("Hello World");
fileStream.close();
```

This function is called once the String has been successfully written to the file:

```
public function handleProgress(e:Event):void { }
```

This function is called as soon as the file stream is closed:

```
public function handleComplete(e:Event):void { }
```

This function is called in the event of an error reading or writing to the file:

```
public function handleError(e:Event):void { }
```

Dragging and dropping

Drag and drop is a user interface convention that is common on desktop applications, with users accustomed to being able to drag files into folders in order to move them around the filesystem. In addition, users can usually drag files onto different applications and have that trigger a response—perhaps loading a file or embedding one into a document.

On the Web, although implemented within Flash and also some JavaScript frameworks, drag-and-drop interactions have never really caught on and do tend to take users by surprise. In many ways, this is most likely because we are only now seeing stable, cross-browser implementations of this functionality, at a time when users are well adjusted to the process of clicking items in order to trigger certain responses and actions.

Now that you are moving across to the desktop, it becomes something that you need to consider within your AIR applications.

You can use the Drag and Drop API within AIR to transport certain types of data into an AIR application, whether that be a file dragged from the desktop or a selection of text from another application. It also supports the dragging of objects from the AIR application to the desktop or other applications.

It provides functionality in order to detect user "gestures" such as dragging an object into or out of a container, hovering over a container, and of course dropping.

Within the context of an AIR application, drag and drop is based upon specific components within the user interface, so rather than simply dragging an object onto the application, the drag-and-drop functionality allows objects to be dragged and dropped onto specific `DisplayList` objects within the application.

This allows for flexibility when developing applications, because you can have many components within the interface that respond differently to objects being dropped on them. It also has the potential to create confusion for users because they now need to be more precise about where they drop items.

Many of these problems can be solved through good user interface design, making it visually obvious how a user can interact with an interface (Figure 13-3).

Figure 13-3. An example of an intuitive interface for a drag-and-drop-based application

The drag-and-drop life cycle

The life cycle of a drag-and-drop interaction involves three stages: initiation, dragging, and dropping.

Initiation

The user initiates this by selecting an object and dragging it while holding the mouse button.

If the object being dragged is an item within the AIR application, then a NativeDragEvent.
NATIVE_DRAG_START event will be dispatched.

Dragging

Once a drag action has been initiated, the user, while keeping the mouse button pressed, can move the mouse cursor around the screen, hovering over components within the AIR application, other applications, or the desktop.

If the object is dragged over a component within your AIR application that can accept drag-and-drop interactions, then once the mouse curser enters the component boundaries, the NativeDragEvent.
NATIVE_DRAG_ENTER event will be triggered.

Similarly, once the mouse leaves the component boundaries, the NativeDragEvent.NATIVE_DRAG_EXIT event will be triggered.

Although the mouse is within the boundaries of a component, the NativeDragEvent.NATIVE_DRAG_OVER event will be triggered.

These events are especially useful if you want to provide visual feedback to users that indicates they are dragging objects over valid drop zones, which becomes helpful when trying to learn how to use a new user interface.

Dropping

The drop occurs when the mouse cursor is over a component that can accept drag-and-drop input and the mouse button is released. At this point, a NativeDragEvent.NATIVE_DRAG_DROP event is dispatched, and the component can access the dropped data through this event object.

If the drag were initiated from within the AIR application, the original container component would dispatch a NativeDragEvent.NATIVE_DRAG_COMPLETE event.

An example drag-and-drop application

In this section, we'll show how to create a simple proof of concept to demonstrate this drag-and-drop functionality.

First, define your application layout using MXML. In the following code, you have a simple List component that will serve as the drop zone and a TextArea that you will use to display output information:

```
<?xml version="1.0" encoding="utf-8"?>
<mx:WindowedApplication xmlns:mx="http://www.adobe.com/2006/mxml"
                        layout="absolute"
                        creationComplete="init()" >

    <mx:TextArea x="10" y="298" width="629" height="230"
                 id="output_txt"/>
    <mx:List dataProvider="{fileList}" x="10" y="10" width="629"
             height="280" id="dragList" backgroundColor="#EDEDED">
    </mx:List>

</mx:WindowedApplication>
```

Second, in an <mx:Script> block, you can add your code—starting with an init() method that is called when the application is first initialized:

```
import flash.desktop.NativeDragManager;
import flash.events.NativeDragEvent;

var fileList:Array = [];

public function init():void{
    dragList.addEventListener(NativeDragEvent.NATIVE_DRAG_ENTER,
                              handleEnter);
    dragList.addEventListener(NativeDragEvent.NATIVE_DRAG_EXIT,
                              handleExit);
    dragList.addEventListener(NativeDragEvent.NATIVE_DRAG_OVER,
                              handleOver);
    dragList.addEventListener(NativeDragEvent.NATIVE_DRAG_DROP,
                              handleDrop);
}
```

Here you are importing the NativeDragManager class that manages the drag-and-drop behavior that you will be implementing and the NativeDragEvent class that defines the events for which you will be listening.

Next, you add event listeners for various drag events to your List component. This will allow it to respond to any drag events that it encounters.

For the handleEnter method, you are outputting some text to the TextArea just so that you know what is happening. You are also looking at what is being dragged, which is stored in the Clipboard object within the drag event.

In this case, you are verifying that the item being dragged is in fact a file and not, for example, a text or bitmap object from another application. If this is the case, you tell the drag manager that the component should accept the drop.

This detection is especially useful should you want to restrict what can and can't be dropped onto an application, and it can provide visual feedback about the error to the user:

```
public function handleEnter(e:NativeDragEvent):void{
    output_txt.text += "DRAG ENTER Event \n";
    if(e.clipboard.hasFormat(ClipboardFormats.FILE_LIST_FORMAT)){
        NativeDragManager.acceptDragDrop(dragList);
    }
}
```

Before any item can be dropped onto an object, the acceptDragDrop method must be called:

```
public function handleExit(e:NativeDragEvent):void{
    output_txt.text += "DRAG EXIT Event \n";
}
```

The exit event simply throws out another line of debug information, but in a proper application, this would be the perfect opportunity to reset any user interface changes made during the enter event to signify that a drag-and-drop interaction was in progress:

```
public function handleOver(e:NativeDragEvent):void{
    output_txt.text += "DRAG OVER Event \n";
}
```

The over event is fired at regular intervals while the user's mouse is within the drop zone. This is another possible point where you can call acceptDragDrop; however, because this method is executed multiple times, it may not yield the best performance.

Once a file is dropped, the handleDrop method is called. Here you are accessing the Clipboard object again in order to get the dropped object.

Now you need to specify the data type of the object, in this case a file that will be returned as an Array of Files; hence, you need to cast the data as an Array.

Now that you have your file, you are simply adding its path to the List component:

```
public function handleDrop(e:NativeDragEvent):void{
    output_txt.text += "DRAG DROP Event \n";

    var droppedFile:File =
(e.clipboard.getData(ClipboardFormats.FILE_LIST_FORMAT) as Array)[0];

    fileList.push(droppedFile.nativePath);
}
```

Figure 13-4 shows the sample application so far.

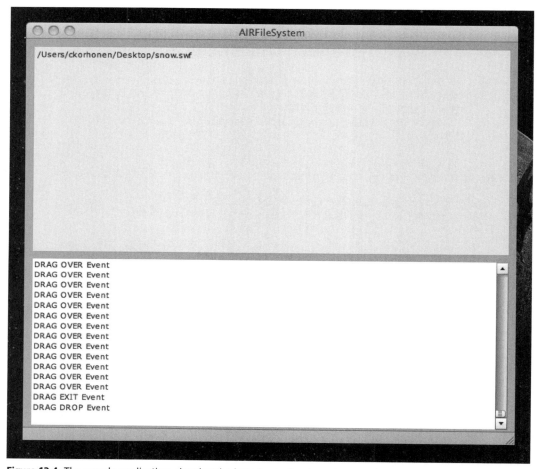

Figure 13-4. The sample application, showing the broadcast of various drag events

Clipboard access

Hand in hand with dragging and dropping is clipboard access, allowing the copying and pasting of rich objects such as formatted text and bitmap data between applications.

Within AIR, this is implemented in a similar way to how you deal with the data transported during a drag-and-drop operation. You have a Clipboard object, through which you can access the clipboard, and you have the ClipboardFormats object, which defines constants for the standard data types you will encounter.

As an example, if you wanted to retrieve an item of text from the clipboard, you would first check to see whether the clipboard contains text, and then you would parse it into a string:

```
if(Clipboard.generalClipboard.hasformat(ClipboardFormats.TEXT_FORMAT)){
    var text:String =
     Clipboard.generalClipboard.getData(ClipboardFormats.TEXT_FORMAT);
}
```

If you wanted to add data to the clipboard, you would first clear it to ensure that any unwanted data is deleted, and then you would use the Clipboard object to add your data:

```
Clipboard.generalClipboard.clear();
Clipboard.generalClipboard.setData(ClipboardFormats.TEXT_FORMAT,
                                "Hello World", false);
```

In the previous example, the text "Hello World" would be added to the clipboard and be available to other applications.

Putting everything together

You have now seen how AIR applications can interact with the local filesystem, drag-and-drop interactions, and the clipboard. Now, it's time to see how to bring all of these techniques together to build a real application.

One of the key desktop applications we discussed for drag-and-drop operations was a companion application for a web application that requires the user to upload files.

Let's take a look at how you would go about building an AIR mashup that utilizes the Flickr API in order to allow a user to upload their photos from the desktop.

The user interface

For the application interface, you will want an area where a user can drag images and also display thumbnails of images that have already been dragged into the application (see Figure 13-5). A user should also be able to edit the title and description metadata, prior to commencing the photo upload.

Figure 13-5. The interface of the Uploadr application

You can define the interface using MXML. Aside from setting the width, height, and visual parameters of your application, you are also calling an onCreationComplete() method once your application's interface has been initialized:

```
<?xml version="1.0" encoding="utf-8"?>
<mx:WindowedApplication
    xmlns:mx="http://www.adobe.com/2006/mxml"
    layout="absolute"
    width="800" height="600"
    backgroundGradientAlphas="[1.0, 1.0]"
    backgroundGradientColors="[#FFFFFF, #9B9393]"
    themeColor="#E4BD35"
    cornerRadius="8"
    showStatusBar="false"
    creationComplete="onCreationComplete( event );" >
```

To allow you to edit images, you are going to create an "edit" state within your application. This allows you to specifically tweak the layout when you are in this mode.

Here, you are modifying the style attributes of your `imageList`, which you will define in a moment, as well as adding labels and text fields for the image title and description, followed by the Save and Cancel buttons, which call the `_onEditComplete` and `_onCancel` methods, respectively.

Finally, you are also using the `<mx:SetProperty>` tag to hide the main application controls (the remove image and upload buttons) while in this mode.

You will also notice that you are using `<hBox>` and `<vBox>` tags to define the interface; these elements allow you to easily ensure that interface elements are horizontally or vertically aligned without having to worry about absolute positioning.

```
<mx:states>
    <mx:State name="edit">
        <mx:SetStyle target="{imageList}" name="top"
                value="214"/>
        <mx:AddChild position="lastChild">
            <mx:Image x="10" y="51" width="150" height="150"
                    source="{photoToEditURL}"
                    id="editPhoto_img"/>
        </mx:AddChild>
        <mx:AddChild position="lastChild">
        <mx:VBox x="168" y="51" width="329" height="155">
                <mx:HBox width="325" height="25">
                    <mx:Label id="title_lbl"
                            text="Title"/>
                    <mx:TextInput id="title_ti"
                        width="100%"
                        text="{photoToEdit.title}"/>
                </mx:HBox>
                <mx:HBox width="325" height="86">
                    <mx:Label id="description_lbl"
                            text="Description"/>
                    <mx:TextArea id="description_txt"
                      width="100%" height="89"
                      text="{photoToEdit.description}"/>
                </mx:HBox>
                <mx:HBox width="200" height="25">
                    <mx:Button id="cancel_btn"
                        label="Cancel"
                        click="_onCancel( event );"/>
                    <mx:Button id="save_btn"
                        label="Save"
                        click="_onEditComplete( event );"
                  />
                </mx:HBox>
            </mx:VBox>
        </mx:AddChild>
```

```
                    <mx:SetProperty target="{delete_btn}"
                                    name="visible" value="false"/>
                    <mx:SetProperty target="{upload_btn}"
                                    name="visible" value="false"/>
              </mx:State>
          </mx:states>
```

The remainder of the interface consists of a label proudly displaying the application title, a TileList where you will be dragging and dropping images, and two buttons (one that is used in order to delete an item from the TileList and one that triggers the upload of photos):

```
      <mx:Label x="10" y="10" text="MashUploadr" fontWeight="bold"
                fontSize="22" fontStyle="italic" fontFamily="Georgia"
                color="#3F3769"/>

      <mx:TileList id="imageList" right="10" left="10" top="51"
                   bottom="40" columnCount="4" paddingBottom="10"
                   paddingLeft="10" paddingRight="10" paddingTop="10"
                   rollOverColor="0xCCCCCC"
                   itemRenderer="ImageFileListRenderer"
                   dataProvider="{images}" />

      <mx:HBox bottom="10" right="10" left="10">
          <mx:Button id="delete_btn" label="Delete"
                     click="_deleteSelectedFile( event )"
                     left="10" bottom="10"/>

          <mx:ProgressBar id="progress_pb" width="100%" visible="false"
                          indeterminate="true"
                          labelPlacement="center"/>

          <mx:Button id="upload_btn" label="Upload Images"
                     right="10" bottom="10"
                     click="_uploadPhotos( event )"/>
      </mx:HBox>
  </mx:WindowedApplication>
```

If you refer to the TileList, you can see you are using a custom item renderer in order to display each item. This is defined in a separate MXML file:

```
<?xml version="1.0" encoding="utf-8"?>
<mx:VBox xmlns:mx="http://www.adobe.com/2006/mxml" width="100%"
         height="100%" horizontalAlign="center"
         verticalAlign="middle">
```

continued

```
<mx:Script>
    <![CDATA[
        import com.mashupload.PhotoData;
        import com.mashupload.events.EditPhotoEvent;
        import mx.events.FlexEvent;
        import mx.controls.Image;
        import mx.utils.ObjectUtil;

        private var _data:Object;
        private var _photoData:PhotoData;
        [Bindable]private var _imageSource:String;
        private function _onDoubleCLick( event:MouseEvent ):void{
            dispatchEvent( new
                EditPhotoEvent( EditPhotoEvent.EDIT_PHOTO,
                            _photoData, true  ) );
            // Set bubbles to true so you can catch it
            // in the main application
        }

        override public function get data():Object{
            return _data;
        }

        override public function set data(p_value:Object):void{
            _data = p_value;
            _photoData = PhotoData( _data );
            _imageSource = _photoData.photo.url;
        }
    ]]>
</mx:Script>

<mx:Image id="displayImage" width="150" height="150"
        horizontalAlign="center"
        verticalAlign="middle"
        doubleClickEnabled="true"
        source="{imageSource}"
        doubleClick="_onDoubleCLick( event )" />
```
`</mx:VBox>`

In the item renderer, you are displaying your image using an `<mx:Image>` tag and also setting up some code that allows you to broadcast an event to your application when it is double-clicked. This will be used to transition between application states when a user wants to edit an item's metadata.

Behind the scenes

Now that you have your interface, you can begin wiring it up and getting things working.

To interface with Flickr in this example, you'll use the ActionScript 3 Flickr library, which is provided by Adobe (http://code.google.com/p/as3flickrlib/). This simplifies the process of working with the APIs and takes care of things such as authentication:

```
<mx:Script>
    <![CDATA[
        import com.adobe.webapis.flickr.AuthPerm;
        import com.adobe.webapis.flickr.AuthResult;
        import com.adobe.webapis.flickr.FlickrService;
        import com.adobe.webapis.flickr.User;
        import com.adobe.webapis.flickr.events.FlickrResultEvent;
        import com.adobe.webapis.flickr.methodgroups.Upload;

        import com.mashupload.PhotoData;
        import com.mashupload.events.EditPhotoEvent;

        import mx.controls.Alert;
        import mx.controls.Image;
        import mx.collections.ArrayCollection;
        import mx.events.ListEvent;
        import mx.utils.ObjectUtil;
```

First, you need to set up several variables; in particular, you need to give the application your Flickr API key so that you can make requests. You also need to create an instance of FlickrService, which you will be using as part of authentication and file upload:

```
        private var _apiKey:String = "xxxxxxxxx";
        private var _secret:String = "xxxxxxx";
        private var _flickrService:FlickrService;
        private var _frob:String;
        private var _uploadFileCount:int;

        [Bindable]public var photoToEdit:PhotoData;
        [Bindable]public var photoToEditURL:String;
        [Bindable]public var user:User;
        [Bindable]public var username:String;
        [Bindable]public var images:ArrayCollection;
```

At this point, you also grab the path of the application storage directory that you will be using to store a temporary copy of any image that is imported into the application:

```
        [Bindable] private var _dir:File =
            File.applicationStorageDirectory.resolvePath( "images" );
        public var file:File;
        private var _imagesDir:String;
```

When you first load the application, the _onCreationComplete method will be called, which initializes the array of images, sets up the NativeDragEvent listeners, and initializes the Flickr service.

You are also listening for EditPhotoEvent, which, as you'll recall, is being broadcast from the ItemRenderer class.

Here, before you can proceed, you need to authenticate with Flickr. The _getFrobResponse method will launch an authentication URL in the user's browser and prompt the user to allow the application access to the data stored in the web application:

```
private function onCreationComplete(p_event:Event=null):void{
        trace( "Initialize Application" );

        images = new ArrayCollection();

        imageList.addEventListener(
                NativeDragEvent.NATIVE_DRAG_DROP,
                _onDragDrop);

        imageList.addEventListener(
                NativeDragEvent.NATIVE_DRAG_ENTER,
                _onDragEnter);

        addEventListener( EditPhotoEvent.EDIT_PHOTO,
                        _onEditPhoto );

        _flickrService = new FlickrService( _apiKey );
        _flickrService.secret = _secret;
        _flickrService.addEventListener(
                FlickrResultEvent.AUTH_GET_FROB,
                _getFrobResponse );

        var flickrCookie:SharedObject =
            SharedObject.getLocal( "FlickrServiceTest" );

        if( flickrCookie.data.auth_token ){
            trace( "Authenticated!" );
            _flickrService.token = flickrCookie.data.auth_token;
        } else{
            trace( "Need to authenticate" );
            _flickrService.auth.getFrob();
        }
}

private function _getFrobResponse(event:FlickrResultEvent):void{
        if ( event.success ) {
            _frob = String( event.data.frob );
            var auth_url:String = _flickrService.getLoginURL(
                _frob, AuthPerm.WRITE );
```

```
                    navigateToURL(new URLRequest(auth_url),"_blank" );

               Alert.show( "This application requires that you
                              authenticate on Flickr.com before
                              proceeding.  Please log in to
                              Flickr in the separate browser
                              window that opened.  After you
                              have successfully logged in,
                              press 'OK' below to continue",
                              "Authentication Required",
                              Alert.OK | Alert.CANCEL, null,
                              _onCloseAuthWindow );
          } else {
               Alert.show( event.data.error.errorMessage,
                              "Error: " +
                              event.data.error.errorCode );
          }
     }

     private function _onCloseAuthWindow(event:*):void {
          if( event.detail == Alert.OK ) {
               _flickrService.addEventListener(
                    FlickrResultEvent.AUTH_GET_TOKEN,
                    _getTokenResponse );
               _flickrService.auth.getToken( _frob );
          }
     }

     private function _getTokenResponse(event:FlickrResultEvent):void
     {
               if( event.success ){
                    var authResult:AuthResult =
                         AuthResult( event.data.auth );

                    _flickrService.token = authResult.token;
                    _flickrService.permission = authResult.perms;

                    var flickrCookie:SharedObject =
                              SharedObject.getLocal(
                                   "FlickrServiceTest" );
                    flickrCookie.data.auth_token =
                              _flickrService.token;
                    flickrCookie.flush();
```

```
                // Store our user data
                user = authResult.user;
                username = user.username;
            } else {
                // Display the error message
                Alert.show( event.data.error.errorMessage,
                            "Error: " +
                            event.data.error.errorCode );
            }
        }
    }
```

You now initialize the image list:

```
    private function _initImageList( p_event:Event=null ):void{
        dir.createDirectory();
        _imagesDir = _dir.nativePath;
    }
```

When a user chooses to edit a photo, you identify the photo you want to edit (the one the user has double-clicked), and you switch the application state to edit:

```
    private function _onEditPhoto( event:EditPhotoEvent ):void{
        photoToEdit = event.photoData;
        photoToEditURL = photoToEdit.photo.url;

        currentState = "edit";
    }
```

If the user chooses to cancel an edit, you simply switch the application state back without saving any data:

```
    private function _onCancel( event:MouseEvent ):void{
        currentState = "";
    }
```

Otherwise, you save the edited title and description before returning to the default application state:

```
    private function _onEditComplete( event:MouseEvent ):void{
        photoToEdit.title = title_ti.text;
        photoToEdit.description = description_txt.text;

        currentState = "";
    }
```

When the user begins dragging an item within the drop area, in this case TileList, then you instruct the application to accept whatever is dropped:

```
private function _onDragEnter(event:NativeDragEvent):void {
    NativeDragManager.acceptDragDrop( imageList );
}
```

On the actual drop event, you get any files that have been dropped on the application, and you check their file format. Provided they are an image format that you can support, then you pass them to the _addDroppedFile method and continue.

If the user attempts to drag and drop something other than a file, such as text or bitmap data, then nothing will happen.

```
private function _onDragDrop( event:NativeDragEvent ):void {
    NativeDragManager.dropAction = NativeDragActions.COPY;

    var files:Array =
      event.clipboard.getData(ClipboardFormats.FILE_LIST_FORMAT)
      as Array;

    for each( var file:File in files ) {
        switch ( file.extension.toLowerCase() ) {
            case "jpg":{
            _addDroppedFile( file.nativePath,
                             file.name );
            break;
        }
        case "gif":{
            _addDroppedFile( file.nativePath,
                             file.name );
            break;
        }
        case "png":{
            _addDroppedFile(file.nativePath,
                            file.name);
            break;
        }
        default:{
            Alert.show( "Unsupported file type!" );
        }
      }
    }
}
```

Dropped files are copied to the application storage directory, which allows you to manage the file while you process and upload it. You then update the master image list:

```
private function _addDroppedFile(nativePath:String,
                                 fileName:String ):void {
    var droppedFile:File =
        File.userDirectory.resolvePath( nativePath );
    var newPhotoData:PhotoData = new PhotoData();

    newPhotoData.photo = droppedFile;

    images.addItem( newPhotoData );

    _uploadFileCount++;
}
```

If the user chooses to upload the photos that they have dragged onto the application, you use the Flickr service to upload each of the images in the image list. You also listen for a completion method so that you can notify the user.

While this is going on, you also show a progress bar so that the user has a visual indication that something is happening in the background:

```
private function _uploadPhotos(p_event:MouseEvent=null):void {
    progress_pb.visible = true;

    var uploader:Upload = new Upload( _flickrService );

    for each( var photoData:PhotoData in images ){
        photoData.photo.addEventListener(
        DataEvent.UPLOAD_COMPLETE_DATA,
        _uploadCompleteHandler, false, 0, true);
    }
}
```

Once a file has been uploaded, you remove it from the image list. If all files have successfully been uploaded, then you remove the progress bar and alert the user:

```
private function _uploadCompleteHandler(p_event:DataEvent):void{
    var file:File = File( p_event.target );

    file.removeEventListener(
        DataEvent.UPLOAD_COMPLETE_DATA,
        _uploadCompleteHandler );
```

287

```
                _uploadFileCount--;

                for each( var photoData:PhotoData in images ){
                    if( file == photoData.photo ){

                        images.removeItemAt(
                            images.getItemIndex(photoData));
                    }
                }

                if( images.length == 0 ){
                    Alert.show("Your photos have been uploaded!",
                                "Upload Complete" );
                    progress_pb.visible = false;
            }
        }
```

If the user chooses to delete a file, you remove it from the image list:

```
        private function _deleteSelectedFile(p_event:MouseEvent=null):void{
            images.removeItemAt(imageList.selectedIndex);
        }


        ]]>
    </mx:Script>
```

To support your application, you have defined two custom ActionScript classes. The first is PhotoData, which simply provides you with a container object in which you can store the file reference, title, and description for each photo, making internal data management simpler and more logical:

```
    package com{

        import flash.filesystem.File;

        [Bindable]
        public class PhotoData{
            public var photo:File;
            public var title:String = "";
            public var description:String = "";
        }
    }
```

The second is EditPhotoEvent, which extends the Event class to pass a PhotoData object to your application when a user has edited a photo:

```
    package com.events{
        import com.PhotoData;

        import flash.events.Event;
```

```
public class EditPhotoEvent extends Event{
    static public const EDIT_PHOTO:String = "editPhoto";
    static public const PHOTO_EDITED:String = "photoEdited";

    public var photoData:PhotoData;

    public function EditPhotoEvent(type:String,
                                  p_photo:PhotoData,
                                  bubbles:Boolean=false,
                                  cancelable:Boolean=false){
        super(type, bubbles, cancelable);

        photoData = p_photo;
    }
}
}
```

Now, when you bring all these pieces together, you should have a functional application that demonstrates the drag-and-drop interactions that are possible in AIR (Figure 13-6) and also manipulates files on the local filesystem (Figure 13-7).

Figure 13-6. The Uploadr application, ready to upload a selection of photos

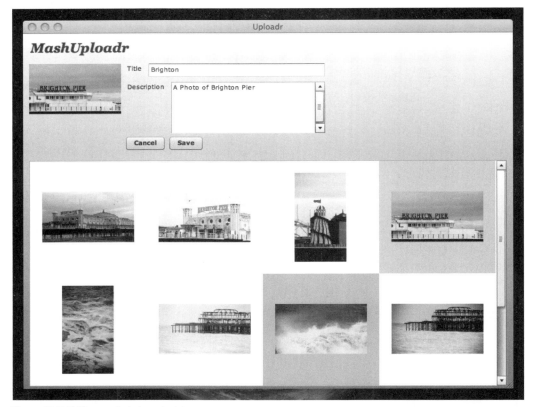

Figure 13-7. Editing a photo's metadata

Summary

You should now be aware of some of the differences in approaches when it comes to building desktop applications. In this chapter, you looked at different forms of application interaction such as drag and drop, which may be a step away from the functionality and interaction patterns available for web applications. You also looked at how you can leverage the local filesystem from within your applications.

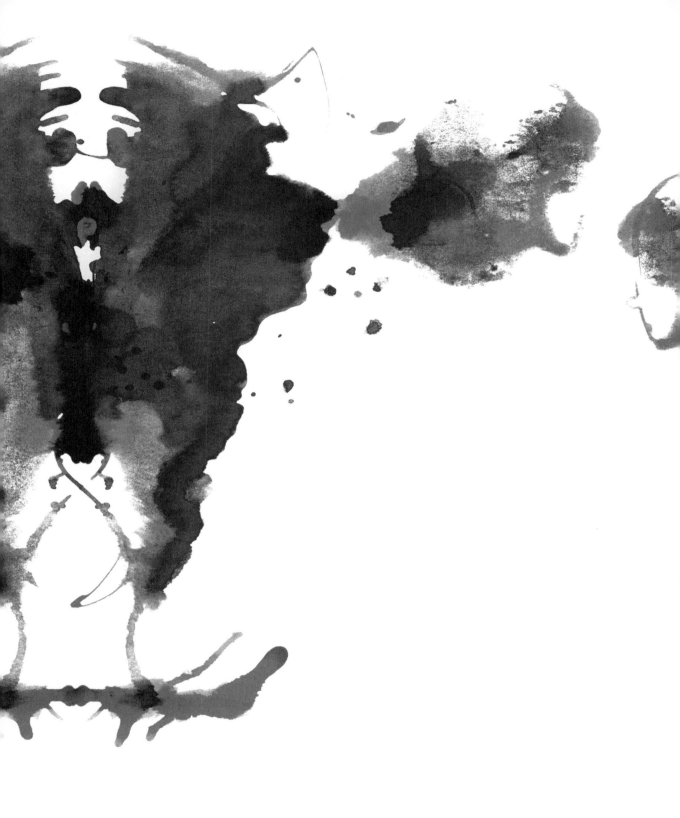

Chapter 14

BUILDING A DESKTOP EXPERIENCE

In this chapter, you'll explore how to create user interfaces using AIR, specifically, how you can use screen real estate and how to skin your applications so that they stand out from the crowd.

By exploiting RSS feeds and APIs, AIR offers many opportunities when developing companion applications and mashups of web applications. As you have seen, accessing the local filesystem offers many opportunities for streamlining the interaction between the web application and the user, which simplifies the process of uploading files and documents.

Of course, the functionality that AIR offers is only part of the development process. Design still plays an important part. From a branding perspective, it is important to create a uniform look and feel across different channels for any given product.

In this chapter, we'll cover some of the usability considerations and specifics of customizing the look and feel of AIR applications.

The desktop jungle

Although many desktop applications carry the look and feel of the host operating system, there is room for creativity within their user interfaces. This can be in the look and feel of an application, in the presentation of toolboxes and secondary windows, or in how a user is expected to interact with the application. From a usability standpoint, there is a lot to be said for consistency within any user interface, especially when compared to other common applications. This helps new users come to grips with how things work and makes them less likely to get frustrated or confused.

Adhering to user interface conventions is also important when building your application. This includes knowing when to leverage many elements of operating system functionality such as drag and drop, menus, windows, and layout and user interface controls. This ensures that the application behaves in a manner consistent with a user's expectations. For example, on Windows, the user probably expects that right-clicking an icon will spawn a contextual menu. It's important to have this consistency across different applications.

> *Apple publishes an excellent set of interface guidelines for Mac OS X, available at* http://developer.apple.com/documentation/UserExperience/Conceptual/OSXHIGuidelines/. *There is no similar official documentation available for Windows, but many of the concepts covered in Apple's interface guidelines are generic across operating systems and are well worth exploring.*

Of course, the approach you will want to take when developing an application also depends on the type of application you are developing and its complexity. Is it a widget or a full-blown desktop application?

Creating an application's user interface

If you look at full-blown applications, you'll see that many utilize the operating system chrome for the look of their primary windows in order to promote consistency and familiarity in the application. However, you'll often see variation in the internal layout of the application and the usage of secondary windows or panels to encapsulate groups of user interface controls or commands logically. For example, Figure 14-1 shows groups of panels, Figure 14-2 shows docked subwindows, Figure 14-3 shows floating windows, and Figure 14-4 shows a custom application look and feel.

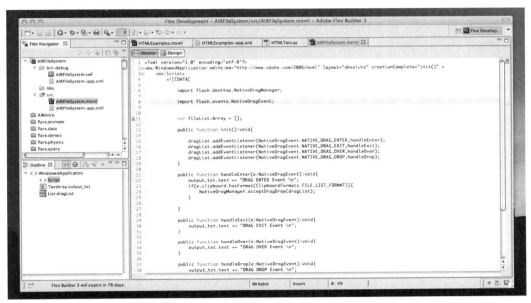

Figure 14-1. Flex Builder's user interface leverages the look and feel of the operating system. Submenus and optional windows appear within the main application window.

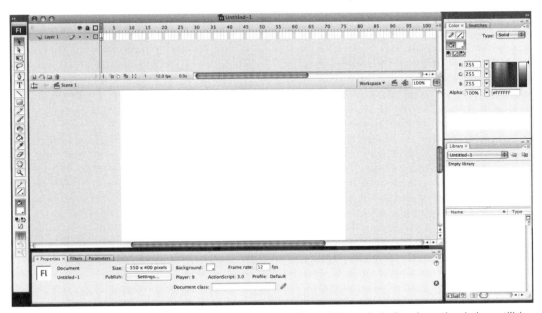

Figure 14-2. In contrast, the Flash CS3 user interface has secondary windows docked to the main window, utilizing a custom, semitransparent styling.

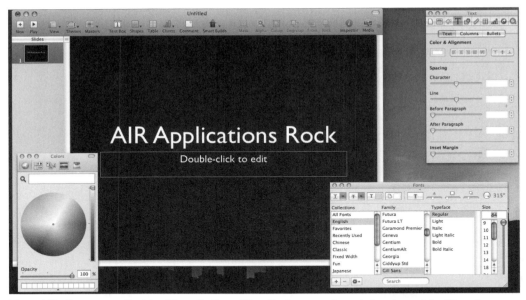

Figure 14-3. Keynote, a native Mac OS application, utilizes floating secondary windows to contain different elements of functionality. These windows conform to the standard "utility window" look and feel that has been defined within the operating system.

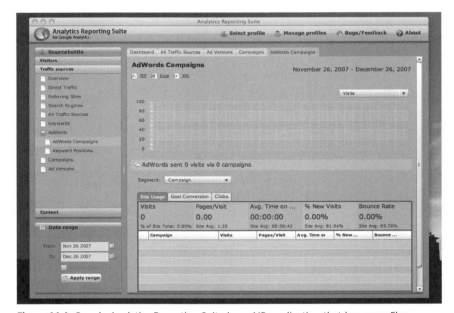

Figure 14-4. Google Analytics Reporting Suite is an AIR application that leverages Flex Charting to help visualize reporting data from Google Analytics. Here you can see the default system chrome being used for the main window, but the user interface of the application takes on the Flex look and feel.

We'll cover how to manage application elements such as secondary windows later in this chapter.

Widgets: the smallest applications

Now, if you turn and look at smaller applications and widgets, you'll see a much greater focus on the look and feel of the application. For these types of applications, developers often choose to ignore the operating system chrome in favor of more visually distinguishing interface elements in order to make their application stand out from the crowd. For example, Figures 14-5, 14-6, and 14-7 all show examples of applications using custom window chrome and transparency in order to increase their visual impact.

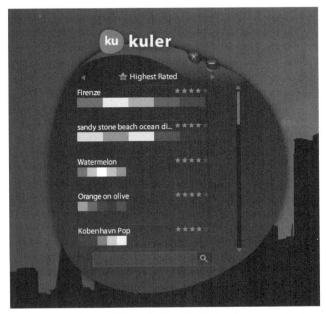

Figure 14-5. Kuler, an AIR application that helps designers select color schemes, demonstrates custom window chrome and transparent elements.

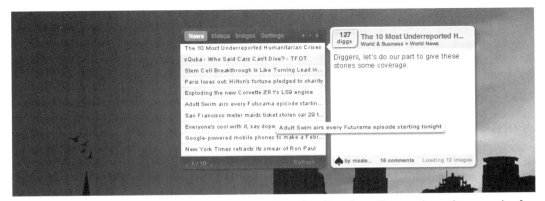

Figure 14-6. Diggtop, an AIR application that displays the latest headlines from digg.com, is another example of a custom application skin and transparency.

Figure 14-7. Snitter, an AIR-based Twitter client, also features a custom window skin and transparency.

This variation in appearance is a lot more acceptable in the case of widgets than it is for larger, full-blown applications. From an interaction standpoint, widgets are often optimized to perform a single task or to serve a single purpose, so usually their interfaces are a lot less complex. Therefore, it should be straightforward for a user to begin interacting with them, without having to spend time familiarizing themselves with how an application works.

In addition, widgets often take up much less screen real estate than other applications. A different look and feel may be more appropriate in this case in order to set them apart for other applications and make the best use of the area available for the user interface.

Managing windows

In many applications, as you have seen, it is often desirable to create secondary windows. You can use these windows to reduce the complexity of the user interface, to create logical groupings of related items, or to display items that may not always be needed when using an application.

Creating windows

Within AIR, it is possible to spawn new windows using either the MXML Window component or the NativeWindow class available within ActionScript. When you create a new window, you also have the opportunity to customize its appearance, size, position, and content just as you would with your main application window.

To spawn a new MXML window, create an instance of the Window component and call the open method to display the window, as follows:

```
var window:Window = new Window();
window.open(true);
```

The boolean passed into the open method determines whether the newly created window has focus. In most cases, opening a new window that has focus can be considered intrusive because it may interrupt the user's activity.

Using NativeWindow, it is a similar process, but this time you are required to pass a NativeWindowObject that contains configuration parameters for the newly created window:

```
var options:NativeWindowInitOptions = new NativeWindowInitOptions();
options.systemChrome = NativeWindowSystemChrome.STANDARD;
var window:NativeWindow = new NativeWindow(options);
```

These code examples will both create a new window similar to that that shown in Figure 14-8.

If the user is currently typing something in another application when the window is created, then focus will move from the field they are typing into, causing keystrokes to be lost.

However, if a user clicks a button within an application, then in this case it is often acceptable to spawn a new window that has focus. It could be a properties panel or confirmation dialog box, with the key difference being that the user has initiated this action while interacting with the application.

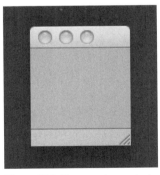

Figure 14-8. Your newly created window, looking a little lonely and vulnerable.

When you create your window, you can also customize its appearance appearance by setting its properties:

```
var window:Window = new Window();
window.maximizable = true;
window.minimizable = false;
window.width = 400;
window.height = 400;
window.resizable = true;
window.transparent = false;
window.alwaysInFront = true;
window.title = "New Window!";
window.type = NativeWindowType.UTILITY;
window.open(true);
```

This code sets several of the properties of the new window, including `alwaysInFront`, meaning that the new window will appear on top of other windows (belonging to your application or other applications).

This code also sets the window's type to be a constant value as defined in the `NativeWindowType` class. You can use this property to define the type of a window, dictating the system chrome that is used and some behaviors. The types correspond to common window types defined by the operating system.

As you begin customizing the window, its appearance will look more like Figure 14-9. Table 14-1 provides an overview of all the available window types.

Figure 14-9. The customized window, now looking a bit less vulnerable!

Table 14-1. Window Types Available Within AIR Applications

Window Type	Description
NORMAL	This window uses the standard system chrome and appears in Mac OS's Window menu and the Windows task bar. This is a typical window in the context of the operating system.
UTILITY	This is a subwindow, often used for toolbars and utilizing a reduced version of the system chrome. Utility windows do not appear in the Window menu or in the task bar.
LIGHTWEIGHT	This type is available only when the systemChrome property is set to none. Much like utility windows, these windows do not appear in the Window menu or in the task bar. They are suitable for toolbars or notifications that do not use the system chrome.

Once you have customized your window's dimensions and positioning, all that remains is to add content to your window. The window can hold any content item that extends the display object, so you are free to use Sprites, UIComponents, and so forth. You simply attach the content to the display list for your window using the addChild method:

```
window.addChild(content);
```

In Figure 14-10, we have created a new MXML component that contains a selection of user interface components. Then we created an instance of the component it and set it as the child.

```
var content:SampleContent = new SampleContent();
window.addChild(content);
```

If you are building an application using ActionScript 3, rather than Flex, you can create your own windows by using the NativeWindow class, which can be instantiated in a similar manner. The key difference is that many of the initialization parameters are passed into the constructor encapsulated within a NativeWindowInitOptions class; they cannot be changed once the window has been created.

> If you want to use Flex components within a window, then you should use the Flex Window component rather than NativeWindow, which does not extend the full range of classes necessary to support the Flex framework and its components.

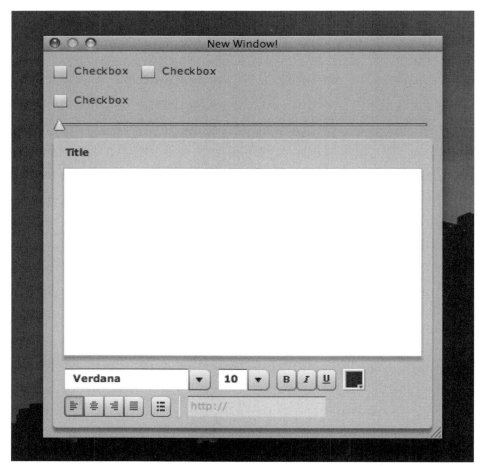

Figure 14-10. The window, now with content

To create the window, first define your initialization parameters, like so:

```
var options:NativeWindowInitOptions = new NativeWindowInitOptions();
options.maximizable = true;
options.minimizable = false;
options.resizable = true;
options.transparent = false;
options.type = NativeWindowType.UTILITY;
```

Then create an instance of NativeWindow:

```
var window:NativeWindow = new NativeWindow(options);
window.width = 400;
window.height = 400;
window.alwaysInFront = true;
window.title = "New Window!";
```

Finally, make the window visible:

```
window.visible = true;
```

Adding content to an instance of NativeWindow also follows a similar approach with a minor difference. Rather than simply adding the content as a child of the window, the newly created window has its own stage element that represents the drawable area where content should be added:

```
window.stage.addChild(content);
```

Now that you have learned how you create windows within AIR applications, we'll show you how to manage them.

Managing windows

Over the lifetime of an application, it is often necessary to manipulate its windows in order to facilitate user interactions so, for example, a user can click a button that brings a particular panel to the front with the focus. Using ActionScript, you can call a variety of methods on a window in order to control it.

These methods should be called on the instance of the window that you want to manipulate, which can usually be found either as a reference on the display list or as the target property of an event dispatched from a window.

Table 14-2 contains a list of methods that are available and can be used to manipulate windows.

Table 14-2. Methods That Can Be Applied to the NativeWindow Class

Method	Description
activate()	Activates the target window, bringing it to the front and giving it focus. This is useful when you require a user's attention, perhaps to solicit input.
close()	Closes the target window.
maximize()	Maximizes the target window.
minimize()	Minimizes the target window.
orderInBackOf(window:NativeWindow)	Moves the target window behind the window specified in the method parameters. This will override any properties set for alwaysInFront.
orderInFrontOf(window:NativeWindow)	Moves the target window in front of the window specified in the method parameters. This will override any properties set for alwaysInFront.
orderToBack()	Moves the target window behind all other visible windows.
orderToFront()	Moves the target window in front of all other visible windows.

One thing to remember before you begin reordering windows is that the window you want to reorder should be visible and not in a minimized state.

You can also read the properties of a window that either have been set during initialization or have been modified by the user while moving and resizing a given window. This can be useful if you want to store the state of a window. So if a user closes a window and then reopens it, the window appears in the same position and with the same dimensions as before. This is a small touch that can make your application more usable.

Window events

Each window manipulation broadcasts a different event, and you can track these by attaching event listeners. Table 14-3 lists the events.

Table 14-3. Window Events

Event	Description
Event.ACTIVATED	Dispatched when the window receives focus.
Event.DEACTIVATE	Dispatched when the window loses focus.
Event.CLOSING	Dispatched when the system chrome Close button is clicked. This is not dispatched when a window is closed by the application itself.
Event.CLOSE	Dispatched when the window has closed.
NativeWindowBoundsEvent.MOVING	Dispatched before the window position changes as the result of a move, resize, or state change.
NativeWindowBoundsEvent.MOVE	Dispatched immediately after the window has moved.
NativeWindowBoundsEvent.RESIZING	Dispatched before the window's dimensions are changed as the result of a resize or state change.
NativeWindowBoundsEvent.RESIZE	Dispatched after the window's dimensions have changed.

When handling NativeWindowBoundsEvent events that correspond to the window being moved or resized, you can extract the new and original size and positions from the afterBounds and beforeBounds properties on the event itself.

If you wanted to capture the size and position of a window prior to the user closing it, you would attach an event listener to the CLOSING event, like so:

```
window.addEventListener(Event.CLOSING,handleClose);
```

In the handleClose method, you can capture the properties relating to the window size and position, prior to storing them either in a configuration file on the filesystem or within a shared object accessible by your application:

```
private function handleClose(e:Event):void{
    var window:NativeWindow = e.target as NativeWindow;

    var height:int = window.height;
    var width:int = window.width;
    var x:int = window.x;
    var y:int = window.y;

    //Store Captured Values Here
    // As an example, let's put them in a shared object
    var so:SharedObject = new SharedObject('position');
    so.data.height = height;
    so.data.width = width;
    so.data.x = x;
    so.data.y = y;
    // Done

}
```

Remember, this function will be triggered only if the user initiates the close of the window. If the application initiates the close, then the CLOSING event is not dispatched.

As a workaround, you could refactor your method to pass the window instance (e.target) to another method that handles the storing of the window properties. You could also use this method prior to any instance where the application closes the window programmatically.

Polishing the chrome

Unless instructed to do otherwise, your AIR applications will use the default operating system user interface elements and settings. In Windows, an AIR application will look like a Windows application, and under Mac OS X, an AIR application will look like a Mac application.

Using the system chrome is often a good choice when you are building larger applications that are functionally similar to standard desktop applications and that should ideally look and feel as if they are native to the operating system. When you create secondary windows and widgets, then you may want to exert a greater degree of customization using transparency, custom window chrome, or both.

Utilizing transparency

You can use transparency in numerous ways within an AIR application:

- Secondary windows can be partially transparent. This allows the user to continue to focus on the primary window.
- The primary window of a smaller widget can be semitransparent, making it less obtrusive to the user when not in use.
- Transparency could be controlled depending on whether a window is active. When inactive, it could blend into the background—again leading to a less obtrusive experience.

To make a window transparent, make sure you're not using the system default interface settings, and then set the transparency property to true:

```
window.systemChrome = NativeWindowSystemChrome.NONE;
window.transparent = true;
```

Now the application window is transparent, as shown in Figure 14-11.

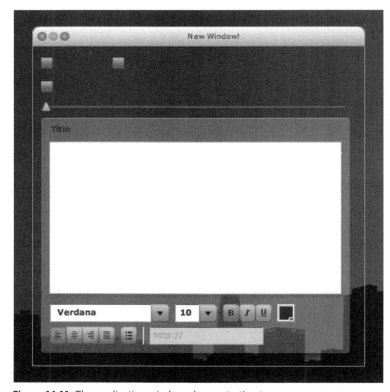

Figure 14-11. The application window, demonstrating transparency

If you are using Flex components, then you should also apply a CSS style to ensure that the window's background is indeed transparent; otherwise, it will take the default background color of the application:

```
<mx:Style>
    Window{
        background-color:"";
        background-image:"";
    }
</mx:Style>
```

You can now go ahead and customize the look and feel of your components, for example, by adding a background color to your canvas and setting a transparency value that will give you a nice semitransparent effect.

The side effect of removing the systemChrome is that there's no longer a drop shadow. If you want to have one, you have to create your own using a filter:

```
var shadow:DropShadowFilter = new DropShadowFilter();
shadow.alpha = 0.75;
shadow.blurX = 10;
shadow.blurY = 10;
shadow.color = 0x000000;
shadow.distance = 5;

window.filters = [shadow];
```

Transparency within AIR applications can be very powerful, especially when creating applications that "stand out" from normal applications. The method we have described here is suitable when creating secondary windows for applications. To take full advantage of the power of transparency, you can use it with application skinning.

Skinning

As you develop widgets and other smaller applications, skinning provides a compelling way to give applications their own unique look and feel. Skinning an AIR application follows the same principles that you used to skin your Flex components in Chapter 4. You can use either image assets or the ActionScript drawing APIs to give your application the look you desire. Because we are discussing desktop applications in this chapter, which may not necessarily remain a fixed size, the following is the code for creating a dynamic skin for an application, which will respond to the application being resized or maximized:

```
<?xml version="1.0" encoding="utf-8"?>
<mx:Application xmlns:mx="http://www.adobe.com/2006/mxml"
                layout="absolute"
                creationComplete="init();">
<mx:Style>
        Application {
            background-color:"";
            background-image:"";
        }
    </mx:Style>
```

You start by defining your application MXML file, triggering an init method upon start-up:

```
<?xml version="1.0" encoding="utf-8"?>
<mx:Application xmlns:mx="http://www.adobe.com/2006/mxml"
                layout="absolute"
                creationComplete="init();">
```

Next, you can ensure that the main window is transparent by setting style rules for your application. You will also need to modify the application descriptor XML; however, we will cover this later in this chapter:

```
    <mx:Style>
        Application {
            background-color:"";
            background-image:"";
        }
    </mx:Style>

<mx:VBox id="app" width="100%" height="100%" x="0" y="0"
         horizontalAlign="center"
         verticalAlign="middle">
        <mx:Button id="minimizeBtn"
                    click="onMinimize(event)"
                    label="Minimize"/>
        <mx:Button id="maximizeBtn"
                    click="onMaximize(event)"
                    label="Maximize"/>
        <mx:Button id="closeBtn"
                    click="onClose(event)"  label="Close"/>
    </mx:VBox>

<mx:Script>
        <![CDATA[
            import mx.events.ResizeEvent;
            public var shadow:DropShadowFilter;

            public function init():void{
                app.addEventListener(MouseEvent.MOUSE_DOWN,
                                        onMouseDown);

                this.addEventListener(
                            NativeWindowBoundsEvent.RESIZE,
                            onResize,true,0,false);
                drawSkin();
                shadow = new DropShadowFilter();
                shadow.alpha = 0.5;
                shadow.blurX = 5;
                shadow.blurY = 5;
                shadow.color = 0x000000;
                shadow.distance = 5;

                this.app.filters = [ shadow ];
            }

            public function drawSkin():void{
                app.graphics.clear();
                app.graphics.beginFill(0xff0000,0.75);
                app.graphics.drawEllipse(0,0,app.width-5,
                                        app.height-5);
                app.graphics.endFill();
            }
```

```
            public function onMouseDown(e:MouseEvent):void{
                stage.nativeWindow.startMove();
            }

            public function onClose(e:Event):void{
                stage.nativeWindow.close();
            }

            public function onMinimize(e:Event):void{
                stage.nativeWindow.minimize();
            }

            public function onMaximize(e:Event):void{
                        stage.nativeWindow.maximize();
            }

            private function onResize(e:Event):void{
                drawSkin();
            }
        ]]>
    </mx:Script>

</mx:Application>
```

For the user interface, we'll show how to define several buttons, contained within a VBox component with the id attribute app that takes care of the layout. Because you won't be using the system chrome for this example, you need to provide your own controls to minimize, maximize, and close the window—this is where buttons come into the picture:

```
<mx:VBox id="app" width="100%" height="100%" x="0" y="0"
        horizontalAlign="center"
        verticalAlign="middle">
    <mx:Button id="minimizeBtn"
                click="onMinimize(event)"
                label="Minimize"/>
    <mx:Button id="maximizeBtn"
                click="onMaximize(event)"
                label="Maximize"/>
    <mx:Button id="closeBtn"
                click="onClose(event)"  label="Close"/>
</mx:VBox>

</mx:Application>
```

With the basics of the application now set up, you can start writing some ActionScript, which will be used to initialize and draw the applications, as well as handle various events:

```
<mx:Script>
    <![CDATA[
        import mx.events.ResizeEvent;
        public var shadow:DropShadowFilter;

        public function init():void{
```

You will want to register an event listener for the mousedown event, which will let you know whether a user clicks the application and attempts to drag it across the screen. Again, because you are not using the system chrome for the example application, there is no "drag bar" defined. Therefore, you will need to implement this functionality.

In this case, the mousedown event is attached to the app element because you will be resizing the layout:

```
app.addEventListener(MouseEvent.MOUSE_DOWN,
                     onMouseDown);
```

Also, this code is listening for events triggered when the user resizes the application window. This is so you can redraw the user interface, making it resolution independent.

```
this.addEventListener(
            NativeWindowBoundsEvent.RESIZE,
            onResize,true,0,false);
```

Next, you draw the application skin by calling the drawSkin method, which we will walk you through in a moment.

```
drawSkin();
```

Finally, add a drop shadow to the application:

```
shadow = new DropShadowFilter();
shadow.alpha = 0.5;
shadow.blurX = 5;
shadow.blurY = 5;
shadow.color = 0x000000;
shadow.distance = 5;

this.app.filters = [ shadow ];
}
```

If you take a look at the drawSkin method, you'll see that you are simply using the drawing API to draw an ellipse that is sized according to the width and height of the application, minus 5 pixels to account for the drop shadow.

When working with the drawing API to define user interface components, it is important to remember to clear the graphics object before you begin drawing in order to remove the previous graphics, which will no longer be valid.

```
public function drawSkin():void{
    app.graphics.clear();
    app.graphics.beginFill(0xff0000,0.75);
    app.graphics.drawEllipse(0,0,app.width-5,
                                 app.height-5);
    app.graphics.endFill();
}
```

All that remains is to add the event listeners that correspond to the various events for which you are listening. All of them access API functions that are defined by the NativeWindow class and so are pretty straightforward:

```
public function onMouseDown(e:MouseEvent):void{
    stage.nativeWindow.startMove();
}

public function onClose(e:Event):void{
    stage.nativeWindow.close();
}

public function onMinimize(e:Event):void{
    stage.nativeWindow.minimize();
}

public function onMaximize(e:Event):void{
            stage.nativeWindow.maximize();
}

private function onResize(e:Event):void{
    drawSkin();
}
        ]]>
    </mx:Script>
```

Within the application descriptor XML file, you also need to set several properties for the application's initialWindow. These properties simply set the window's properties to transparent and instruct AIR not to use the system chrome:

```
<initialWindow>
    <title>Skinned App</title>
    <content></content>
    <systemChrome>none</systemChrome>
    <transparent>true</transparent>
    <visible>true</visible>
    <minimizable>true</minimizable>
    <maximizable>true</maximizable>
    <resizable>true</resizable>
</initialWindow>
```

Now, if you compile and run the application, you should see the skinned application (Figure 14-12). When you click the Maximize button, the skin should automatically be redrawn to accommodate the window's new shape and position (Figure 14-13).

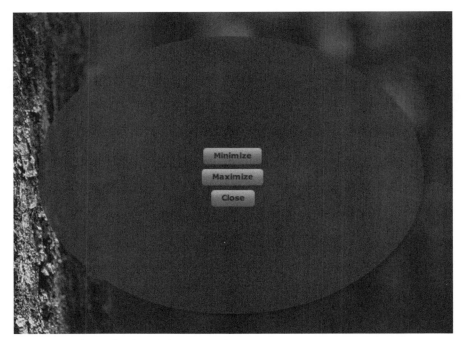

Figure 14-12. The application window and its skin

Figure 14-13. A maximized window, with the skin redrawn to fit

To make the application window resizable, create a button or other element to serve as a drag handle:

```
<mx:Button id="resizeBtn"
           mouseDown="startResize(event)"  label="Resize"/>
```

You can also define a function that calls the startResize method on the NativeWindow class. In its parameters, you can specify the size or the corner you will be resizing from—in this case, the bottom right—allowing you to restrict the resize to the horizontal or vertical dimension:

```
private function startResize(e:Event):void{
    stage.nativeWindow.startResize(NativeWindowResize.BOTTOM_RIGHT);
}
```

When it comes to application skinning, like cats, you can approach things in many different ways. Much of this depends on the nature of the application. If you are developing a fixed-size widget, then using a graphical asset is likely easier than using the drawing APIs.

For larger and dynamic applications, then the drawing APIs make more sense. However, for complex interfaces, this process can be a time-consuming one. The other thing to remember is that Flex-based AIR applications support the same scale-nine grids that we touched on in Chapter 4, making things much easier.

Summary

In this chapter, we covered the steps associated with creating new application windows and skinning them in a manner where you can create unique applications. By creating a distinct look and feel, you can make your applications stand out on a user's desktop and also effectively use the available screen real estate.

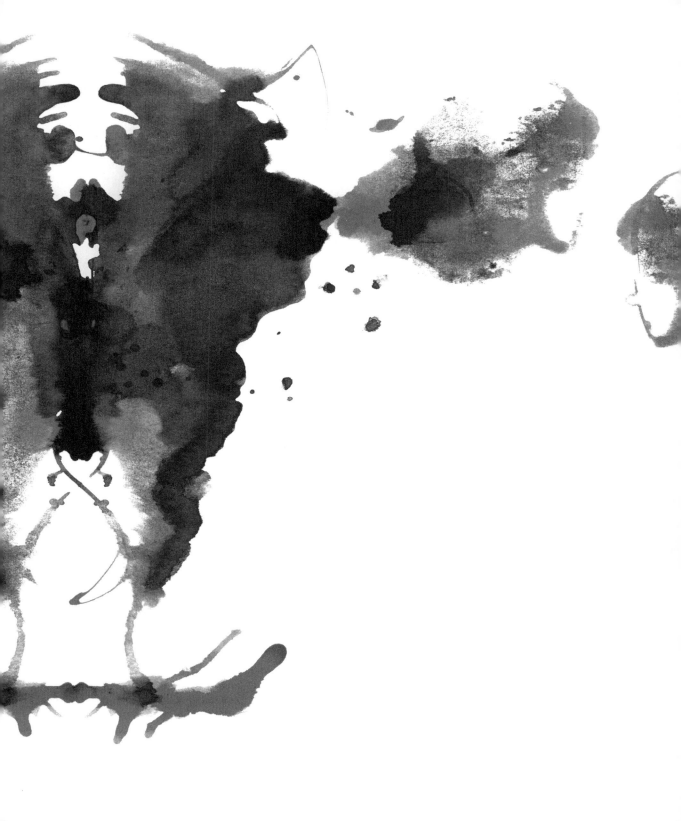

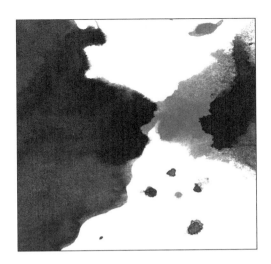

Chapter 15

COMPLETING THE EXPERIENCE

You've learned how you can use AIR to build desktop applications and about some of the features that are especially useful when building widgets and mashups; however, AIR still has a lot more to offer that can make all the difference in your applications.

AIR makes taking existing web applications and transferring them to the desktop a breeze, presenting the developer with many opportunities to reuse existing code as is. However, if this is all you do when creating an AIR application, then you might be missing out on delivering a truly special and integrated user experience. Many of the desktop integration features are the key distinguishers between AIR and the other solutions you looked at in Chapter 10.

Over the course of this chapter, you'll learn about some of the features that help AIR applications stand out from traditional Flex application and that help leverage more of the functionality that is available on the desktop.

Rendering HTML richly

Often when building an application, especially one that consumes dynamic data from feeds and web services, it is often desirable to be able to render HTML tags in order to preserve the formatting of text elements. Otherwise, your options become very limited as to how you can render your data to the user—either restricting the presentation to plain text or fitting data into rigid templates.

Unfortunately, HTML rendering is an area where Flash has traditionally been quite weak by supporting a limited subset of HTML tags and even fewer CSS styles. In addition, requirements to support common elements such as subscript and superscript text cause further headaches, often requiring the developer to customize fonts or develop separate components in order to render them correctly because they are not supported natively.

To sum it up nicely, the current state of text and HTML layout and rendering within Flash and Flex applications sucks! And although Adobe is focusing on text rendering and layout in future releases of Flash Player, for web-based content there is currently no elegant solution.

One would be forgiven for thinking that this spells doom and gloom for AIR applications, but fortunately that would be wrong, because the AIR runtime includes a full web browser–rendering engine that can be utilized as a Flex component.

And if that weren't enough, the rendering engine in question is WebKit, the same technology used in Apple's Safari web browser and that is common on mobile devices such as the iPhone and some newer Nokia phones.

What this means is that we, as developers, do not need to worry about how our web pages will render in yet another web browser. If a page looks and functions correctly in Safari, it will look and function correctly within an AIR application (see Figure 15-1).

Figure 15-1. The *New York Times*, rendered within an AIR application, displaying HTML-based and Flash-based content

AIR also has full support for CSS and JavaScript content, so there really is very little difference in rendering capabilities between viewing a page within an AIR application and viewing it within a regular web browser. The only items of content that may not display are those that are dependent on additional browser plug-ins; however, both Flash content and PDF-based content are supported.

So, when might you want to use the HTML component?

- If you are developing a desktop companion for a web-based application, then you may want to allow users to register a new user account while keeping them within the desktop experience.
- If you are dealing with RSS feeds, you may want to allow the user to drill down into the feed's content through a web interface.
- If you have a great deal of content in either HTML or PDF that you want to make available within your application but perhaps don't have the budget to reformat that content, then you'd want to use the HTML component.
- If you are asking the user to enter HTML-formatted content and want to offer a live preview of the entered data, then you'd want to use the HTML component.

Using the HTML component

If you want to use the HTML component within your application, you can instantiate it in several ways.

From MXML, it can be defined quite simply, using the location attribute in order to specify the web page to load:

```
<mx:HTML id="browser" left="10" bottom="10" right="10" top="10"
        location="http://www.nytimes.com" />
```

This can be useful if the HTML component is intended to occupy a fixed location within the user interface of an application or one of its constituent states in the case of a Flex application.

Of course, sometimes you may want to do a bit more with the HTML component. Because it implements the UIComponent class, it can be manipulated in the same way as any other user interface or graphical element using ActionScript.

You can add a filter to it, scale it, squeeze it, stretch it, rotate it, adjust the alpha transparency, and do a lot more to it. And, while you perform all these visual manipulations to the component, the HTML content within remains gloriously interactive. You too can now experience what it is like to fill in an HTML form that is upside down and slightly blurred!

This of course opens the door for developing much more creative interfaces and visualizations, which are often well suited to the development of mashups and showcase applications, such as ApolloBook, shown in Figure 15-2.

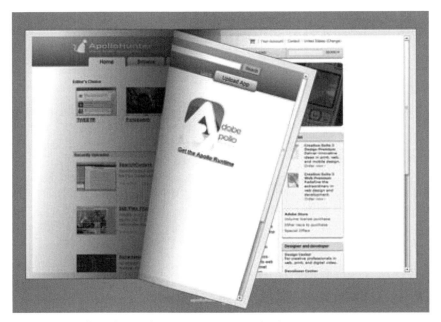

Figure 15-2. ApolloBook, transforming web pages into books!

As you do more with your HTML component, it becomes useful to be able to manipulate it using ActionScript.

To instantiate the component, you simply create an instance with the desired parameters and add it as a child on the display list:

```
var browser:HTML = new HTML();
    browser.width = 400;
    browser.height = 400;
    browser.x = 10;
    browser.y = 10;
    browser.location = "http://google.com";
    addChild(browser);
```

Obviously, if you are using the component for anything complex, such as a page of an animated book, then it makes sense to create a custom class to encapsulate the HTML component. This keeps your code neat and avoids you having to expend unnecessary effort setting parameters on the individual component.

In the example, you are specifying the page to load using the location property. It is also possible to render an HTML string, which can be useful if you want to generate a live preview of user-entered data. In that case, you would assign a value to the htmlText property of the HTML component.

To implement as-you-type rendering (see Figure 15-3), you just need to attach an event listener to the text field that will be receiving the user input and use that to update your HTML component.

In the following example, you are simply creating a text area and instance of the HTML component shown in Figure 15-3 by using MXML and then attaching the liveUpdate function to the text area's change event, meaning that it will execute following every keystroke:

```
<mx:TextArea x="10" y="10" width="629" height="218" id="htmltext_txt"
             change="livePreview();"/>
<mx:HTML x="10" y="236" width="629" height="292" id="browser" />


<mx:Script>
    <![CDATA[

        private function livePreview():void{
            browser.htmlText = htmltext_txt.text;
        }

    ]]>
</mx:Script>
```

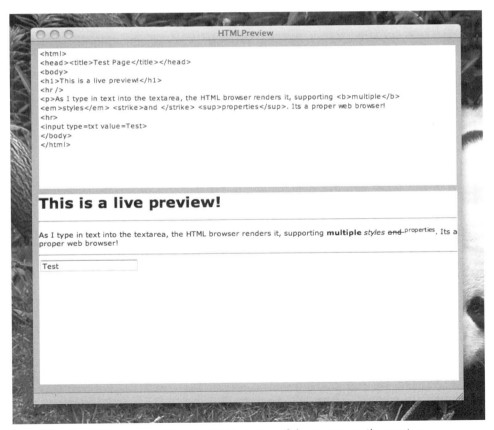

Figure 15-3. The HTML component, rendering the content of the text area as the user types

Working with events

The application will also trigger certain events based on the current status of the HTML component. You can use event listeners to listen for these events in the normal manner. Table 15-1 lists the events.

Table 15-1. Events Dispatched by the HTML Component

Event	Description
Event.HTML_BOUNDS_CHANGE	Denotes that the dimensions of the HTML component have changed
Event.HTML_D_O_M_INITIALIZE	Fired when the HTML DOM has been created but before rendering of the actual page
Event.HTML_RENDER	Fired when the page rendering has completed
Event.LOCATION_CHANGE	Fired when the location property of the HTML component is changed (for example, the user has navigated to another page)
Event.SCROLL	Triggered by scrolling within the HTML component
HTMLUncaughtScriptExceptionEvent.UNCAUGHT_SCRIPT_EXCEPTION	Fired if there are any JavaScript errors when executing scripts within the HTML component

Rendering PDF content

You can also use the HTML component to load and render PDF content provided that the user has Adobe Acrobat Reader version 8.1 or newer installed.

You would load the PDF in the same way you would load a web page, except this time you'd specify the URL of the PDF document you want to open.

Because PDF may not be supported, it makes sense to perform a check before attempting to load a document. PDF capability checking is managed through the pdfCapability property of the HTMLLoader class. This will return one of the five results listed in Table 15-2.

Table 15-2. Events Dispatched When Working with PDF Content

Property	Description
HTMLPDFCapability.STATUS_OK	The user has Acrobat Reader 8.1 or newer installed, allowing PDF content to be displayed.
HTMLPDFCapability.ERROR_CANNOT_LOAD_READER	The user has Acrobat Reader installed; however, there was an unspecified error instantiating the plug-in.
HTMLPDFCapability.ERROR_INSTALLED_READER_NOT_FOUND	No version of Acrobat Reader can be found on the user's system.

continued

Property	Description
`HTMLPDFCapability.` `ERROR_INSTALLED_READER_TOO_OLD`	A version of Acrobat Reader prior to 8.1 has been detected.
`HTMLPDFCapability.` `ERROR_PREFERRED_READER_TOO_OLD`	The user has Adobe Reader 8.1 or newer installed; however, they also have an earlier version that is set up as the default handler for PDF files. This version is too old.

Because PDF viewing is done through the WebKit plug-in rather than natively within the AIR runtime, developers should be aware of several limitations.

Specifically, PDF content can be rendered only if the application window is fully opaque. Filters and other visual transformations applied to the HTML component will also prevent the content from being rendered. In addition, the PDF viewer will take on the frontmost z-index within the AIR application's display list, so overlapping content is out of the question.

Finally, advanced features of the PDF format such as reviewing forms and documents may not function within the AIR runtime.

Operating system–specific functionality

In addition to advanced features such as HTML rendering, the AIR runtime also contains functionality that allows the developer to take advantage of operating system–specific functionality.

This is often necessary because of the differences between various operating systems and the user interface metaphors used to represent items such as menus and running applications.

System tray icons

Under Mac OS, an application's icon appears in the Dock when it is active. From the Dock icon, application developers can choose to display a custom application menu where users can access items of functionality (see Figure 15-4). In addition, an application can make the Dock icon "bounce" as a means of attracting the user's attention.

Figure 15-4. The Mac OS X Dock, with the blue "lights" underneath individual icons denoting running applications

This functionality can be particularly useful in the instance of a music player application that exposes the basic functionality to control playback from a Dock icon menu. Similarly, bouncing the Dock icon could signify that fresh application content has been downloaded.

On Windows, similar concepts exist, but they are implemented slightly differently. Although running applications are shown in the task bar, menus are not available there. An application may define an additional icon that appears in the system tray area of the taskbar (see Figure 15-5). From there, a user can access application functionality by right-clicking.

Figure 15-5. The Windows taskbar, with the running applications shown in the center area and the system tray to the right

To notify the user, you have two options under Windows. If you want to present a simple notification, you can flash the taskbar icon. This is the equivalent of bouncing the Dock icon on a Mac.

The second option for notifying a user is to display a tooltip on a system tray icon. This appears over the tooltip icon and can be used to display a small amount of text to the user. Unfortunately, this functionality is not available on Mac OS.

Detecting system capabilities

If you want to detect the capabilities of the user's machine, several properties within the NativeApplication class will return a boolean value depending on the capability in question, as listed in Table 15-3. If you attempt to invoke capabilities that are not supported by an operating system, a runtime exception will be thrown.

Table 15-3. Properties Used to Determine Whether a Capability Is Supported

Property	Description
supportsDockIcon	Does the current operating system support Dock icons?
supportsSystemTrayIcon	Does the current operating system support system tray icons?

Notifying the user

If you want to notify the user by bouncing the Dock icon under Mac OS and flashing the taskbar icon under Windows, then you would check the capabilities and run the appropriate method:

```
if(NativeApplication.supportsDockIcon){
    var dock:DockIcon = NativeApplication.nativeApplication.icon
        as DockIcon;
    dock.bounce(NotificationType.INFORMATIONAL);
} else if (NativeApplication.supportsSystemTrayIcon){
    stage.nativeWindow.notifyUser(NotificationType.INFORMATIONAL);
}
```

When you invoke a notification, you have two different types you can use, as defined in the NotificationType class:

You can use `NotificationType.CRITICAL` to signal an important event that requires the user's immediate attention. Here the taskbar entry will flash repeatedly, or the Dock icon will bounce repeatedly, until the user brings the window to the foreground.

- If the notification is purely for information only and requires no immediate response from the user, then `NotificationType.INFORMATIONAL` is preferred. This will highlight the applications taskbar entry or bounce the Dock icon only once.

> *By default, the icon image used for system tray and Dock icons will be the one of the icon images specified in the* `app.xml` *file when the application was installed. If you want to change this (if, for example, you want to create an animated icon), you can do so within the* `NativeApplication` *class:*
>
> `NativeApplication.nativeApplication.icon.bitmaps = [icon.bitmapData]`
>
> *Multiple images can be supplied in the* `bitmaps` *array if you want to provide images that are different sizes. AIR will automatically select the closest-sized image and perform scaling if necessary.*

As you can see, if you want to animate the Dock or system tray icon, you can set a new array of images in every frame.

Should you want to remove the Dock or system tray icon, you can set the bitmaps array to [ ], clearing its contents.

Menus

You can control several types of menus within an AIR application; some are operating system dependent, and others are generic across different platforms. All are customizable by the AIR menu APIs.

Mac OS has the application menu, which is accessible from the title bar at the top of the screen, as shown in Figure 15-6. By default, it contains functionality to hide and exit the application.

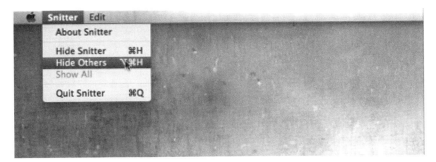

Figure 15-6. The default application menu under Mac OS

Using the AIR APIs, you can customize this by adding items and submenus. In addition, you can remove or add custom event handlers for the default functionality in this menu. This can be especially useful if you want to run cleanup functions when a user chooses to exit an application.

On Windows, you have a similar type of menu that appears under the title bar of an application (Figure 15-7). In a similar way to how you customize the Mac application menu, the AIR menu APIs provide functionality for you to add items and submenus to this location. The only caveat with these window menus is that, being an operating system component rather than specifically part of your application's user interface, this functionality is not available to applications that use custom window chrome.

Figure 15-7. An application's menu bar on Windows Vista

Across both platforms, there is functionality that allows you to enable context menus. These come in a variety of forms.

An alternative to using the Mac application menu or the Windows window menu could be to use the menu components that exist within the Flex framework. This is essential if you are creating an application that uses its own custom chrome.

Standard in text fields are context menus that apply to any selected text, allowing cut/copy/paste operations to be performed (Figure 15-8). This is common across Flash and Flex applications in general, though can be disabled on a per-component basis if desired.

Figure 15-8. An example of a context menu within an AIR application

You also have the ability to define your own custom right-click menus for your application.

Creating a menu structure

Within your applications, you can view menus as what are essentially tree structures. You have the root, which is defined by the NativeMenu class. From here you can add menu items, separators, and submenus as you build up the hierarchy.

When a menu item is selected, a select event for which you can write your own custom event handlers is dispatched.

If you wanted to create the menu shown in Figure 15-9 with six items, separated by a divider, with a submenu containing a further two items, then you would build it as follows:

```
var menu:NativeMenu = new NativeMenu();

var item1:NativeMenuItem = new NativeMenuItem("First Item",
                                              false);
var item2:NativeMenuItem = new NativeMenuItem("Second Item",
                                              false);
var item3:NativeMenuItem = new NativeMenuItem("Third Item",
                                              false);
var item4:NativeMenuItem = new NativeMenuItem("Forth Item",
                                              false);
var item5:NativeMenuItem = new NativeMenuItem("Fifth Item",
                                              false);
var item6:NativeMenuItem = new NativeMenuItem("Sixth Item",
                                              false);
var item7:NativeMenuItem = new NativeMenuItem("SubmenuItem 1",
                                              false);
var item8:NativeMenuItem = new NativeMenuItem("SubmenuItem 2",
                                              false);

menu.addItem(item1);
menu.addItem(item2);
menu.addItem(item3);
menu.addItem(item4);
menu.addItem(new NativeMenuItem("Separator",true));
menu.addItem(item5);
menu.addItem(item6);

var submenu:NativeMenu = new NativeMenu();
submenu.addItem(item7);
submenu.addItem(item8);

menu.addSubmenu(submenu,"Submenu");
```

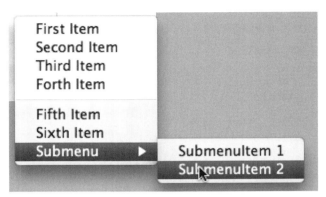

Figure 15-9. The example menu

You can also insert items at specific positions within your menu, using the addItemAt and addSubmenuAt methods, meaning that you are in no way restricted to creating your menus sequentially. These methods take one additional parameter: an integer representing the position where an element can be inserted.

Once you have created your menu, you now need to decide where to use it and assign it to the appropriate element.

If you wanted to create a menu for our application, either in the Mac OS menu bar or in the window frame of a Windows application, you would first check what is supported on the user's system and then set either the application or window's menu to be your NativeMenu instance:

```
if(NativeApplication.supportsMenu){
    nativeApplication.menu = menu;
}

if(NativeWindow.supportsMenu){
    window.menu = menu;
}
```

Similarly, if you wanted to set an icon for a Dock or system tray icon, you would first check to see which (if any) is supported on the user's machine and assign your menu to the appropriate element:

```
if(NativeApplication.supportsDockIcon){
    DockIcon(NativeApplication.nativeApplication.icon).menu = menu;
}

if(NativeApplication.supportsSystemTrayIcon){
    SystemTrayIcon(NativeApplication.nativeApplication.icon).menu
        = menu;
}
```

The final option for you is to utilize your newly created menu as a right-click context menu. You can do this with any class that extends `InteractiveObject`, which covers most user interface components and anything else you might be using. In this case, you would simply set the `contextMenu` property:

```
element.contextMenu = menu;
```

To trigger actions whenever one of your menu items is selected, you need to add event listeners to your menu items:

```
var item1:NativeMenuItem = new NativeMenuItem("First Item",
                                              false);
item1.addEventListener(Event.SELECT,handleItem1);
```

For complex menus, attaching listeners to each and every `NativeMenuItem` may become tedious. One option here is to add the event listener to the `NativeMenu` itself:

```
var menu:NativeMenu = new NativeMenu();
menu.addEventListener(Event.SELECT,menuHandler);
```

When the `Select` event is dispatched, its target property is the `NativeMenuItem` that was selected. By examining the `label` property, you can decide what command to execute:

```
private function menuHandler(e:Event):void{
    var item:NativeMenuItem = e.target as NativeMenuItem;

    switch(item.label){
        case "First Item":
            handleItem1();
            break;
        case "Second Item":
            handleItem2();
            break;
        case "Second Item":
            handleItem3();
            break;
    }
}
```

Although with this method you may not end up with less code being written, it should result in the menu handlers being easier to read and maintain.

Launching, detecting, and updating AIR applications

Other key functionality within the AIR runtime governs how an application interacts with the operating system, sets up file associations, detects user activity, and performs autoupdates.

Launching on start-up

Often when developing smaller applications and widgets, it is desirable for an application to be persistent, running in the background even when a user may not be directly interacting with it. In such cases, a desirable feature is to have the application launch when a user first logs into their computer.

Within AIR you have the capability to set this through the NativeApplication class, which provides functionality for handling application-wide events and functionality. To apply this setting, you simply need to set the startAtLogin property:

```
NativeApplication.nativeApplication.startAtLogin = true;
```

This will remain in effect until either the property is set to false or the user changes this setting manually in a tool outside the application, such as MSConfig or the Mac OS X user preferences.

> *You cannot set this setting during the application install process—only during runtime.*

Another gotcha is that you can set this setting only if an application is installed, meaning that if you are testing the application within Flex Builder or another IDE, you will get a "Feature is not available at this time" error message during runtime.

File associations

During the installation process, you can associate a particular application with any given file type by adding an entry in the app.xml file.

For example, if you were developing an RSS reader and wanted to associate it with .opml files, then you would add the following XML snippet within the <application> node:

```
<fileTypes>
    <fileType>
        <name>OPML File</name>
        <extension>opml</extension>
        <description>XML Outline Document</description>
        <contentType>text/x-opml</contentType>
        <icon>
            <image16x16>icons/opml16x16.png</image16x16>
            <image32x32>icons/opml32x32.png</image32x32>
            <image48x48>icons/opml48x48.png</image48x48>
            <image128x128>icons/opml128x128.xml</image128x128>
        </icon>
    </fileType>
</fileTypes>
```

name is what is displayed by the operating system in a given file's properties. description is also used in operating system dialog boxes and preferences listings.

extension and contentType identify instances of a given file, either by file extension or by MIME type. Including a MIME type is optional; however, this often helps the operating system identify a file. But it is worth noting that some file types may be served under multiple different MIME types.

In addition, during installation, an icon may be specified for a given file type. These should be provided within the .air file as PNG images with the dimensions of 16×16, 32×32, 48×48, and 128×128.

Once an application has been installed, there also exists the functionality to check whether it is registered as the default application for a specific file type.

You access these capabilities through the NativeApplication class. If you wanted to check whether your application is currently set as the default and, if not, set it up as the default, then you would use code similar to the following snippet:

```
if(!NativeApplication.isSetAsDefaultApplication("opml")){
    NativeApplication.setAsDefaultApplication("opml");
}
```

In addition, you can also remove a file association by calling the NativeApplication.removeAsDefaultApplication() method.

If you want to get the path of the application that is currently set up as a handler for a given file type, you can use the NativeApplication.getDefaultApplication("opml") method, which will return a path in string format.

> From a user experience perspective, it can often be considered impolite and frustrating to change the default application for a particular file type without asking the user.
>
> You can handle this in several different ways, including performing a check during the start-up of an application and presenting the user with an option to make the current application the default application (Figure 15-10).
>
> It is also important to give the user an option to "opt out" of this check, which is a great relief for a user who has no intention of making the application the default and doesn't want to be hassled!

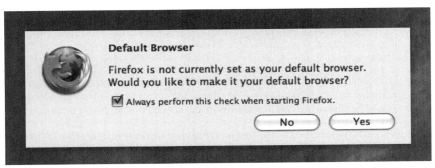

Figure 15-10. An example of asking the user whether they want to change their default application

Detecting user activity

An application can respond to a user's activity or inactivity in a number of ways. For example, if the user does not interact with the mouse or keyboard for a period of time, an operating system will often activate a screen saver, turn off monitors, or put the computer to sleep. Video games respond to similar events; if a user does not interact with the controller for a period of time, you often see Mario or Sonic respond by crossing their arms and impatiently tapping their foot!

When you consider applications and mashups, you may want to do several things in this instance:

- In the case of multiuser applications such as collaboration tools or instant messengers, you may want to notify other users of this inactivity by setting your status to Away.
- For data-consuming applications, you may be interested in when a period of inactivity ends so that you can update your data feeds once a user has returned.
- If CPU-intensive processing is required by your application, you may want to wait until the user is inactive so that you do not interfere with their normal computer usage.

As with other application-level functionality, within the NativeApplication class exists a means to detect a user's activity, firing events when the user is believed to be idle and when they return.

A developer can also set an idleThreshold property, which is the threshold value that is used to determine the presence of a user.

For example, if you want to execute the method handleIdle after three minutes of inactivity and execute another method called handleReturn upon the commencement of interaction, you can use the following code snippet:

```
NativeApplication.nativeApplication.idleThreshold = 180;
NativeApplication.nativeApplication.addEventListener(Event.USER_IDLE,
                                    handleIdle);
NativeApplication.nativeApplication.addEventListener(Event.USER_PRESENT,
                                    handleReturn);
```

The NativeApplication class also provides the timeSinceLastUserInput method, which will return the time in seconds from the last mouse or keyboard input. You can also use this when reacting to the user's presence (or lack of).

Updating applications

AIR makes the process of installing applications relatively painless compared to native applications. However, once an application is installed, what happens if a new version is released?

Most users tend to install applications and continue to use them provided they continue to work satisfactorily. If a new version is released, unless you spend time promoting it through e-mail and website marketing, many users, oblivious that the old version is now out of date, will continue to use it.

When you are developing applications with dependencies on web-based content and functionality, this can present a problem. If a service URL or API changes, then you will want to distribute an updated version to your user base immediately. If you don't, you may find that older versions of the application

COMPLETING THE EXPERIENCE

become unusable. In addition, if you discover security vulnerabilities, then it becomes desirable to distribute them to your user base as quickly and painlessly as possible.

Within AIR, you can use the Updater class to ease the pain of this process. But first you need to retrieve the updated version of your application from the Internet.

Usually, you would query a web service of some description, which would tell the application whether a newer version was available, possibly also returning the URL of the updated .air file. Using a server-side technology such as PHP, a developer can easily put together a service like this, or alternatively a static text file hosted on a web server containing both the latest version number and a URL would be sufficient for an application to determine whether it was indeed the latest version.

If there is a newer version of your application available, you run the downloadUpdate() method. This method creates a URLStream object that downloads the update:

```
var urlStream:URLStream;

private function downloadUpdate():void{
    urlStream = new URLStream();
    urlStream.addEventListener(Event.COMPLETE, downloadComplete);

    var url:URLRequest = new URLRequest(
            "http://yourserver.com/yourapp.air");
    urlStream.load(url);
}
```

Once the file has been downloaded, you need to write it to disk. In this instance, you are placing it on the user's desktop:

```
private function downloadComplete(event:Event):void {
    var fileData:ByteArray = new ByteArray();

    urlStream.readBytes(fileData, 0, urlStream.bytesAvailable);

    var file:File = File.desktopDirectory.resolvePath("yourapp.air");

    var fs:FileStream = new FileStream();
    fs.addEventListener(Event.CLOSE, update);
    fs.openAsync(file, FileMode.WRITE);
    fs.writeBytes(fileData, 0, fileData.length);
    fs.close();
}
```

Now that your file has been written to disk, you can now update your application by creating an updater instance and passing it the location of your updated AIR file and the new version number:

```
private function update(e:Event):void{
    var updater:Updater = new Updater();
    var file:File = File.desktopDirectory.resolvePath("yourapp.air");
    updater.update(file, "1.12");
}
```

331

This will cause the running instance of the application to exit while the AIR runtime performs the update. When complete, the application will relaunch as normal.

> *For the* Updater *to work as intended, both the old and new versions of the application should have the same* appId *property (defined in the application XML descriptor file).*

Summary

In this chapter, you learned about many of the often-overlooked features of a successful application that can have a significant impact on the experience of interacting with an application. These include the smaller aspects of integration that is expected between a desktop application and an operating system, including file associations, icons, menus, and notifications. As you move from the Web to the desktop, it's important that you do not forget these and that you devote sufficient time in your application's development to "polish the chrome."

We also covered some of the additional functionality provided by AIR, specifically, the HTML-rendering capabilities and the framework in place that allows you to easily update your applications and ensure that your users are always running the latest version.

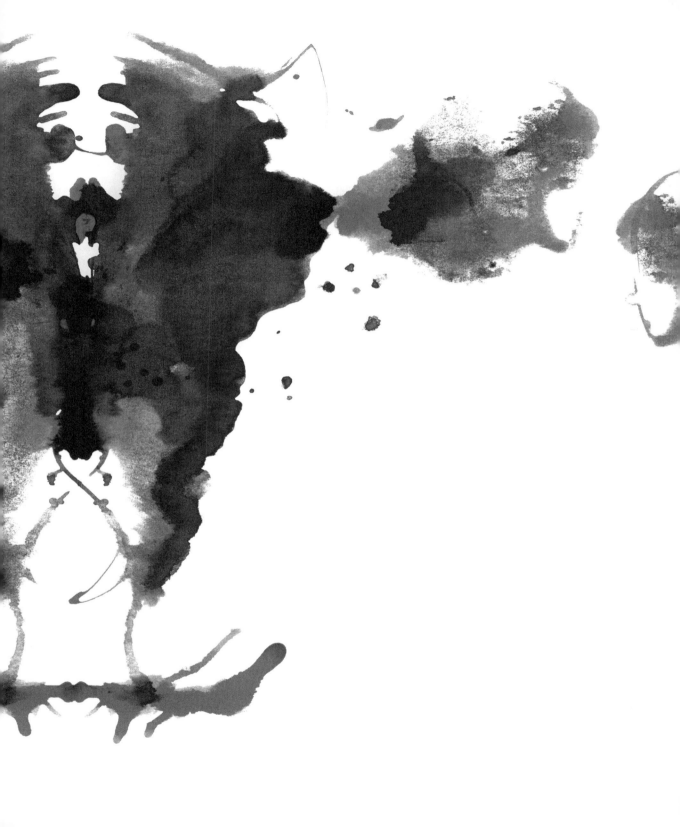

INDEX

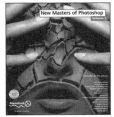

friendsofed.com/forums

Join the friends of ED forums to find out more about our books, discover useful technology tips and tricks, or get a helping hand on a challenging project. *Designer to Designer*™ is what it's all about—our community sharing ideas and inspiring each other. In the friends of ED forums, you'll find a wide range of topics to discuss, so look around, find a forum, and dive right in!

■ Books and Information

Chat about friends of ED books, gossip about the community, or even tell us some bad jokes!

■ Flash

Discuss design issues, ActionScript, dynamic content, and video and sound.

■ Web Design

From front-end frustrations to back-end blight, share your problems and your knowledge here.

■ Site Check

Show off your work or get new ideas.

■ Digital Imagery

Create eye candy with Photoshop, Fireworks, Illustrator, and FreeHand.

■ ArchivED

Browse through an archive of old questions and answers.

HOW TO PARTICIPATE

Go to the friends of ED forums at **www.friendsofed.com/forums**.

Visit **www.friendsofed.com** to get the latest on our books, find out what's going on in the community, and discover some of the slickest sites online today!